ENGLISH PASTORAL POETRY

FROM THE BEGINNINGS TO MARVELL

English Pastoral Poetry

FROM THE BEGINNINGS
TO MARVELL

EDITED BY

FRANK KERMODE

Lord Northcliffe Professor of English Literature
University College, London

The Norton Library
W · W · NORTON & COMPANY · INC ·
NEW YORK

ORIGINALLY PUBLISHED 1952
FIRST PUBLISHED IN THE NORTON LIBRARY 1972

W. W. Norton & Company, Inc. also publishes *The Norton Anthology of English Literature*, edited by M. H. Abrams et al; *The Norton Anthology of Poetry*, edited by Arthur M. Eastman et al; *World Masterpieces*, edited by Maynard Mack et al; *The Norton Reader*, edited by Arthur M. Eastman et al; *The Norton Facsimile of the First Folio of Shakespeare*, prepared by Charlton Hinman; and the Norton Critical Editions.

Library of Congress Cataloging in Publication Data

Kermode, John Frank, ed.
   English pastoral poetry, from the beginnings to Marvell.

   (The Norton library)
   Original ed. issued in series: Life, literature, and thought library.
   Bibliography: p.
   1. Pastoral poetry, English.   I.   Title.
II.   Series: Life, literature, and thought library.
PR1195.P3K4   1972   821'.008'014   72-7044
ISBN 0-393-00612-3

PRINTED IN THE UNITED STATES OF AMERICA
1 2 3 4 5 6 7 8 9 0

PREFACE

THIS book is meant primarily for readers who experience discomfort when confronted with literary shepherds, nymphs, mazers, sheep-hooks, and the rest of the properties of pastoral poetry. Three hundred and sixty years ago a professor of rhetoric pugnaciously asked the literary world whether pastoral poetry was not at best a trifling, and at worst a dangerous thing; the modern reader may not feel in any moral danger, but he has been known to concur in the view that this kind of poetry is tedious and trivial. Because it is not, and because as a consequence of this misapprehension a large quantity of fine verse is misunderstood and neglected, it would appear to be at least a virtuous undertaking to present it in a light favourable to more sympathetic reading. This is what I have attempted. The apparatus is intended as a guide to such reading, and not as a survey of a field in which vast learning has been expended. The short bibliography should facilitate more specialized inquiry.

The translations from classical and foreign poets are included because no real understanding of the English Pastoral is possible without some acquaintance with them. It should, however, be observed that English translators of this period (and no version later than 1660 has been admitted) treated their originals with considerable freedom.

As to the text, it has been thought desirable to retain the old spelling, though a few words have been modernized where there seemed to be a danger of confusion. The punctuation has been more freely emended.

My thanks are due to the following publishers, who have very kindly granted me permission to use copyright material: Basil Blackwell (Nos. 35 and 36); the Cambridge University Press (Nos. 24, 48, 49, 50, 51, and 60); the Harvard University Press (Nos. 4, 5, 6, 28, 29, 37, and 45); the Manchester University Press (Nos. 13 and 55); Messrs Oliver and Boyd, Ltd

(No. 2); the Oxford University Press (Nos. 1, 46, 47, 53, 54, 67, 68, 74, 75, 76, 77, 78, and 79); Penguin Books, Ltd, for the lines quoted on page 20; and the Editor of *Anglia* (No. 3).

The General Editor has given me the benefit of his experience and learning, and saved me from some mistakes; those that doubtless remain are not to be laid at his door.

F.K.

CONTENTS

INTRODUCTION

Jove, Jove! this shepherd's passion
Is much upon my fashion.
       As You Like It, II, iv, 56–57.
Hast any philosophy in thee, shepherd?
       Ibid., III, i, 21.

PASTORAL is one of the 'kinds' of poetry, like Epic, Tragedy, and Satire. We still know what these 'kinds' are, though we probably attach less importance to them than earlier readers did. To an Elizabethan critic they were natural; men had discovered, not devised, them. A poet who wrote in some novel form not recognized as a 'kind' was liable to be called to account, and accused of a breach of decorum, which is an offence against nature. Pastoral, though it ranked below some of the other 'kinds' of poetry, had, during the period which most concerns us, this official protection, and the Elizabethan schoolboy learned its laws as part of his rhetorical training. Yet to Dr Johnson it was a form "easy, vulgar, and therefore disgusting"—he was writing about *Lycidas*—and to us it probably suggests the word 'artificial' rather than the word 'natural.'

We can perhaps learn something from the use of the word 'artificial' in this connexion. For us it suggests mannerism, triviality, lack of seriousness, possibly even the *ersatz*. But for the Elizabethan it was usually high praise. "Our vulgar Poesie," says Puttenham, a good critic,

> cannot shew it selfe either gallant or gorgious, if any lymme be left naked and bare and not clad in his kindly[1] clothes and coulours,[2] such as may convey them somewhat out of sight, that is from the common course of ordinary speach and capacitie of the vulgar iudgement, and yet being artificially handled must need yeld it much more bewtie and commendation.

And Puttenham is speaking, not merely of Pastoral, but of all poetry. He is recommending the poet to be as 'un-natural'

---

[1] *I.e.*, Appropriate to its kind, or *genre*.   [2] *I.e.*, Figures of rhetoric.

as possible, though he would not have used that word. He meant that to do the work of Art the poet must be artificial; and the work of Art was no less than the improvement or development of Nature. There are great difficulties in this word 'Nature,' as the Elizabethans themselves realized. They would argue, for example, that Art itself is an instrument of Nature. But the chief meaning, as it concerns us here at the moment, may best be expressed as 'the antithesis of Art,' the wild or savage as opposed to the cultivated, the material upon which Art works. And this opposition is nowhere so evident and acute as in Pastoral, for in this 'kind' the cultivated, in their artificial way, reflect upon and describe, for their own ends, the natural life. For reasons we shall have to consider, this natural life was normally associated with shepherds.

At first sight it must seem odd that so considerable a proportion of European literature should concern itself with rustics, and even odder that it should concentrate on a small class of rustics. It will probably be easier to understand if we devote a little time to the history of the kind, and its critical justification. It must not be forgotten that when a new kind is founded its literary momentum may carry it far beyond the particular situation from which it took its origin; that is to say, the literary tradition is carried on by one writer imitating another despite the fact that the world of the second is different from that of the first. He is asking his readers to judge him by a purely literary criterion, and his mind is working in accordance with one of the laws of literary history which lays it down that to imitate a classic writer is the same as imitating Nature. Nature and Homer, so Pope tells us, are the same. The theory of Imitation has for good or ill a great deal to do with pastoral poetry, and it needs to be expounded in connexion with our present purposes. It seems, therefore, that this approach to the Pastoral of the English Renaissance involves three main considerations, which are in fact closely related to each other: we must look at the history of the kind, at its critical and philosophical background, and at the general theory of Imitation as it affects Pastoral. But first, we must try to understand its scope and fertility.

THE NATURE OF PASTORAL POETRY

Some modern writers use the term 'Pastoral' to describe any work which concerns itself with the contrast between simple and complicated ways of living; its method is to exalt the naturalness and virtue of the simple man at the expense of the complicated one, whether the former be a shepherd, or a child, or a working-man. This is perfectly justifiable, although the title given to the kind emphasizes that the natural man is conventionally a shepherd. There were reasons for this, but when the old feeling about shepherds, about which I shall be speaking shortly, faded, the preoccupation of the Pastoral with them tended to increase its 'artificiality.' A necessary result of this is that there is much pastoral poetry which must be sympathetically read with reference to the convention in which it is written; otherwise it will certainly seem a barren or frigidly ornamental literary exercise, as *Lycidas* did to Johnson. Milton could not impress *him* by claiming that he and King "drove a field" and 'battened their flocks with the fresh dews of night'; "we know," says Johnson, "that they never drove a field, and that they had no flocks to batten."[1] And to Johnson it seemed that Pastoral was useful only to give young poets something to cut their teeth on. "It seems natural for a young poet to initiate himself by Pastorals, which, not professing to imitate real life, require no experience . . ."[2] If we are to avoid Johnson's mistake we must be aware of what the poets who wrote artificially about shepherds were trying to do; clearly they had in mind a great deal of earlier pastoral writing which had established the conventions within which they worked, and assumed in their readers a knowledge of the history of the kind. That is why our historical inquiry must be directed, not only upon the general situation which produces significant contrasts between the natural and the cultivated, but upon the tradition of literary Pastoral which is carried on by one poet's

[1] *Lives of the Poets:* "Life of Milton" (World's Classics edition, I, 116; Oxford University Press, 1906).
[2] *Lives of the Poets:* "Life of Pope" (*ibid.*, II, 324). The tradition that poets profitably commence their careers with Pastoral developed from Virgil's *Eclogues*.

imitating another. But first, the more general topic of the scope of Pastoral.

The first condition of pastoral poetry is that there should be a sharp difference between two ways of life, the rustic and the urban. The city is an artificial product, and the pastoral poet invariably lives in it, or is the product of its schools and universities. Considerable animosity may exist between the townsman and the countryman. Thus the 'primitive' may be sceptical about the justice of a state of affairs which makes him live under rude conditions while the town-poet lives in polite society. On the other hand, the town- or court-poet has a certain contempt for the peasant (sometimes very strong); and both primitive and court-poet write verse which reflects these attitudes. Occasionally there is a certain similarity of subject. Townsman and rustic alike may consider the idea that at a remote period in history nature gave forth her fruits without the aid of man's labour and worship. Perhaps, somewhere, she still does so. This idea that the world has been a better place and that men have degenerated is remarkably widespread, and a regular feature of pastoral poetry. We have abused Nature, by breaking its laws or falling into sin, and we are therefore steadily deteriorating so that our only hope is for a fresh start, after some kind of redemption. The restoration of the Golden Age is a theme of Virgilian Pastoral, and was naturally taken over in the Pastoral of the Christian era. All such ideas are more ancient than the pastoral convention, but they naturally became attached to it in the course of time. They occur in primitive poetry as well as in the poetry of the cultivated, but this should not deceive us into thinking that there can be primitive Pastoral. The first condition of Pastoral is that it is an urban product.

Nevertheless, it is as closely connected with earlier poetry as the Epic is with the lays of the 'heroic age.' For example, although the literary tradition of the Golden Age is securely rooted in Virgil, Ovid, Seneca, Juvenal, and Boëthius, we may be sure that the primary impulse, human resentment at the conditions and struggles of life, vitalizes the myth in its literary form and establishes its kinship with similar primitive myths which occur in almost every recorded culture from Mycenæan to American Negro. Something better must have existed, and for some folly or sin we can easily recognize in ourselves we have been turned out of the garden and can only hope to return.

Satire, also an urban 'kind,' assumes that in its own milieu, the metropolis, it discovers the extremest forms of degeneracy, which it exposes by contrasting it with some better way of life—that is, some earlier way of life; the farther back you go the better. One would expect Satire to get better and better, as the conditions grow more odiously stimulating; and in Rome this happened, for from being a comparatively good-humoured affair it took over various rights from other forms, including that of direct and vigorous attack on the vices of society and individuals, and culminated in the fierce and gloomy Juvenal, who is the genuine prototype of European Satire, though the last of the considerable Roman practitioners. In the heyday of English Pastoral the satirist, with Juvenal never far from his thoughts, is always at hand, flogging away with his scourge of untrimmed decasyllables; sometimes, by a pardonable etymological confusion, imagining himself a satyr, but never to be reconciled to the loss of virtue always entailed in wresting a metropolis out of the gentler countryside. *Pietas*, *gravitas*, *virtus*—these are qualities which wither in acquisitive communities; leisure increases, and with it the arts and the vices. By contrast the rural nation of a few generations back appears as free of vice as it is of culture in the narrow sense of a refined minority pursuit. Society outside the town walls is still comparatively simple, and still natural—especially in properly pastoral areas, where the country has to be rich and fresh—whereas the town has viciously supplied imagined wants in nature with the art of brick and stone. Obviously there is common ground between Pastoral and Satire; but Pastoral—here I limit the meaning of the word to literature which deals with rural life, and exclude other 'versions' of Pastoral—Pastoral flourishes at a particular moment in the urban development, the phase in which the relationship of metropolis and country is still evident, and there are no children (as there are now) who have never seen a cow.

Heroic poetry celebrates the achievements of an age of heroes in the verse of sophisticated poets like Homer. "The result," writes Professor G. Thomson,[1] "was a dynamic tension between them [the poets] and their material, and so deeply had they absorbed their material that this tension appears as something internal in the heroes of the story." He then quotes a speech of Sarpedon's which certainly justifies the comment that it is "not the voice of a robber chief."[2] The heroic poet, believing in his right, and that of his patrons, to the heroic life, and yet experiencing a complex response to the recounting of that life which the heroes themselves could not have imagined, is under extraordinary pressure. The position of the pastoral poet is even less simple than that of the heroic poet; although his rustics are in a way contemptible in their simplicity and coarseness, they have a way of life which is admirable because it is natural, and are, in fact, a local and contemporary version of Golden Age humanity, without the intrigues of the Court and the money-grubbing of the city. The shepherd in particular leads a deliciously idle life and whiles away the time playing a pipe. He became the type of the natural life, uncomplicated, contemplative, and in sympathy with Nature as the townsman could never be. He is the measure of the cultivated man's unnaturalness: he has plenty of time for thought; when he weeps the Nature with which he lives in such sympathy weeps also. Unlike the townsman, he does not meddle with Nature. (Of course, one believes this only in a certain frame of mind, or when striking a certain attitude, like that adopted by Marvell in *The Mower against Gardens*, or by the seventeenth-century French poet Théophile when he said:

> La nature est inimitable
> Et dans sa beauté véritable
> Elle éclate si vivement
> Que l'art gaste tous ses ouvrages,
> Et luy fait plustost mille outrages
> Qu'il ne luy donne un ornement.[3]

[1] *Æschylus and Athens* (Lawrence and Wishart, 1941), p. 66.   [2] *Iliad*, XII, 310–328.
[3] "Nature is inimitable; and in her real beauty she bursts forth with such vigour that Art can merely spoil all her works, committing upon her a thousand outrages for every ornament it manages to bestow." This is the opinion that is orthodoxly confuted by Polixenes in *The Winter's Tale*.

Unlike the townsman, he lives a contemplative and not an active life. This, as everybody knew from the story of Cincinnatus, and as Cicero had said of Scipio Africanus, was the best preparation for virtue. God preferred Abel before Cain, the contemplative life of the shepherd before the active life of the farmer. In Hesiod as well as in the Gospels a divine nativity is announced to shepherds. Their craft endows them with a kind of purity, almost a kind of holiness.

The simplest kind of pastoral poetry assumes that the quiet wildness of the country is better than the cultivated and complex life of the hurrying city and court. These places are unfortunate islands of luxury in a green sea of simplicity; Nature's handmaid, Art, has driven Nature out, and at best the city is a garden, tortured by artist-gardeners who

> . . . the cherry vex
> To procreate without a sex;

while, in the fields beyond,

> Every mower's wholesome heat
> Smells like an Alexander's sweat.

It does not concern itself with the subtleties which Polixenes offers to the reluctant Perdita. Living in his city garden with its sophisticated philosophies, its exotic plants, its cultivated music, the poet contemplates the life he has rejected, the life of the healthy countryside, with its simple manners, natural flowers, and rude pipings. The die is cast; in the great no man's land of the fields even the grasshoppers will mock him— as Marvell said in his lines on Nun Appleton House. There is no going back; the Golden Age is a moving fiction, the *vendange* and the hock-cart are charming and interesting, and upon them one may construct the amusements of a polite society; but the gentleman is now committed to another way of life. And always at the back of this literary attitude to Nature is the shadow of its opposite; the knowledge that Nature is rough, and the natural life in fact rather an animal affair; by long cultivation men have improved the natural breed, and the difference between the cultivated and the natural is the difference between a Ferdinand and a Caliban.[1] It is surely inevitable that in such a situation the poet should allow his complexities to colour his talk of the rustic subject, as the Epic poet projected his intellectual tensions on to the hero. Sarpedon appeared as a man of extraordinary sensibility; the shepherd appears as philosopher and poet.

Provided, then, that one does not allow the hard view of Nature as crude and rough to overset the dreamier view of it as uncorrupt,[2] one may well find that the rustic, and in particular the shepherd, has fascinating possibilities for the cultivated poet. A natural piper and singer, he is easily made to stand for the poet. It may be that the cultivated poet at a very early date learned his themes from the rustic primitive. In Ancient Greece and in the Europe of the Middle Ages the women at the corn-mills sang their *cantilenæ molares*, songs which told of a former Age of Gold, under the reign of a peaceful king whose sudden death brought it to an end; they dreamed of rest as a hungry man does of food. Another theme of the peasant singer was the encounter of rustic and courtier, in which the rustic triumphed. This was a kind of song which certainly had its origin in sheep-country, as modern French scholars have shown. Both of these themes, sophisticated and given a new orientation, belong to the stock of the pastoral poet. He will also observe that the figures of the shepherd and the shepherd-king have accumulated through the ages new and deeper meanings; if the pastoral poet is late enough in time he will never be unconscious of the persistent pastoral imagery of Christ,[3] in sermon and parable, or of the manner in which the Church has adapted that imagery. (The connexion between this imagery and that of the formal Pastoral was made explicit by Petrarch.) The Christian Pastoralist will also remember that the Song of Solomon, with all its unfathomable significance

[1] This is a topic of endless discussion. The reader might consult Castiglione, *The Courtier*, for a characteristic debate upon it. Shakespeare's *Tempest* treats the theme allusively but very fully.

[2] This hard view is as old as the soft one; both are pre-Christian, though Christian views on Nature tend to prefer the hard view, when by Nature is meant that which Adam's fall corrupted, and which is opposed to Grace. But this is a complicated subject.

[3] See, for example, John X, 11–16.

to the allegorical divine, is an epithalamium cast in the form of a dream-Pastoral. The poet's language is therefore capable of venturing close to, and across, that vague frontier which in the great periods of poetry separates secular and religious imagery.

These are merely a few random hints as to the complexity of Pastoral, treated abstractly. In the England of 1600, which produced most of the poetry in this collection, the relationship between the poet and his theme was governed in these and in many other ways, and affected by more specific religious, political, and economic tensions. Evidently it cannot be properly understood in isolation from the 'kind' within whose conventions it is written.

These general remarks might be summed up as follows. Pastoral depends upon an opposition between the simple, or natural, and the cultivated. Although this opposition can be complex, the bulk of pastoral poetry treats it quite simply, and assumes that natural men are purer and less vicious than cultivated men, and that there exists between them and Nature a special sympathy. The natural man is also wise and gifted in a different way from the cultivated man. By reason of his simplicity he is a useful subject for cultivated study, since his emotions and virtues are not complicated by deterioration and artificiality. The themes of the cultivated poet may be connected with those of the primitive poet, much as the garden is related to the open countryside, but the cultivated poet sophisticates them and endows them with learned allusions. Thus the Pastoral can become a vehicle for poetic speculation on religious mysteries, on the hierarchy of the Church, and also on poetry itself.

ORIGINS AND DEVELOPMENT OF THE 'KIND'

There are extant very old songs concerning shepherds, which may be connected with pastoral poetry. One dates from the early (i.e., Sumerian) civilization of Mesopotamia; in it a girl prefers a farmer (socially superior because economically more highly organized) to a shepherd:

> Never shall the shepherd marry me;
> Never shall he drape me in his tufted cloth;
> Never shall his finest wool touch me.
> Me, the maiden, shall the farmer,
> And he only, take in marriage—
> The farmer who can grow beans,
> The farmer who can grow grain.[1]

The shepherd spurned here is quite like the rejected swain in the Twentieth Idyll of Theocritus. The simplicity which accompanies the poverty of the shepherd is celebrated in many pre-Pastoral myths; in particular, there is the myth of the royal child (to the Christian, the type of Christ), cast away or exiled in infancy, who "receives the ministrations of shepherds, and is reared by a foster-father of humble birth";[2] a myth later treated in pastoral poetry by many poets, and especially by Spenser and Shakespeare.

The connexion between myth of this kind and the beginnings of Pastoral is obscure. Little is known about the sources of Theocritus, the first pastoral poet, who was born in Syracuse about 310 B.C., and lived in Alexandria under the patronage of Ptolemy Philadelphus. These sources may have had local characteristics which Theocritus generalized when he established the form. It is impossible to guess what these might have been. It may, however, be supposed that some pastoral themes, like those of gift-bringing and song-contest, originated in the sheep-pastures of Sicily. It is known that Theocritus, in those Idylls which deal with country life, made a fairly thorough attempt to write in rustic language, 'placing' his rustics socially by using the Doric dialect, and allowing their hexameters to be occasionally the vehicles of coarse or bawdy expressions. Theocritus found that the country folk were interesting in themselves, and worth recording in these relaxed hexameters. He did not himself do much by way of refining the poetic-philosophic potentialities of the Pastoral, but simply offered a courtly version, presumably substantially accurate, of certain rustic activities as he had observed them in

[1] Frankfort, Frankfort, Wilson, and Jacobsen, *Before Philosophy* (Penguin, 1949), p. 180.
[2] See A. J. Toynbee, *A Study of History*, abridged D. C. Somervell (Oxford University Press, 1946), pp. 219 ff.

Sicily and on the island of Cos. This in itself was an achievement related to, and in a sense bred out of, the needs of his time. "Theocritus," says Professor Jackson Knight, "brought the country itself out from the mere relief of the choric ode, and normal, active love out from the background of a story, on to the central stage, where highly complex urban communities needed it most."[1]

We find in Theocritus the court-poet, dependant of tyrants, habitué of the advanced literary communities of Alexandria, many signs of the typical pastoral attitude. In his First Idyll he celebrates the death of the shepherd-hero Daphnis, which in folklore had represented the annual death of Nature itself. Thus the "pathetic fallacy," as Ruskin called the convention by which Nature is made to share human sorrow, enters the pastoral tradition at the very beginning. From this Idyll developed the whole elaborate convention of the Pastoral Elegy, which perhaps reached its climax in Milton's *Lycidas* and in his *Epitaphium Damonis*. Yet Daphnis could have meant little to Theocritus except in the vicarious way in which the townsman enjoys the serious rites of the countryside. The pastoral flute was an instrument not of utility but of nostalgia, the nostalgia of a sophisticated poet for an art which was not yet a matter for hair-splitting and casuistry. And although Theocritus was more content than any pastoral poet up to the time of the Elizabethans to give his readers a straightforward account of the simple completeness of bucolic culture, and let them draw from it the conclusions to which he himself had come, he did not always avoid that projection of his own values and interests on his characters which we have noted as being characteristic of Pastoral. In the Seventh Idyll, for instance, the emphasis in the description of the harvest festival in Cos is on the fact that the city poets are playing at shepherds in this rich and authentic autumn setting. Actual poets are discussed under fancy names.

So 'shepherd' can on occasion mean 'poet'; to sing or play in shepherd fashion is to write or publish poetry. . . . The first step had been taken towards the days when, if anyone was called a

---

[1] *Roman Vergil* (Faber and Faber, 1944), p. 31.

shepherd in poetry, it would have been a startling discovery to find that he really was a country fellow who got his living by looking after actual sheep and had never published or tried to publish anything in his life.[1]

Kinds of poetry are not unchangeable entities, though the Renaissance found that easy to believe. Theocritus is obviously a pastoral poet, and in some ways the most accomplished of all who explore the form; but conditions which later became inseparable from the kind are only sketched and hinted at in its earliest exponent.[2] The work of developing these hints fell to a line of comparatively undistinguished poets who were writing between the time of Theocritus and the time of Virgil. For these poets Theocritus was the model, and from him they derived authority for the manner of their writing, giving him the status of a classic. Their themes, their metre (the hexameter), and their dialect (the Doric) they derived from him.

The position of Theocritus thus resembles in some respects that of Homer. He is the acknowledged classic of pastoral poetry, though his influence upon the tradition is less direct and in the long run less formative than that of Virgil. But he quickly became a true classic, the subject of imitation by later poets working in the same line.

Imitation is one of the fundamental laws of literary history, for it arises whenever a poet contemplates poetry. It is the function which gives literary history a meaning in terms of itself, and provides the channels of literary tradition. It is a wide concept, covering many related aspects of literary activity, and when used dogmatically it has often had very damaging and confusing consequences. But when that is said it must still be remembered that Imitation, in so far as it implies the need for an awareness of the best that has been thought and said, and the best ways of thinking and saying it, an awareness of what a classic is and how it should modify later work, is a doctrine of prime import for the study of literature,

---

[1] H. J. Rose, *The Eclogues of Vergil* (Cambridge University Press, 1942), p. 11.
[2] Some scholars believe that Theocritus found in Cos a school of pastoral poets, whom he imitated; but none of these poets has survived.

and particularly of modern literature; for it was during the Renaissance that the characteristic modern attitude to the ancients (the classics) was adopted and defined.

The critics of the Renaissance sometimes named the poet's chief requirements as being Art, Imitation, and Exercise; these requirements relate to the knowledge, study, and practice of the best models and methods of their medium. Another requirement, that of native genius, is also mentioned; unfortunately, not all practitioners of poetry have this, and the result was a good deal of poetry which depended upon critical laws and the pedantic imitation of detail. The consequence is a degree of tedium which has tended to bring the whole doctrine into disrepute as a dreary rhetorical substitute for poetry. This bad kind of Imitation is not confined to poetry; two great, but very different, humanists, Politian and Erasmus, were driven to complain of the absurdities into which those neo-Latinists fell who insisted upon the closest imitation of Cicero's style down to the last *esse videatur*. If we consider the degree to which Imitation penetrated the educational systems of the Renaissance and shaped the minds of all its writers we shall not be surprised that it occasionally had such dull and mechanical consequences. But not with the true scholar and poet who had laboured to understand it in ancient criticism and ancient literature—who understood that, although the letter may kill, the spirit will always give life, and that the doctrine was, among other things, a rational interpretation of the true relationship between the ancient and the modern world. Not, in fact, with Jonson, whose many and close imitations of Horace, Juvenal, and other poets require far more explanation than that they happened to have said already whatever it was he proposed to say. They were his guides, he said, not his commanders. Like Pope and Milton, he distinguished between the essence and the accident in his model; like Pope, he inhabited the critical and moral environment of the classic civilization without forfeiting citizenship of his own. He understood Imitation, and I have sometimes felt that it is through Jonson that we, in a rather different world, might hope best to understand it, and to understand how it can be held responsible on the one hand for mountains of dullness and on the other for *Volpone* and *Lycidas*. To conclude this digression, it may be said that a measure of the importance of the doctrine historically is the possibility of maintaining that the great seventeenth-century war of Ancients and Moderns was really fought on divergent interpretations of Imitation, in the widest sense of the term.

But Imitation, even in its narrowest rhetorical sense, is not a modern doctrine; it was current in the schools of Alexandria and Rome. The imitators of Theocritus did not, so far as is known, explore, using him as a guide; they reproduced. The best-known Greek pastoral poem outside Theocritus is the elegy written for Bion, a second-century Alexandrian poet, which was formerly, but it seems incorrectly, attributed to Moschus, under whose name it still goes. This poem is the next link in the chain connecting the First Idyll of Theocritus with Milton.[1] It is written in literary Doric, with many allusions to Theocritus. Its connexion with rustic life is purely formal. Bion is a shepherd-poet who had gladdened Pan with his pipe and his songs; pastoral details are given allegorical significances by now very obscure. These details, however, themselves descended from Theocritus, who was already an edited classic, and perhaps the subject of commentary not merely philological but of the laboured and far-fetched sort that Virgil was later to receive. In Moschus there are in full measure those artifices of allegory and myth and language which, when they are separate from the genuine emotional and intellectual interests of Pastoral, give the kind its reputation as a matter of frigid ornament. His *Lament* is, in fact, the kind of poem Johnson thought *Lycidas* was.

There is no need, for our purposes, to say any more of post-Theocritean Greek pastoral poetry, or, indeed, of the dependent Latin tradition. "It would seem," says H. J. Rose, "that by the time of Nero one of the stock rhetorical exercises, a thing of which every passman was supposed to be capable, was to describe a country feast or praise the life of the countryman."[2]

---

[1] It is not included here, for lack of a suitable English translation.
[2] *The Eclogues of Vergil* (Cambridge University Press, 1942), p. 16.

But meantime Virgil had intervened to change the merely rhetorical tradition.

Virgil seems to have gone straight to Theocritus for the model of his Imitation. He used him as a guide, not as a commander, and the result is poetry which it would be impossible to study as merely part of a rhetorical tradition. It is pastoral poetry which, for the first time, complicates the simple town-country contrast with serious reflections upon that contrast; which cultivates simplicity in decorated language; and which uses the country scene and rustic episode for allegorical purposes.

Robert Graves speaks of "the Virgilian pseudo-shepherd,"[1] and there would be no objection to the phrase if its tone were not slightly disparaging. The pastoral figures of the youthful Virgil are as sophisticated as his later Trojan emigrants. He places them in a remote paradise which he calls Arcadia, though in fact Arcadia was and is a rugged and unparadisial place; he could not use Sicily, as Theocritus had done, because it was over-familiar, though his Muses are the Pastoral Muses of Theocritus—*Sicelides Musæ*. Some of his most exquisite passages refer, as Mr Graves suggests, to vulgar and unpoetic contemporaries; he discusses contemporary agrarian questions; he flatters powerful men; he celebrates in exalted language homosexual love (though it should be remembered that this passion was not at the time regarded as peculiarly vicious). In fact, Virgil develops the hints of Theocritus in a very thorough way; he is derivative, and often translates (sometimes, it has been argued, even mistranslates) his master. Indeed, there seems to be a case for dismissing Virgil as a particularly 'artificial' writer of Pastoral, who simply "used the pastoral situation as a convenient rostrum for moral philosophy"[2] and for other even less reputable purposes. If the charge is fair it is a poor look-out for the remainder of the European bucolic corpus, in which Virgil is by far the most potent influence; one of the eclogues, the fourth, has perhaps the best claim of all pagan poetry to be considered, with respect to the whole culture of Christian Europe, seminal. Clearly this account of Virgil is incomplete.

[1] *The Common Asphodel* (Hamish Hamilton, 1949), p. 253. [2] Graves, *op. cit.*, p. 252.

Daphnis, the figure whom Virgil borrowed from Theocritus to do duty for Gallus, a friend lamenting his desertion by professional mistress, had a place in the Sicilian mythology that corresponds to that of various more familiar figures like Thomas the Rhymer, who took fairy brides under odd and stringent conditions. The similarity between the Greek Daphnis and the sensitive but worldly Gallus is of course somewhat remote, and Virgil does not force it, preferring to convey it by delicate allusion to the Theocritean character. But it is surely wrong to suggest that he was indifferent to the ultimate propriety of the analogy. A soldier-poet distressed by the defection of "an actress in low comedy who has left him to go off with a soldier"[1] may very well be celebrated in these terms, as the scheming monopolists of Elizabeth's court were glorified in great poetry as knights of chivalry. There is a basic similarity in the situation of Gallus and Daphnis. Again, the lament for the dead Daphnis in Eclogue V may be about Julius Cæsar; both were gods, and both were shepherds— Cæsar of his people. To adherents of Octavian Cæsar was also a saviour. The Pastoral is a leveller—it has to assume that "you can say everything about complex people by a complete consideration of simple people."[2] But in order to do so you must project polite complexities on the rude pastoral situation. When the peasant is nothing but a courtier in disguise, when the sillabubs are, as it were, pasteurized, there is nothing left but an emptily artificial Trianon masquerade. Despite Virgil's polite projections and his well-groomed hinds, he has not done this; he has left the situation intact, and the characteristically urban plight of Gallus, as well as the political murder of Julius Cæsar, yield a fuller significance when they are appraised in terms of a world schematically simple and sensitive to magic and poetry.

Virgil's is the supreme achievement of classical Pastoral; the virtues of his English rivals derive from a revaluation of the relationship between the actual town-country situation and the poetic tradition. He is perhaps as far removed from the facts of

[1] Graves, *op. cit.*, 253.
[2] W. Empson, *Some Versions of Pastoral* (Chatto and Windus, 1935), p. 137.

rural society as it is safe to go; his imitators support this suggestion by adopting a sterile pose even farther removed Virgil's influence is therefore not without its dangers; it is easier to reproduce the letter than the spirit. The best of later pastoral poetry arduously achieved the Virgilian feat of rediscovering the true impulse of the classical form.

The most influential of Virgil's eclogues is the fourth. This poem, with its hundred problems for the scholar, has a hundred virtues for the poet. It conquers new and legitimate territory for the Pastoral, and gives licence for a new and more authoritative tone—*paulo maiora canamus*. Above all, it suggests to other poets an unsuspected complexity in the 'pseudo-shepherd' and his associated imagery, a suggestion partly responsible for the profundity characteristic of so many later poems. The view of this eclogue generally held during the formative period of modern Pastoral was that, by employing the dicta of the Cumæan sibyl, Virgil had been enabled to prophesy the birth of Christ a few decades later, and some modern scholars have found traces of evidence that he was in fact indebted to the sibylline remains. But that does not matter. The enormous influence of Virgil in the Renaissance derives in some degree from his strange medieval reputation as a mage and pre-Christian prophet, and this reputation is undoubtedly dependent to some extent on the acceptance of the 'Messianic' Eclogue as a pagan prophecy of Christ—an acceptance made with the authority of St Augustine. In the official hierarchy of kinds Pastoral was always classed as one of the lower manifestations of poetry on account of the ostensible meanness of its milieu and characters; the Fourth Eclogue authorized an occasional 'unkindly' majesty of diction, of which later poets were to take advantage. The influence of this poem extends far beyond the pastoral kind, but within that kind it is often at work when there is no explicit reference to Virgil. It is the point at which the Golden Age of Saturn, the return of which the poet foresees, mingles with the Christian vision of man in paradisial state before Adam's sin, and after redemption is complete.

Virgil may therefore be regarded as a liberator of the Pastoral. The immensity of his achievement did nevertheless induce in his imitators a servility which, if unaccompanied by a proper sense of the fullness of that achievement and an awareness of what each poet needs to do again for himself, gave rise to the bad kind of imitation, which imitated the letter and not the spirit. This was not Virgil's fault. He did for Theocritus what he was to do for Homer; he established the classical poem and suggested many of its recognized variant forms. These remarks, which must conclude the scanty appraisal of the Eclogues which is all we have space for here, really say no more than that Pastoral would have been another, and a lesser, thing had Virgil never applied himself to the exploration of its problems and possibilities.

THE MODERN PASTORAL

The Middle Ages did not quite let the classical Pastoral die, for there were some clerkly imitations of the Virgilian eclogue.[1] But these were evidence only of the half-life which the memory of classical civilization led until the Renaissance. From the time of Petrarch we may say that the Pastoral experienced a revival characteristic of this movement in European history. Ancient Pastoral was studied and imitated, as the Apollo Belvedere was studied and imitated; it was not reproduced in facsimile, but modified by preconceptions, æsthetic and historical, and by medieval habits of thought. Virgil in particular, though the Renaissance is distinguished by its sense of his historical greatness, had not lost all those magical attributes credited him by the Middle Ages. Nor had the allegorical way of reading poetry yet succumbed to rationalist criticism and new, unmagical ways of looking at the world. Spenser's epic poem is "a continued allegory and dark conceit" partly because he believed that Virgil wrote thus, and partly because, for all his modernity, he was sufficiently of the Middle Ages to believe that the poet should hide his meaning under fair shows and even in obscurities. Pastoral was a genre critically regarded as

[1] W. W. Greg, *Pastoral Poetry and Pastoral Drama* (Sidgwick and Jackson, 1906), pp. 22 ff.

allegorical by nature and tradition, and as particularly apt for
veiled personal and ecclesiastical references. In this respect it is
like enough to Virgil, but even if we limit our attention to
work which is evidently imitative we find that the total
impression is quite un-Virgilian, as a sculpture by Michelangelo
is quite un-Greek. Even in close imitation the centuries hang a
deceptive veil between the artist and the object of his scrutiny.
And when the Pastoral becomes fully acceptable, a congenial
mode of Renaissance expression, it naturally broadens, changes,
takes on new tasks and neglects old ones, assumes the colours
and forms of new scenes and different peasants, absorbs the
tributes paid by primitive singers to Muses not Sicilian. It is
not my object to trace these developments historically, but to
describe as simply as may be the complex situation of Renais-
sance Pastoral. The best way to do this is to consider the theory
of the genre in relation to the practice of it, the modifications
due to related aspects of contemporary thought and society, and
the achievement of some of the great exponents of pastoral
poetry. The third of these objects should be achieved inciden-
tally in the course of working out the other two. Let us there-
fore consider briefly some of the things said about Pastoral by
the critics of the Renaissance.

RENAISSANCE THEORIES OF PASTORAL

A reasonable idea of the normal Renaissance definition of
Pastoral may be derived from Puttenham's remarks on the
Eclogue in his *Arte of English Poesie*:[1]

> the Poet devised the *Eglogue* . . . not of purpose to counterfait
> or represent the rusticall manner of loves and communication:
> but under the vaile of homely persons, and in rude speeches to
> insinuate and glaunce at greater matters, and such as perchance
> had not bene safe to have disclosed in any other sort, which may
> be perceived by the Eglogues of *Virgill*, in which are treated by
> figure matters of greater importance then the loves of *Titirus* and
> *Corydon*. These Eglogues came after to containe and enforme

[1] Edited by G. D. Willcock and A. Walker (Cambridge University Press,
1936), pp. 38–39.

morall discipline, for the amendment of mans behaviour, as be those of *Mantuan*[1] and other modern poets.

Puttenham, as usual, displays considerable common sense. He avoids the doctrine that the Pastoral is the oldest of genres because of its association with primitive rustic communities, and confines himself to a description of what it was really like in the hands of authors like Mantuan, who imitated Virgil and included topical references and ecclesiastical allegories. He insists on the paradox inherent in the kind; though rudely written, it deals with great matters. Decorum insists that the proper style for Pastoral is low, or rude, though there is precedent (invoked by Spenser and Milton) for higher flights. Sidney, who in his own *Arcadia* wrote a heroic Pastoral, a blend of two kinds, pretends in his *Apologie for Poetrie* that Pastoral is a possible weak point in the defences of poetry, where its opponents may choose to assault it, "for perchance where the hedge is lowest they will soonest leap over." Webbe says that, despite its lowness, the Pastoral can offer much profit-able delight, and in this he includes both flattery and inveighing against abuses. Although poets preferred to use a decorative licence, decorum nevertheless insisted that Pastoral, like Satire, belonged to the base style, "to be holden within their tether by a low, myld and simple maner of utterance, creeping rather then clyming, & marching rather then mounting upwardes." This tenet explains in a general way the provincialisms and archaisms conscientiously used by Spenser in his Eclogues. Although they descend ultimately from the Doric of Theocritus, it is not even certain that Spenser knew the Greek poet at first hand; he is showing his familiarity with the laws of poetry and the practice of the best modern French poets.

The most thorough examination of the status of the kind was

[1] The *Eclogues* of Baptista Spagnuoli, known as Mantuanus, were published in 1498, and won him a great reputation as a Latin poet. His bucolics were standard in the Renaissance; when Holofernes misquotes him in *Love's Labour's Lost*, IV, ii, 95-96, the implication is that Holofernes is a dunce. Mantuan was one of Spenser's many models in *The Shepheardes Calender*, and hundreds of other eclogues are indebted to him. He is one of the authorities for the attack on unworthy pastors in *Lycidas*. The earliest English writers to be affected by him were Barclay and Googe. He is represented in this book by one of his Eclogues in the translation of Turberville.

Such arguments are of little interest save in that they show a certain concern about the historical justification of this apparently somewhat arbitrary form. Although Guarini shows some independence of the strict classicist interpretation of the kind, he is a poet of the second or third rank, and shows no real understanding of the true philosophic importance of the kind, or of the peculiar contribution which his age was able to make to it. His countryman Tasso, in his *Aminta*, is much closer to such an understanding, and in France the kind was patiently and successfully investigated; but it is not until we consider English Pastoral that we can recognize an appreciation, almost intuitive and certainly remarkably complete, of pastoral poetry as it was shaped by the pressure of the age's thought and sensibility. For this understanding we look not to critics, but to poets.

EARLY ENGLISH PASTORAL FORMS

One might expect that, just as Theocritus found in Sicily or in Cos shepherd-songs which strongly appealed to his sophistication, so later poets, reviving the tradition of Theocritus, would be aware of a native and primitive song which seemed already to be touching upon the pastoral theme.

The Twenty-seventh Idyll of Theocritus is, by modern standards, indecent, and in Dryden's version coarse (but amusing, as Dryden frequently is in his music-hall mood); like most of Dryden's editors, I have refrained from reprinting it, but chiefly because it is a mere travesty of the original. The importance of the poem lies in its resemblance to the later *pastourelle*, and it has, though with doubtful justice, been called the model of that medieval form. It is, however, interesting to speculate on the possible rustic origins of this saucy love-encounter, and permissible to guess that they were similar to those of the *pastourelle*.

The *pastourelle* is a lyric of courtly origin; in it a poet describes how, as he was riding in the country, he met a shepherd-girl (not an Arcadian nymph, but a real peasant) and made love to

that undertaken by the Italian dramatist Guarini, his supporte
and his opponents, in a long controversy about Guarin
pastoral drama, *Il Pastor Fido*, towards the end of the sixteen
century. Guarini had been challenged by a certain Jasone
Nores, who held that pastoral drama was socially and mora
useless, and also that it contravened the ancient laws of poeti
Pastoral, said de Nores, was not only useless to town-dwellei
but might even do harm by inducing them to live in tl
country; if the pastoral life was unfavourably treated, the
harm was done to the rustics as well. He thought shepherd
particularly poor subjects for drama, since they were lazy an
lacking elaborate manners and customs. The Ancients avoide
these difficulties; for one thing, their pastoral poems were a
short eclogues which did not infringe the laws of probability
or make shepherds talk like princes or philosophers. Guarini'
reply is interesting because he was forced to make explicit th
rationale of Pastoral. He relies upon the historical argument
that the pastoral society is the earliest of all, and that when
every one was a shepherd there must have been shepherd kings,
shepherd poets, shepherd warriors, and so on, so that in
writing about shepherds one can write freely about the con-
cerns of the modern world. They are all reflected in a very
simple form in the hypothetical pastoral community. He is at
some pains to explain that love, a special concern of Renaissance
Pastoral, can be easily and pleasantly studied in this context.[1]

[1] Pastoral drama as such has been excluded from this collection; it is too
bulky to be properly represented. But it is none the less an important Renaissance
development of Pastoral. When an extract from it seems to make an important
point about Pastoral I have not hesitated to use it.

The other great formal development of Renaissance Pastoral was the prose
verse-and-prose romance. The chief writers in this kind were Sannazaro (14
1530), in Italian; Montemayor (1520–61), in Spanish; and Sidney in Engl
Their starting-point was the Hellenistic romance, and generally speaking they
more concerned with narrative values than with specifically pastoral values. T
have their place in the history of the novel, and in the history of Epic, as Sidn
comments in the *Apologie* suggest. Sannazaro, with his polished melancholy
his insistence on the "pathetic fallacy" whereby he makes the whole of Na
lament with the unhappy lover, was enormously fashionable, and Sidney i
borrowed his title, *Arcadia*. He was probably very well known in Eng
So was Montemayor, who provided Shakespeare with at least one, and prol
two, plot-ideas. Sidney was likewise used, but was equally thought of
pastoral poet, and his death stimulated a large number of pastoral elegies i
tradition of Theocritus, Moschus, and Virgil.

her, sometimes successfully and sometimes not, often bringing the whole of the girl's family into action against him.[1] In fact, the poem is a knightly *vante*, a boastful account of the poet's amorous triumph, gained sometimes by his overwhelming attractiveness, sometimes by the promise of reward, and sometimes by force. Occasionally the girl resists and overthrows her seducer; this may be a piquant courtly variant, or, more probably, a survival from an older form. The best surviving *pastourelles* are Provençal, but they occur also in French, Italian, and English. In all languages they preserve certain easily recognizable structural characteristics, of which the most obvious is the opening device: "As I was riding along, I met . . ." But they display a great variety of style; in Provençal they are very sophisticated, and prone to deal with the metaphysics of love; in French they are more versatile, and coarser; in English disappointingly few survive,[2] but there were probably large numbers of them, and their influence can be seen in much popular poetry of the Elizabethan and later periods, down to the present time. I have included in the present selection several examples of the original *pastourelle*, of Elizabethan popular adaptations, and of literary versions, from Henryson to Drayton.

There are good grounds for supposing that this form originated with the rustics themselves, and described an encounter between a clever maiden and a knightly or royal would-be seducer, whom she baffles either by a trick or in debate. The court poet appreciated the latent indecencies in the form, and exploited it with the defeat of the courtier transformed into a victory. Later the form reverted to the folk. It began as a rustic revenge on the rich, developed into a

---

[1] This account of the *pastourelle*, the importance of which form is probably still underrated in the history of Pastoral, is very compressed, and omits to mention that authorities have disagreed fundamentally on the question of its origins ever since the publication of Jeanroy's *Origines de la Poésie Lyrique en France* (1904) and Gaston Paris's vast review of the book. There is a good account of the situation in W. P. Jones's *The Pastourelle* (Oxford University Press, 1931).

[2] Any reader interested in pursuing the English *pastourelle* should consult H. E. Sandison's *The Chanson d'Aventure in Middle English* (Bryn Mawr, 1913). See also E. K. Chambers, *Sir Thomas Wyatt and other Studies* (Sidgwick and Jackson, 1933), pp. 46–97, 146–180.

courtly *vante* at the expense of the ignoble, and survived as a poetic theme interesting in itself to the primitive and the cultivated alike. In its original form it would scarcely concern itself with a pastoral *décor*, or with the ethics of love, but in its courtly transmutation it emphasized the contrast between cultivated and natural behaviour (as all Pastoral does) by comparing the high-flown love-affairs of the court with the easy gratifications to be found among the peasantry; and it took on a townsman's interest in pastoral scenery. The *pastourelle* is a manifestation of a characteristic movement of European culture which once produced the Idylls of Theocritus, and later the unclassical, independent, medieval Pastoral of Northern Europe. Its importance (and in this it is not alone among medieval song-forms) cannot be measured in terms of its visible effect upon later forms of Pastoral; its vitality, its continued existence in popular song, and its close relationship to the social status of the countryman provide pastoral poetry in the Elizabethan age with harmonics which greatly increase its quality and range.

Nor is this the whole story of the *pastourelle*.

> Ase I me rod this ender day
> By grene wode to seche play,
> Mid herte I thohte al on a may,
> Swetest of alle thinge.

This 'may' is the Virgin Mary. The *pastourelle* was often adapted to her worship. Some examples survive in both secular and religious forms.[1] Some are, so to speak, religious parodies of secular poems, working on the assumption that the imagery of physical love applies by analogy to spiritual love. "Let us sing," says one poet, "not of Mariette, but of Mary. Let us leave these old *pastourelles*, and make new songs of the flower whose praises angels sing night and day." Sometimes the religious versions derive from a minor variant of the *pastourelle* in which the narrator is merely a spectator, and sometimes they have obvious connexions with the learned Latin lyric, but there is no doubt that they are closely connected with

[1] See E. K. Chambers and F. Sidgwick, *Early English Lyrics* (Sidgwick and Jackson, 1937), p. 287.

a literary form which has for its most distinctive feature an aristocratic contempt for the serf. Love is a main pastoral theme, and it is already complex because of the implied contrast between natural love and love regulated by artificial codes; this complexity is further deepened when physical love can, with so little adaptation, figure forth spiritual love. During the Renaissance this well-established convention is strengthened by Neo-Platonic teaching, which systematizes the relationship between spiritual and physical love and beauty, as Spenser does in his Hymns; and, further to enrich it, there was always in men's minds the *Song of Solomon*, which provided all the necessary authority for expressing mystical love in erotic imagery. The influence of this work, and the vast amount of devout and ingenious commentary which it had accumulated during the centuries, is evident throughout the Renaissance, and particularly in pastoral poetry, though often it is very subtle; a matter of the suggestiveness of language rather than of explicit reference.

The most remarkable poet to blend the language of Pastoral and its primitive analogues with the erotic imagery of mysticism was St John of the Cross, a sixteenth-century Spanish poet whose work does not appear in English translation during our period, though it may have been familiar in the original to many English poets who could read Spanish, like Sidney and his friends, Drummond, Vaughan, Lord Herbert, Marvell, and others. It was also available in a very fine French translation. St John's *Cantico Espiritual* might be taken as demonstrating the full powers of Renaissance Pastoral when it used the advantages conferred by its special vocabulary.[1] It is worth noticing that St John was susceptible not only to the influence of Andalusian folk-song and allegorical readings of the *Canticles*, but also to that of courtly poets like Garcilaso de la Vega, the young Spanish poet who is sometimes compared with Sidney, and who was in his turn under Italian influence. This blend of interests is not essentially different from that of

[1] For a literal translation see E. Allison Peers, *Complete Works of St John of the Cross* (3 vols.) (Burns Oates, 1943). There is a good recent verse translation by Roy Campbell (Harvill Press, 1951). The best short study of this poet in English is, I think, that by Gerald Brenan in *Horizon*, 89 (June 1947), pp. 324-356.

the Elizabethan writers of Pastoral, despite the dominance of more secular concerns in their work. It is not until we come to Marvell that we find among the English a poet whose talent (however different in other respects) lent itself to the exploration of the ambiguities in the imagery of love with anything like the intensity of St John, and even then we think of Marvell primarily as an exquisite master of tone and imagery rather than as a religious poet. But although there is no one like St John, he does demonstrate, as I say, the extraordinary range and power of the revived Pastoral in the hands of a master.

The interchangeability of secular and religious poetry was known in the Middle Ages, and affected the early *pastourelle*. But this is not the only point at which pastoral images may assume religious significance. I have already mentioned that the pervasive pastoral language of the Gospels, which has been embodied in the nomenclature of the Church's officials and responsibilities, early led to the use of the Eclogue as a means of criticizing the administration of the Church. Petrarch, Mantuan, Spenser, Milton, and many others availed themselves of this convenient coincidence. The simplicity of shepherds, which was so evident in their loves, had won for them the distinction of being the first men to hear of a divine birth. That this honour was not forgotten by English shepherds is proved by the exquisite nativity play of the Wakefield Shepherds (*Secunda Pastorum*), and by the charming little poem which appears as No. 3 in this collection. The existence of such work, side by side with the *pastourelle* tradition and the religious use of pastoral imagery, might have ensured that the modern world would develop its own version of Pastoral. In fact it did so, and blended these elements with the classical tradition. The Renaissance, which saw the beginning of the change to something like a modern town-life, had its own nostalgia for simplicity, its own deep though ambiguous feelings about the countryside and its inhabitants, its own myth of the natural man, and his special sympathy with created Nature. Some of these ideas and feelings were very ancient; but some of them were distinctively modern, and this complex of old and new we must now consider.

NATURE IN THE RENAISSANCE PASTORAL

When Marvell, at the end of our period, wrote about a mower's hatred of gardens, he was representing the world of Nature, the uncultivated, the pure, by the untamed, uncorrupted fields; and the world of Art, the civilized, the cultivated, the sphere in which men had meddled with Nature, by the garden. He was, of course, simplifying for his own purposes a difficult philosophical opposition between Art and Nature, but he is none the less putting, with considerable subtlety, a point of view which was frequently expressed in the Renaissance, and which recurs with some persistence in the history of our literature. Probably the contrast between town and country—the social aspect of the great Art-Nature antithesis which is philosophically the basis of pastoral literature—was more poignant at that time than it has been since. London was becoming a modern metropolis, with a distinctively metropolitan ethos, before the eyes of its citizens, who were by tradition and even by upbringing much more rural than any town-dweller can now be. The plays of Jonson, and some of Shakespeare's too, contain many references to the new morality, the new men, the new social standing of the commercial classes, the growth of wealth not based upon the soil; and the death of an old order which hated usury and did not imagine that cakes and ale were hostile to virtue. The great Astrophel himself, like many other courtiers, was deeply in debt, and consciously living the life of a dead and lamented epoch—a kind of golden age of chivalry—in the age which saw the inauguration of modern capitalist finance. Puritanism, at its best a way of life and worship worthy of fine minds, was legitimately associated, by Jonson and others, with a tendency to hypocritical self-aggrandizement and to a mean interference with the traditional pleasures and customs of others. Essentially an urban growth, it was suspicious of country matters, and its hatred for the maypole and its associated sports, which Puritans rightly conjectured to be descended from pagan religious rites, was logical in a religious attitude which also condemned the drama. The satirist looked about him in a town which was turning into a metropolis, and observed that its citizen body was stratifying into new classes, actively discontented with the old dispensation, and living under a municipal authority predominantly Puritan. The court was held to be corrupt and affected; the increase in luxury and artificiality visible in the lives of courtier and burgher alike deeply troubled Jonson, who found that the language was imitating "the public riot." When Jonson turned from Satire to Pastoral, at the end of his career, he lamented the death of an order as old, he thought, as the countryside; a way of life in which generosity, in the fullest sense of that word, accompanied a purity of life and pleasure which the Juvenalian town had exchanged for disease, obscurantism, affectation, and bigotry.[1] The moving passage from his *Sad Shepherd* which I have included in this collection is one of the themes which occur frequently in Elizabethan Pastoral.

The contrast between town and country is frequently expressed in the literature of the period. There was a tendency to laugh at country folk, and this was a traditional activity; but there was also a tendency to idealize them. Overbury writes of a milkmaid:

> The golden ears of corn fall and kiss her feet when she reaps them, as if they wished to be bound and led prisoners by the same hand that felled them. Her breath is her own, which scents all the year long of June, like a new made haycock. She makes her hands hard with labour, and her heart soft with pity: and when winter evenings fall early (sitting at her merry wheel) she sings a defiance to the giddy wheel of fortune. . . . The garden and bee-hive are all her physic and chirurgery, and she lives the longer for it. . . . Thus lives she, and all her care is she may die in the spring-time, to have store of flowers stuck upon her winding-sheet.[2]

Something of the Elizabethan sense of the urgent beauty of the

[1] Characteristically, Jonson chose the Robin Hood legend as the theme of his *Sad Shepherd*. This hero of the dead golden world of England echoes throughout Elizabethan Pastoral.

[2] This Character, with others of the same kind, may be found in J. Dover Wilson's *Life in Shakespeare's England* (Cambridge University Press, 1925; Penguin, 1949).

country life emerges in Nicholas Breton's dialogue, "The Courtier and the Countryman." The Countryman speaks:

> Now for the delight of our eyes, we have the May—painting of the earth, with flowers of dainty colours, and delicate sweets: we have the berries, the cherries, the peas and the beans, the plums and the codlings, in the month of June: in July the pears and the apples, the wheat, the rye, the barley and the oats, the beauty of the wide fields, and the labours with delight and mirth, and merry cheer at the coming home of the harvest cart. We have, again, in our woods the birds singing: in the pastures the cow lowing, the ewe bleating, the foal neighing, which profit and pleasure makes us better music than an idle note and a worse ditty, though I highly do commend music, when it is in the right key. Again, we have young rabbits that in a sunny morning sit washing their faces, while as I have heard there are certain old conies that in their beds sit painting of their faces. . . .

To all this, the worsted Courtier replies, "I can the better bear with your humour because it is more natural than artificial, yet could I wish you would not so clownify your wit, as to bury your understanding under a clod of earth." Which earns him the reproof, "Now for your Nature and Art, I think better of a natural Art than an artificial Nature"; for this is a pastoral countryman, who understands the terms of the town. We might note what he has to say about love, the passion which occupies so much space in Elizabethan pastoral poetry:

> And for love, if it be in the world, I think it is in the country, for where envy, pride, and malice and jealousy makes buzzes in men's brains, what love can be in their hearts, howsoever it slip from their tongues? No, no, our turtles ever fly together, our swans ever swim together, and our loves live and die together. Now if such love be among you, it is worthy to be made much of, but if you like today and loathe tomorrow, if all your love be to laugh and lie down, or to hope of gain or reward, that is none of our love. . . .

Here is the Golden Age envisaged in the countryside, all the more poignantly because the countryside is still very near one's own doorstep. This tension between town and country seems to be productive of the special kind of literature we call Pastoral. Poets were interested in the contrast between the wild and the cultivated. But their interest was not dependent entirely upon social changes and the discovery of ancient Pastoral; the interest of Renaissance poets in Nature was stimulated by the discovery of countries in which men were living in a state of nature, unaffected by Art, and outside the scope of Grace. Anyone who turns to Montaigne's essay *Of Cannibals* may read an account of one sensitive and subtle reaction to the news from the New World. The travellers came back with their accounts of the natives, or even brought the savages back with them—Montaigne conversed with some. But, because there were two opinions about natural men, one holding that they were virtuous because unspoilt, and the other that they were vicious because they belonged to what the theologians called the state of nature as opposed to the state of grace, the travellers emphasized the evidence which suited the theory they favoured; some reported the New World savages to live in perfect concord and happiness (as Montaigne says they did), but others found them treacherous and devil-worshipping. Both these views fell in neatly with preconceptions already held and already expressed in literature and philosophy. On the one hand there is the classic expression of Golden Age happiness in the much-imitated chorus of Tasso's *Aminta*; this could easily be extended to the 'naturalist' libertine poetry of Donne and Carew and Randolph, which Marvell subtly countered in his poetry. On the other hand there is the deeper examination of Nature and its true relationship to Art and Grace which Spenser in *The Faerie Queene*, Shakespeare in his last comedies, and Milton in *Comus* undertook. Each of these poets sometimes presents Nature for what it is—that state from which men, by nurture and grace, have been led away. The generous 'salvage man' in Spenser is so by reason of the cultivated stock from which he sprang; his nature is improved by the action of grace. The King's sons in *Cymbeline* cannot suppress their nobility, and Caliban is natural and vile in contrast with Miranda, who has the virtues of nobility; *nobile*, it was believed, was a contraction of *non vile*. Comus rules over the realm of Nature, and attempts to deprave the lady, who is clad in the magical armour of nobility and chastity, by using the very arguments of the 'naturalist.'

This is only a very hurried glimpse of the serious philosophic element which penetrates the English Pastoral of the Renaissance. In the longer poems, and in the plays, it is rarely far from the surface—as, for example, in Fletcher's *The Faithful Shepherdess*. It mingles with serious attempts to reproduce the ancient tradition in the modern Eclogue by inventing a native Doric and adapting the equipment of the Sicilian shepherd to his English equivalent; with studious adaptations and translations of modern authors like Mantuan, Sannazaro, Marot, Ronsard, Montemayor, Tasso, and Guarini. Every device of literary Pastoral is found in some form or other in the poetry of this period; every use to which the kind can be put is exploited, from the ecclesiastical allegory which Googe derived from Mantuan to the elegies which Bryskett and Milton derived from Moschus. All the moral and scientific interests of the time found expression in the form, and the age's passion for allegory found the Pastoral a particularly congenial form of expression. In Spenser alone one may study almost every aspect of Renaissance Pastoral.[1] It is generally acknowledged that the publication of *The Shepheardes Calender*, in 1579, was one of the most important events in the history of English poetry, and not only in the history of Pastoral. In this work Spenser, while not ignoring the charms of the English pastoral scene, which often gave the work of his contemporaries a fresh, unstudied charm, brought into the tradition of English poetry the influence of every great pastoral poet of the past, from Theocritus to the modern French poets. As E.K. says, after a roll-call of the bucolic poets of the past, Spenser follows their "footing" everywhere, "yet so as few, but they be wel sented, can trace him out." Spenser's imagination worked freely within the classical tradition, which he explored in depth, but he was also capable of sustained efforts in heroic Pastoral of a sort not contemplated by the ancient poets. In the Sixth Book of the *Faerie Queene*, which is the Legend of Courtesy, we have the richest and most impressive example of a distinctively English development of the pastoral tradition, which was later imitated by Shakespeare and Milton.

[1] See the very valuable appendices in Volume I of the Minor Poems in the *Variorum Spenser* (ed. Greenlaw and others) (Oxford University Press, 1933–47).

But it is not only the great who engage us. Hundreds of poets wrote Pastoral in one form or another, and the general level of achievement was almost incredibly high; never had Pastoral seemed a more natural mode of song. And when its summer had passed, and poets had for a while contented themselves with re-examining the formal Eclogue, there came Herrick, who seemed to look back on all the richness of the Elizabethan Pastoral and distil from it a nostalgic essence, and Marvell, whose handful of poems seem to sum up the whole story of the English Pastoral, inexhaustibly rich in their solemn undertones.

With Marvell the story really ends, for the later Pastoral lived in a quite different atmosphere, and in a quite different relationship to its readers. Marvell's lyrics, whenever they were written, were not published until the tradition in which they existed was already being forgotten. Dryden's translations of Theocritus are pert, as Theocritus never was; the true impulse of rustic Pastoral petered out; it was something the Giant Race had understood. The Pastorals of Pope show how much and how little the new poetry could do in this kind; in Pope there is a union, impossible a century earlier, between the practice and the academic theory of Pastoral. The eighteenth century excelled in the mock-Pastoral, which is a kind of pantomime following the great play. The Augustans were often conscious of their defects, and Pope understood the significance of his addiction to mock-Epic; the *Dunciad*, he said, was a kind of satyr-play appended to the great trilogy of Homer, Virgil, and Milton. It is not too difficult to see an analogy with mock-Pastoral. Human needs had, perhaps, not changed; but certain things of importance had reduced the relevance of the old Pastoral. London had lost the country; its maypole, as Pope observed, had been taken down. The literary and philosophical preoccupations of the Renaissance poets had largely given way to a new, or newly expressed, set of problems. The old poetry, and everything that gave it its peculiar richness, had been largely forgotten by the time Johnson expressed his rational objections to *Lycidas*.

CONCLUSION

To some extent, the conditions under which the pastoral poetry of the English Renaissance was written were similar to those which give rise to the first pastoral poetry in Theocritus; but many other factors worked upon it to make it different, though of the same 'kind.' For one thing, the Renaissance poets were aware of their great ancient progenitors, as Virgil had been aware of Theocritus. Not only was Imitation a part of their accepted rhetorical and educational system; it was also a leading principle in their poetic, it controlled their attitude to their Art. The best poets would imitate the spirit which gave life, and adapt the work of their masters to a new world. This new world was not unconscious of the ages of poetry which filled the time between Theocritus and itself; during that time there had been other kinds of poetry relevant to the pastoral kind, and the language of shepherds had been applied variously to greater concerns, notably to the government of the Church, and the worship of God and the Blessed Virgin. Pastoral poetry concerns itself with the relationship between Nature and Art, and Renaissance views of Nature had been enlarged by new knowledge. The object of the pastoral poet's contemplation was no longer merely the happy peasant or shepherd, but the true natural man of the New World. Old modes of thinking about Nature and Art did, however, survive, and led a lively existence in the thought of the Renaissance. Montaigne's reaction to the accounts he had heard of the New World and its inhabitants were conditioned by all he knew of the old pastoral myths of the Golden Age. A 'naturalist' philosophy induced poets to portray that age as hedonistic and sinless, though wanton; in reply, the more moral poets asserted supernatural values, and described Nature as corrupted by the sin of Adam. Furthermore, even more keenly than Theocritus, perhaps, the English poets of the Renaissance found a pure though nostalgic pleasure in contemplating the life of the countryside. This is, in essence, the same delight that all ages know, and which is so keenly expressed in Chaucer. Country sports and country loves were interesting for their own sake, as well as being a kind of comment on the sophistication of the city. Flowers were valued not only as decorations for the laureate hearse of a dead shepherd-poet, but for their own beauty. Although, in thoughtful mood, the poet might think of Nature as God's Book of the Creatures, the more usual reaction of the Elizabethan poet is one of spontaneous pleasure. This pleasure, and the nostalgia of which I have spoken, combine with the critical and philosophical elements in the pastoral tradition to produce the rich profundity of English pastoral poetry. It may be that mere fashion had something to do with the extraordinary profusion of pastoral lyrics; many of the poems in *Englands Helicon*, which is heavily represented in this collection, were converted into Pastoral for the purpose of the miscellany. But it should not be assumed that such tinkering must be written off as a simple commercial concession to fashion. The poems are changed in tone, and the demand for the change is an interesting comment on the function of Pastoral in the Elizabethan poetic world. Doubtless there are many poems which would do as well were the properties and the speakers not in the least Pastoral; but we cannot condemn the worthier poets because lesser men abused the form.

The poems printed below are intended to give some impression of that lost richness, of that complexity and range of interests, which characterized the heyday of the English Pastoral. I have taken Henryson and Dryden as my limits; consequently I have had to omit some poems I wanted to include—on account of the lack of translations of desirable works during this period. The advantages, however, are clear; there may be one or two doubtful cases, but there are very few poems here which do not belong in their own right to the finest period of English pastoral poetry. No one could complain that there is too little to choose from. There are as many varieties of Pastoral as, in the catalogue of Polonius, there were varieties of drama—heroic, imitative, ecclesiastical, medieval, romantic—all of them turning upon the poles of Art and Nature. There is much great poetry, and a copious supply of elegant and mellifluous minor poetry. I have tried to represent all the varieties of English pastoral poetry, great and small, in this book.

NOW SPRINKES THE SPRAI

Nou sprinkes the sprai,
Al for love icche am so sick
That slepen I ne mai.

Als I me rode this endre dai
   O mi playinge,
Seih I hwar a litel mai
   Bigan to singge:
     "The clot him clingge!
Wai es him i love-longinge
A Sal libben ai!"
   Nou sprinkes etc.

Son icche herde that mirie note,
   Thider I drogh;
I fonde hire in an herber swot,
   Under a bogh,
   With joie inogh.
Son I asked: "Thou mirie mai,
Hwi sinkestou ai?"
   Nou sprinkes etc.

endre dai, Just passed.
mai, Maiden.
The clot him clingge! May the clay cling to him. (I wish he were dead.)
Wai es him i love-longinge
A Sal libben ai!   (Paraphrase) Unhappy is he who must always live in
                love-longing.
Son icche herde, As soon as I heard.
herber swot, Scented arbour.
Hwi sinkestou ai? Why do you sing so?

Then answerde that maiden swote
    Midde wordes fewe:
"Mi lemman me haves bihot
    Of love trewe:
    He chaunges anewe.
    Yif I mai, it shal him rewe
Bi this dai."
        Nou sprinkes etc.
            ANONYMOUS (fourteenth century)

Mi lemman me haves bihot, My love promised me.   *Yif*, If.

2

ROBYN AND MAKYNE

Robene sat on a gud grene hill,
    Kepand a flok of fe:
Mirry Makyne said him till,
    "Robene, thow rew on me;
I haif thee luvit lowd and still,
    Thir yeiris two or thre;
My dule in dern bot gif thow dill,
    Dowtless but dreid I de."

Robene ansert, "Be the Rood,
    Nathing of lufe I knaw,
But keipis my scheip undir yone wude,
    Lo! quhair thay raik on raw;
Quhat hes marrit thee in thy mude,
    Makyne, to me thow schaw?
Or quhat is lufe, or to be lude,
    Fane wald I leir that law."

Kepand, Keeping.   *fe*, Sheep.   *him till*, To him.
thow rew on me, Have pity on me.   *lowd and still*, Aloud and silently.
My dule in dern bot gif thow dill, Unless you assuage my secret woe.
Dowtless but dreid I de, Without doubt I shall die.
Rood, Cross.   *Lo! quhair thay raik on raw*, Range in row.
Quhat hes marrit thee in thy mude, What is on your mind?
lude, Loved.   *leir*, Learn.

"At luvis lair gife thow will leir,
　Tak thair ane A, B, C;
Be heynd, courtass, and fair of feir,
　Wyse, hardy, and fre:
So that no denger do thee deir,
　Quhat dule in dern thow dre;
Preiss thee with pane at all poweir,
　Be pacient, and previe."

Robene answerit hir agane,
　"I wait nocht quhat is lufe;
Bot I haif mervell incertane,
　Quhat makis thee this wanrufe.
The weddir is fair, and I am fane,
　My scheip gois haill aboif,
And we wald play us in this plane,
　They wald us bayth reproif."

"Robene, tak tent unto my taill,
　And wirk all as I reid,
And thow sall haif my hairt all haill,
　Eik and my maidinheid.
Sen God sendis bute for baill,
　And for murnyng remeid;
In dern with thee, bot gif I daill,
　Dowtles I am bot deid."

"Makyne, to morne this ilka tyde,
　And ye will meit me heir,
Peraventure my scheip ma gang besyd,
　Quhill we haif liggit full neir;
Bot mawgre haif I and I byd,
　Fra thay begin to steir;
Quhat lyis on hairt I will not hyd;
　Makyne, than mak gud cheir."

---

lair, Lose.　　*heynd*, Gentle.　　*feir*, Demeanour.　　*deir*, Daunt.　　*dre*, Suffer.
Preiss, Exert.　　*wanrufe*, Uneasy.　　*My scheip gois haill aboif*, Healthy on the hills.
And, If.　　*tak tent*, Pay attention.　　*And wirk all as I reid*, Do exactly as I say.
bute for baill, Remedy for loss.
In dern with thee, bot gif I daill, Have dealings with thee in secret.　　*liggit*, Lain.
mawgre, Ill-will.　　*Fra thay begin to steir*, If I stay when they begin to stray.

"Robene, thou reivis me roiff and rest,
    I luve bot thee allone."
"Makyne, adew! the sone gois west,
    The day is neir hand gone."
"Robene, in dule I am so drest,
    That lufe wilbe my bone."
"Ga lufe, Makyne, quhair evir thow list,
    For lemman I luve none."

"Robene, I stand in sic a styll
    I sicht, and that full sair."
"Makyne, I haif bene heir this quhyle,
    At hame God gif I wair."
"My huny, Robene, talk ane quhyll,
    Gif thow will do na mair."
"Makyne, sum uthir man begyle,
    For hamewart I will fair."

Robene on his wayis went,
    Als licht as leif of tre;
Mawkyne murnit in hir intent,
    And trowd him nevir to se.
Robene brayd attour the bent;
    Than Makyne cryit on hie,
"Now ma thow sing, for I am schent,
    Quhat alis lufe at me?"

Mawkyne went hame withowttin faill
    Full wery eftir cowth weip:
Than Robene in a ful fair daill
    Assemblit all his scheip.
Be that sum parte of Mawkynis aill
    Out-throw his hairt cowd creip;
He fallowit hir fast thair till assaill,
    And till hir tuke gude keep.

reivis me roiff, Robbest me of peace.   *drest*, Woeful.   *bone*, Bane.
lemman, Lover.   *styll*, Condition.
sicht, Sigh.   *intent*, Desire.   *brayd attour the bent*, Strode over the brake.
schent, Destroyed.   *Quhat alis lufe at me?* What has love against me?
cowth weip, Did weep.   *Be that*, By that time.   *aill*, Pain.
thair till assaill, To encounter her.   *tuke gude keep*, Paid heed.

"Abyd, abyd, thow fair Makyne,
    A word for ony thing;
For all my luve it salbe thyne,
    Withowttin departing.
All haill! thy harte for till haif myne,
    Is all my cuvating;
My scheip to morne, quhill houris nyne,
    Will neid of no keping."

"Robene, thow hes hard soung and say,
    (In gestis and storeis auld,)
'The man that will nocht quhen he may,
    Saill haif nocht quhen he wald.'
I pray to Jesu, every day
    Mot eik thair cairis cauld,
That first preissis with thee to play,
    Be firth, forrest, or fawld."

"Makyne, the nicht is soft and dry,
    The weddir is warme and fair,
And the grene woid rycht neir us by
    To walk attour all quhair:
Their ma na janglour us espy,
    That is to lufe contrair;
Thairin, Makyne, bath ye and I,
    Unsene we ma repair."

"Robene, that warld is all away,
    And quyt brocht till ane end,
And nevir agane thairto perfay,
    Sall it be as thow wend:
For of my pane thow maid it play,
    And all in vane I spend:
As thow hes done, sa sall I say,
    Murne on, I think to mend."

quhill, Until ('while' in modern Scots).   *gestis*, Romance.
Mot eik, Might increase.   *preissis*, Attempt.
firth, Enclosure.   *fawld*, Open pasture.   *quhair*, Everywhere.
Their ma na janglour us espy, No gossip can see us there.
erfay, Parfois, by my faith.

"Makyne, the howp of all my heill,
    My hairt on thee is sett,
And evir mair to thee be leill,
    Quhill I may leif but lett;
Never to faill, as utheris feill,
    Quhat grace that evir I gett."
"Robene, with thee I will nocht deill;
    Adew! for thus we mett."

Makyne went hame blyth annewche,
    Attour the holttis hair;
Robene murnit, and Makyne lewche;
    Scho sang, he sichit sair;
And so left him, bayth wo and wreuch,
    In dolour and in cair,
Kepand his hird under a huche,
    Amangis the holtis hair.

ROBERT HENRYSON (fifteenth century)

heill, Health.	*leill*, True.	*lett*, Without cease.
annewche, Enough.	*holttis hair*, Grey hills.	
lewche, Laughed.	*sichit*, Sighed.	*wreuch*, Dejected.	*huche*, Cliff.

3

CAN I NOT SYNG BUT 'HOY'?

Can I not syng but 'Hoy,'
Whan the joly shepard mad so mych joy?

The shepard upon a hill he satt;
He had on hym hys tabard and hys hat,
Hys tarbox, hys pype and, hys flagat;
Hys name was called Joly Joly Wat,
    For he was a gud herdes boy.
        Ut hoy!
For in hys pype he mad so mych joy
Can I not syng but hoy!

tabard, Short coat.	*flagat*, Flagon.

The shepard upon a hill was layd;
Hys dog to hys gyrdyll was tayd;
He had not slept but a lytill brayd,
But '*Gloria in excelsis*' was to hym sayd.
        Ut hoy!
  For in hys pype he mad so mych joy.
                Can I not, etc.

The shepard on a hill he stode;
Round about hym hys shepe they yode;
He put hys hond under hys hode,
He saw a star as rede as blod.
        Ut hoy!
  For in hys pype he mad so mych joy.
                Can I not, etc.

The shepard sayd anon ryght,
'I will go se yon farly syght,
Wher as the Angell syngith on hight,
And the star that shynyth so bryght.'
        Ut hoy!
  For in hys pype he mad so mych joy.
                Can I not, etc.

'Now farewell, Mall, and also Will!
For my love go ye all styll
Unto I cum agayn you till,
And evermore, Will, ryng well thy bell.'
        Ut hoy!
  For in hys pype he mad so mych joy.
                Can I not, etc.

'Now must I go there Crist was born;
Farewell! I cum agayn to morn.
Dog, kepe well my shep fro ye corn,
And warn well 'Warroke' when I blow my horn!'
        Ut hoy!
  For in hys pype he mad so mych joy.
                Can I not, etc.

braid, While.   *ode*, Went.   *farly*, Wonderful.

Whan Wat to Bedlem cum was,
He swet, he had gone faster than a pace;
He found Jesu in a sympyll place,
Betwen an ox and an asse.
        Ut hoy!
    For in hys pype he mad so mych joy.
                Can I not, etc.

'Jesu, I offer to thee here my pype,
My skirt, my tarbox, and my scrype;
Home to my felowes now will I skype,
And also loke unto my shepe.'
        Ut hoy!
    For in hys pype he mad so mych joy.
                Can I not, etc.

'Now farewell, myne owne herdes man Wat!'
'Yea, for God, lady, even so I hat;
Lull well Jesu in thy lape,
And farewell, Joseph, wyth thy rownd cape!'
        Ut hoy!
    For in hys pype he mad so mych joy.
                Can I not, etc.

'Now may I well both hope and syng,
For I have bene at Crystes beryng;
Home to my felowes now wyll I flyng.
Cryst of hevyn to hys bliss is bryng!'
        Ut hoy!
    For in hys pype he mad so mych joy.
                Can I not, etc.
            ANONYMOUS (fifteenth century)

Bedlem, Bethlehem.   *scripe*, Wallet.   *hat*, Hight, am called.

4

A PLEASANT COUNTREY MAYING SONG

To the tune of "The Popes Machina"

In this merry Maying time,
Now comes in the Summer prime,
Countrey damsels fresh and gay,
Walke abroad to gather May:

In an evening make a match,
In a morning bowes to fatch.
Well is she that first of all
Can her lover soonest call,

Meeting him without the towne,
Where he gives his Love a gowne.
Tib was in a gowne of gray,
Tom he had her at a bay.

Hand in hand they take their way,
Catching many a rundelay,
Greeting her with a smile,
Kissing her at every stile.

Then he leades her to the Spring,
Where the Primrose reigneth king.
Upon a bed of Violets blew,
Downe he throwes his Lover true.

She puts finger in the eye,
And checkes him for his qualitie.
She bids him to her mothers house,
To Cakes & Creame & Country souce.

He must tell her all his mind,
But she will sigh and stay behind.
Such a countrey play as this,
The maids of our town cannot mis.

They will in a morning gay,
Decke themselves and gather May.
Then they will goe crop the flowers,
Mongst the leaves and Country bowers.

When our maidens meet together,
There is praying for faire weather.
Glad are they to see the Sunne,
That they may play when work is don.

Some at Dancings make a show,
If they can get leave to goe.
Young men will for maidens sakes,
Give them Sugar, Creame & Cakes

With a cup of dainty Wine,
And it must be neate and fine.
Some of them for their good cheare,
Playes three quarters of a yeare.

Thou at the first I liked well,
Cakes and Creame do make me swell.
This pretty maiden waxeth big:
See what 'tis to play the Rig.

Up she deckes her white and cleene,
To trace the medowes fresh and green:
Or to the good towne she will wend
Where she points to meet her friend.

Her gowne was tuckt above the knee,
Her milkwhite smock that you may see.
Thus her amorous Love and she,
Sports from eight a clocke till three:

Playes, Probably 'Pays.'

All the while the Cuckow sings,
Towards the evening home she flings,
And brings with her an Oaken bow,
With a Country cake or two.

Straight she tels a solemne tale,
How she heard the Nightingale,
And how ech medow greenly springs:
But yet not how the Cuckow sings.

In the merry Maying time,
Love is in her chiefest prime.
What for Gentlemen and Clownes,
Our country maids can want no gownes.

Sillibubs and dainty cheare,
Yong men lacke not all the yeere.
All the maidens in the street,
With the bonny Yonkers meet.

All the while the grasse is greene,
And the Dasies grow betweene;
Dicke and Tom doe walk the fields,
Still to trip up maidens heeles.

Thus the Robin and the Thrush,
Musicke make in every bush.
While they charme their prety notes,
Young men hurle up maidens cotes.

But 'cause I will do them no wrong,
Here I end my Maying song,
And wish my friends take heed in time.
How they spend their Summers prime.

ANONYMOUS (1625 ?)

5

THE GOLDEN AGE; OR, AN AGE OF PLAINE-DEALING

To a pleasant new Court tune:
Or, *Whoope doe me no harme good man*

Come grant me, come lend me
   your listning ears:
The golden Apple now againe
   plainely appeares.
Carowse away sorrow,
   and fling away feares,
Leave your wife wealthy,
    Shee'l never shed teares:
    Oh this is a golden Age,
    Oh this is a Joviall Age.

The bountifull Lawyer
   that never doth wrong,
To plead poor men's cases
   for price of a song,
Who is by bright Angels
   still guided along,
For twenty two shillings,
    Hee'le lend you his tongue,
    To plead in this golden Age,
    Oh this is a Joviall Age.

The Ladies have put away
   painting and pride,
The foolish French fashion
   they cannot abide;
Without Maske or Caroches
   they civilly ride,
And to the poore people
    Their purses ope wide:
    Oh this is a bountifull Age,
   . *Oh this is a liberall Age.*

Angels, Coins worth 10s. 6d.

Base dealing is banisht,
    and women growne chaste,
And by their owne Husbands
    will scarce be embrac'd,
And will not their times
    in idleness waste,
For fear in their carriage
    They should be disgrac'd:
    Oh this is an honest Age,
    Oh this is a hopefull Age.

Your Cittizens bounty
    is growne now of late,
To raise a poore Gallants
    decayed estate,
Hee'l utter his wares
    at a reasonable rate,
And unto all commers
    Keepe open his gate:
    Oh this is a bountifull Age,
    Oh this is a liberall Age.

The valourous Souldiers
    stout manhood is spred,
With armes on his backe
    and Helmet on's head;
With Pike and with Musket
    to the field they tread,
While the base Coward
    Lyes sleeping in bed:
    Oh this is a valourous Age,
    Oh this is a warlike Age.

The Courtier, his Taylor
    doth pay with good will,
The Taylor he thinketh,
    his payment is ill.

But yet if he yeerely
   doe cancell his Bill,
His onely desire is
   To deale with him still;
    Oh this is a ventering Age,
    Oh this is a trusting Age.

The Usurer that lent out
   his money before,
Hath burned his Bonds,
   and lendeth no more,
Because his broad conscience
   oppresseth him sore,
The Divell still for him
   Stood gaping at's doore:
    Oh this is a mending Age,
    Oh this is an honest age.

ANONYMOUS (1621)

6

THE LOVING VIRGINS COMPLAINT.
OR, HER DESIRE
TO OBTAINE THE LOVE OF A YOUNG MAN

To the tune of " Walking of late abroad"

One morning when bright *Sol*
Did first ith East appeare,
   abroad I walked,
   abroad I walked,
the Nightingale to heare.

Close by a pleasant Grove,
I heard a Maiden cry,
   with sobs of sorrow,
   with sobs of sorrow,
she wept most heartily.

O fie on *Cupids* Chaine,
That hath my heart in hold,
　to endlesse bondage,
　to endlesse bondage,
I am for ever sold.

Was never silly lasse
tormented with such paine,
　I long have loved,
　I long have loved,
and all alack in vaine.

Ill fortune sure had I
to dote thus on a boy,
　the more I love him,
　the more I love him,
the more the foole is coy.

Like *Venus* Queene of Love,
I woo my sweet *Adonis*,
　but he is bashfull,
　but he is bashfull,
all comfort from me gone is.

I dote upon his face.
I more respect his sight,
　then did that virgin,
　then did that virgin,
who wooed Hermaphradite.

So beautifull is he,
and of so rare complexion,
　his eyes like lodestones,
　his eyes like lodestones,
have drawne me to subjection.

His lockes of lovely browne
are every one a snare,
    to binde poore Maidens,
    to binde poore Maidens,
to sorrow, griefe, and care.

Would I had never seene
those honey smiles so sweet,
    which did inthrall me,
    which did inthrall me,
when first we two did meet.

Methought he to mine eye
did seeme so pleasant rare,
    that sure a creature,
    that sure a creature,
he was without compare.

But all that breeds my care,
is that he is so young,
    he hardly knowes yet,
    he hardly knowes yet,
what doth to love belong.

When he and I by chance
in any place doe meet,
    from me he turneth,
    from me he turneth,
with rosie blushes sweet.

I doe more then my sex
will give me leave to doe,
    yet he is silent,
    yet he is silent,
and knowes not how to woo.

ANONYMOUS (1626)

7

IDYLL VIII

(*Theocritus*)

With lovely Netehearde DAPHNIS on the hills, they saie,
Shepeherde MENALCAS mett, upon a summers daie.
Both yuthfull striplings, both had yeallow heades of haire;
In whistling both, and both in singing skilfull were.
MENALCAS first, behoulding DAPHNIS, thus bespake:

MENALCAS

Wilt thou in singing, Netehearde DAPHNIS, undertake
To strive with me? For I affirme that, at my will,
I can thee pass. Thus DAPHNIS aunswerde on the hill.

DAPHNIS

Whistler MENALCAS, thou shalt never me excell
In singing, though to death with singing thou shouldst swell.

MENALCAS

Then wilt thou see, and something for the victor wage?

DAPHNIS

I will both see, and something for the victor gage.

MENALCAS

What therefore shal we pawne, that for us maie be fit?

DAPHNIS

Ile pawne a calfe; a wennell lambe laie thou to it.

MENALCAS

Ile pawne no lambe: for both my Syre and Mother fell
Are verie hard; and all my sheepe at even they tell.

DAPHNIS

What then? What shall he gaine that winns the victory?

MENALCAS

A gallant Whistell which I made with notes thrise three,
Joinde with white waxe, both evne below and evne above;
This will I laie. My Fathers thinges I will not move.

DAPHNIS

And I a whistle have with notes thrise three arowe,
Joinde with white waxe, both evne above and evne belowe.

wennell, Newly weaned.

I latelie framde it; for this finger yet doth ake
With pricking, which a splinter of a reede did make.
But who shall be our Judge, and give us audience?

MENALCAS

What if we call this Goteheard here, not far from hence,
Whose dog doth barke harde by the kids?

The lustie boies
Did call him, and the Goteheard came to heare their toies.
The lustie boies did sing, the Goteheard judgement gave.
MENALCAS first, by lot, unto his whistle brave,
Did sing a Neteheards song; and Neteheard DAPHNIS than
Did sing, by course: but first MENALCAS thus began:

MENALCAS

Yee Groves and Brookes divine, if on his reede
MENALCAS ever sung a pleasant laie;
Fat me these Lambs! If DAPHNIS here wil feede
His Calfes, let him have pasture too I praie.

DAPHNIS

Yee pleasant Springs and Plants, would DAPHNIS had
    As sweete a voice as have the Nightingales;
Feede me this heard, and if the Sheepeheards lad
    MENALCAS cums, let him have al the dales.

MENALCAS

Tis ever spring; there meades are ever gaie;
    There strowt the bags; there sheepe are fatly fed,
When DAPHNE cums; Go she awaie,
    Then both the sheepheard there, and grasse is dead.

DAPHNIS

There both the Ewes and Gotes bring forth their twins;
    There Bees do fil their hives; there Okes are hie
Where MILO treades when he awaie begins
    To goe, both Neteheard and the Nete waxe drie.

MENALCAS

O husband of the Gotes! O wood so hie!
    O kids! come to this brooke, for he is there!
Thou with the broken hornes, tell MILO shie,
    That PROTEUS kept Sea-calfes, though God he were.

strowt, Swell.

DAPHNIS

Nor PELOPS kingdom may I crave, nor gould;
    Nor to outrunne the windes upon a lea:
But in this cave Ile sing, with thee in hould,
    Both looking on my sheepe, and on the sea.

MENALCAS

A tempest marreth trees; and drought, a spring:
    Snares unto foules, to beastes, netts are a smarte;
Love spoiles a man. O JOVE, alone his sting
    I have not felt; for thou a lover art!

Thus sang these boies, by course, with voices strong;
MENALCAS then began a latter song:

MENALCAS

Wolfe, spare my kids: and spare my fruitful sheepe!
    And hurt me not; though, but a lad, these flockes I guide.
Lampur my dog, art thou indeede so sound asleepe?
    Thou should'st not sleepe when thou art by thy Masters side.
My sheepe, fear not to eate the tender grasse at will,
    Nor when it springeth up againe, see that you faile;
Goe to, and feede apace, and al your bellies fill,
    That part your Lambes may have; and part, my milking
    paile.

Then DAPHNIS in his turne sweetly began to sing:

DAPHNIS

And me, not long agoe, fair DAPHNE whistly eyed
    As I drove by; and said, I was a paragone:
Nor then indeede to her I churlishlie replide;
    But, looking on the ground, my way still held I on.
Sweet is a cowcalfes voice, and sweet her breath doth smell;
    A bulcalfe, and a cow, doe lowe full pleasantlie;
'Tis sweete in summer by a spring abrode to dwell;
    Acornes become the Oke; apples, the Appletree;
And calfes, the kine; and kine, the Neteheard much set out.

Thus sung these yuthes. The Gotehearde thus did ende the
dout.

GOTEHEARDE

O DAPHNIS, what a dulcet mouth and voice thou hast!
'Tis sweeter thee to heare than honie-combes to tast.
Take thee these pipes, for thou in singing dost excell.
If me, a Gotehearde, thou wilt teach to sing so well,
This broken horned Goate, on thee bestowe I will,
Which to the verie brimm the paile doth ever fill.

So then was DAPHNIS glad, and lept and clapt his handes;
And danst, as doth a fawne, when by the damm he standes.
MENALCAS greevd, the thing his mind did much dismaie:
And sad as Bride he was, upon the marriage daie.

Since then among the Shepeheards, DAPHNIS chiefe was had,
And took a Nimph to wife, when he was but a lad.

Anonymously translated (1588)

8

IDYLL XXI

(*Theocritus*)

ARGUMENT

A Neteheard is brought in, chafing that EUNICA, a Maid of the cittie, disdained to kisse him. Whereby it is thought that THEOCRITUS seemeth to checke them that thinke this kinde of writing in Poetry to be too base and rustical. And therefore this Poeme is termed NETEHEARD.

NETEHEARD

EUNICA skornde me, when her I would have sweetly kist,
And railing at me said, Goe with a mischiefe, where thou list!
Thinkst thou, a wretched Neteheard, mee to kisse? I have no will
After the Countrie Guise to smouch; of Cittie lips I skill.
My lovely mouth so much as in thy dreame thou shalt not touch.

How dost thou look! How dost thou talke! How plaiest thou
    the slouch!
How daintilie thou speakst! What courting words thou
    bringest out!
How soft a beard thou hast! How faire thy locks hang round
    about!
Thy lips are like a sickmans lips! thy hands, so black they bee,
And rankely thou dost smel, awaie, lest thou defilest me!
    Having thus sed, she spatterd on her bosome twise or thrise;
And, still beholding me from top to toe in skorneful wise,
She mutterd with her lips, and with her eies she lookte aside,
And of her beutie wondrous coy she was; her mouth she wride,
And proudly mockt me to my face. My blud boild in each vaine,
And red I woxe for griefe as doth the rose with dewye raine.
Thus leaving me, awaie she flung, since when, it vexeth me
That I should be so skornde of such a filthie drab as she.
    Ye Shepeheards, tel me true, am not I fair as any swan?
Hath of a sodaine anie God made me another man?
For well I wote, before a cumlie grace in me did shine,
Like ivy round about a tree, and dekt this bearde of mine.
My crisped lockes like Parslie, on my temples wont to spred;
And on my eiebrowes black, a milke white forhed glistered:
More seemelie were mine eies than are MINERVAS eies, I know.
My mouth for sweetnes passed cheese, and from my mouth did
    flow
A voice more sweete than hunniecombes. Sweete is my
    rundelaie,
When on the whistle, flute or pipe, or cornet I do plaie.
And all the weemen on our hills, do saie that I am faire,
And all do love me well: but these that breathe the citty air
Did never love me yet. And why? The cause is this, I know,
That I a Neteheard am. They heare not how, in vales below
Fair BACCHUS kept a heard of beastes. Nor can these nice ones
    tell
How VENUS, raving for a Neteheards love, with him did dwell
Upon the hills of Phrygia; and how she lovde againe
ADONIS in the woods, and mournde in woods when hee was
    slaine.

What was ENDYMION? Was he not a Neteheard? Yet the
   Moone
Did love this Neteheard so, that from the heavens descending
   soone,
She came to Latmos grove where with the daintie lad she laie.
And RHEA, thou a Neteheard dost bewaile, and thou, al daie
O mighty JUPITER but for a shepeheardes boy didst straie.
EUNICA only, dained not a Neteheard for to love:
Better, forsooth, than CYBEL, VENUS, or the Moone above.
And VENUS, thou hereafter must not love thy faire ADONE
In cittie nor on hill, but all the night must sleep alone.

EMBLEM
Habitarunt Dii quoque sylvas.
Anonymously translated (1588)

[This poem is reckoned as Idyll XX in modern editions.]

9

ECLOGUE IV

(*Virgil*)

Sicilian Muses, sing we greater things;
All are not pleas'd with shrubs and lowly springs;
More fitly to the consull, woods belong.
Now is fulfild Cumaean sibyl's song:
Long chaines of better times begin againe;   5
The Maide returnes, and brings backe Saturne's raigne;
New progenies from lofty Heav'n descend;
Thou chaste Lucina, be this Infant's friend,
Whose birth the days of ir'n shall quite deface,
And through the world the golden age shall place;   10
Thy brother Phoebus weares his potent crowne.
And thou—O Pollio—know thy high renowne—
Thy consulship this glorious change shall breed,
Great months shall then endeavour to proceed:

Thy rule the steps of threatening sinne shall cleare, 15
And free the Earth from that perpetuall feare.
He with the gods shall live, and shall behold,
With heavenly spirits noble souls enroll'd;
And, seene by them, shall guide this worldly frame,
Which to His hand His father's strength doth tame. 20
To Thee—sweet child—the Earth brings native dowres,
The wandring ivy, with faire bacchar's flowres,
And colocasia, sprung from Egypt's ground,
With smiling leaves of greene acanthus crown'd;
The goats their swelling udders home shall beare, 25
The droves no more shall mighty lions feare:
For Thee, Thy cradle, pleasing flowres shall bring;
Imperious Death shall blunt the serpent's sting;
No herbes shall with deceitfull poyson flow,
And sweet amomum ev'ry where shall grow. 30
But when Thou able art to reade the facts
Of worthies, and thy father's famous acts,
To know what glories Vertue's name adorne,
The fields to ripeness bring the tender corne;
Ripe grapes depend on carelesse brambles' tops, 35
Hard oakes sweat hony, form'd in dewy drops.
Yet some few steps of former fraudes remaine,
Which men to trie, the sea with ships constraine,
With strengthening walles their cities to defend,
And on the ground long furrows to extend; 40
A second Tiphys, and new Argo then,
Shall leade to brave exploits the best of men;
The war of Troy that town againe shall burne,
And great Achilles thither shall returne:
But when firm age a perfect man Thee makes, 45
The willing sayler straight the seas forsakes;
The pine no more the use of Trade retaines;
Each country breeds all fruits, the Earth disdaines
The harrowes weight, and vines the sickle's strokes;
Strong ploughmen let their bulls go free from yokes; 50

bacchar, Valerian.   *colocasia*, The Egyptian bean-flower.
amomum, Balsam-shrub.   *facts*, Deeds.   *steps*, Footsteps; traces.

Wooll feares not to dissemble colours strange,
But rams their fleeces then in pastures change
To pleasing purple, or to saffron dye,
And lambes turn ruddy, as they feeding lie.
The Fates—whose wills in stedfast end agree,   55
Command their wheeles to run such daies to see—
Attempt great honours, now the time attends;
Dear Childe of Gods, whose line from Iove descends.
See how the world with weight declining lies;
The Earth, the spacious seas, and arched skies: 60
Behold againe, how these their grief asswage
With expectation of the future age:
O that my life and breath so long would last
To tell Thy deeds! I should not be surpast
By Thracian Orpheus, nor if Linus sing,   65
Though they from Phœbus and the muses spring:
Should Pan—Arcadia judging—strive with me,
Pan by Arcadia's doome would conquer'd be.
Begin Thou, little Childe; by laughter owne
Thy mother, who ten months hath fully knowne   70
Of tedious houres: begin, Thou little Childe,
On Whom as yet thy parents never smil'd;
The God with meate hath not Thy hunger fed,
Nor goddesse laid thee in a little bed.

              Translated by SIR JOHN BEAUMONT (1629)

                              10

                        ECLOGUE VII

                          (*Virgil*)

                          MELIBŒUS
All underneath a tall straight Holme, whyleere
    Sate *Daphnis*: whilst *Thyrsis* and *Coridon*,
Their simple sheep, & milk-stuffed Goates, yfeere,
    (Their severall flocks) compelled into one:
Arcadians both, and both of equall yeeres,
    In answers prompt; and both in singing Peeres.

As I from cold the tender Myrtles save,
    The Goate (the husband of the heard) did stray;
I *Daphnis* spyde: hee mee: and mee did wave,
    And cryde; (*Melibe*) thy Kids are well: away
Come; heere's thy Goate too: if thou maist be staide
Of fellowship, come rest thee in this shade.

Heere all the heards doon leave their meadow-feede,
    To come to drink: here quiet *Mincius* bounds
The verdant flowrie bankes with tender reed,
    And sacred Oak with buzzing swarmes, resounds.
What should I doe?
Not having *Phillis*, nor *Alcippe*, whom
To send shut up my weaning lambs at home:

And much to doo, was like to be (God know)
    Twixt *Thyrsis* and *Coridon*; yet foolish I
Did for their toyes, my business for-slow:
    Tho, both by turns, their verses gan to vye,
And each with turning songs invoke their *Muse*,
First *Coridon*; next *Thyrsis* his course ensues.

CORIDON

Lybethrian Nymphes, my joy, my deere delight,
Or doon mee help sike ditties to endite,
As *Codrus* erst ye taught: (for none so nie
As hee to *Phoebus*-selfe can versifie;)
Or, if wee cannot all so happy bee,
Ile hang my Pipe on this Pine-sacred tree.

THYRSIS

Crowne your new Poet, yee Arcadian Swaines,
With ramping Ivie: that so *Codrus* raines
And very guts may crack, with fell despite:
Or if he praise him more, than is his right,
With Berryes bynd his front: that his ill tong
Heere after may not doo your Poet wrong.

CORIDON

This Bores rough head, *Micon* (my little wagg)
And branched hornes of a long-lyved Stagg,

Doth heere present (fayre *Delia*) unto thee:
Which if he find them faire accepted bee,
Of finest marble thou shalt stand upright,
Thy Calves lapt all in Punick—Buskins light.

THYRSIS

Thow but an Orchard-Keeper art; no more,
Poor *Priapus!* inough is thee therefore
This bowle of Milke, and wafers every yeere:
Now, for the while, allbee I make thee heere,
But of coarse marble, yet if once my Fold
Double my stock, Ile carve thee all of Gould.

CORIDON

Nereus' deere daughter, *Galatea* myne,
More sweete to mee than *Hybla's* pretious Tyme,
More than white Ivie smooth; than Swans more fayre,
When once the Bulls from feede returned are
Unto their stalls, if that thy heart be right
To thine own *Coridon* come bless him with thy sight.

THYRSIS

Let mee be held more sowr than *Sardian* grass,
Rougher than brushwood, abject and more base
Than the Seas weedy wrack, if not to mee
Long as a yeere this one day seeme to bee:
My Bullocks, having fedd, no farther rome;
For shame, if yee have any shame, goe, hie you home.

CORIDON

Yee mossy Fountaines, and yee Hearbes which bee
Softer than sleepe: And, oh, thou Strawberry-tree,
Who thy thinn shade doth over all extend,
From the Solstitium doon my beasts defend:
The soultry Summer gins his broyling heate,
And the Vine buds doon burgeon broade and greate.

THYRSIS

Wee Chimnyes heere, and Torches dropping fat;
And Fires nose-high wee have; and unto that,
Posts, with continuall smoake as black as Jet:
Heere wee by *Boreas* could no more doe set,

Than one woolfe feares whole flocks of sheepe: no more
Than tumbling Tides reaken the severall shore.

CORIDON

The Juniper, and rough-ryn'd Chessunt stand,
And under every Tree, each-where on hand,
The Apples ready lye: and every thing
Doth laugh for joy: but if my deere darling
Alexis from these Mountaines chance to stray
Soone shall you see the Floods quite dride away.

THYRSIS

The Field doth wither, and the dying Grass
By th'ayres distemper doth to nothing pass;
The Vine envies the Hills her branched shade;
But all the woods full goodly been arayd
At my fair *Phillis* coming, and self-*Jove*
In pretious showres descendeth from above.

CORIDON

Most is the *Popler* to *Alcides* leefe,
The Vine, to *Bacchus*; *Venus*, myrtles cheefe
Affects: and *Phoebus* Laurels most approves:
And *Phillis* Hazels: which (whiles *Phillis* loves,)
Nor Myrtles can the Hazels paralell,
Nor *Phoebus*-laurels ever them excell.

THYRSIS

The Ash is glory of all Timber woods,
The Pine, of Orchards; Popler, in the Floods:
The Firr is beauty of the Hills so high:
But (would my *Licidas* continually
Come visit mee) both Firr, and Ash, and Pine
To thee, my Lief, the Guarland must resigne.

MELIBŒUS

These I remember, and that after long
Contention vaine, *Thyrsis* was laid along:
And ever since that time is *Coridon*
My noble *Coridon* and *Paragon*.

Translated by W[ILLIAM] [LISLE] (1628)

II

THE GOLDEN AGE

(from "Ovids Metamorphoses Englished," Book I)

The *Golden Age* was first; which uncompeld,
And without rule, in faith and Truth exceld.
As then, there was nor punishment, nor feare;
Nor threatning Lawes in brasse prescribed were;
Nor suppliant crouching pris'ners shooke to see
Their angrie Iudge: but all was safe and free.
To visit other Worlds, no wounded Pine (*a*)
Did yet from Hills to faithlesse Seas decline.
Then, un-ambitious Mortals knew no more,
But their owne Countrie's Nature-bounded shore.
Nor Swords, nor Armes were yet: no trenches round
Besieged Townes, nor strifefull Trumpets sound:
The Souldier, of no use. In firme content
And harmlesse ease, their happy daies were spent.
The yet-free Earth did of her own accord
(Untorne with ploughs) all sorts of fruit afford.
Content with Natures un-enforced food,
They gather (*b*) Wildings, Strawb'ries of the Wood,
Sowre (*c*) Cornels, what upon the Bramble growes,
And Acornes, which (*d*) Iove's spreading Oke bestowes.
'Twas alwaies Spring; (*e*) warme *Zephyrus* sweetly blew
On smiling flowres, which without setting grew.
Forth-with the Earth corne, unmanured, beares;
And every yeere renewes her golden Eares:

a. Whereof masts are made for ships: a part of the ship here taken for the whole.

b. Arbuteus fœtus—which I have rather rendred in a familiar word, nor lesse agreeable to the subiect.

c. A red fruit with a hard shel growing on a thick shrub, for the most part in mountainous places.

d. Either that the Symboll of Empire: or because he first introduced the feeding upon Acornes.

e. Therefore the fained husband of Flora.

With (*f*) Milke and Nectar were the Rivers fill'd;
And Hony from (*g*) greene Holly-okes distill'd.
    But, after *Saturne* was throwne downe to Hell,
Iove rul'd; and then the *Silver Age* befell:
More base then Gold, and yet then Brasse more pure.
Iove chang'd the Spring (which alwayes did indure)
To Winter, Summer, Autumne hot and cold:
The shortned Springs the year's fourth part uphold.
Then, first the glowing Ayre with fervor burn'd
The Raine to icicles by bleake winds turn'd.
Men houses built; late hous'd in caves profound,
In plashed Bowres, and Sheds with Osiers bound.
Then, first was corne into long furrowes throwne:
And Oxen under heavy yokes did groane.
    Next unto this succeeds the *Brazen Age*;
Worse natur'd prompt to horrid warre, and rage:
But not yet wicked. Stubborn *Yr'n* the last.
Then blushlesse crimes, which all degrees surpast,
The World surround. Shame, Truth, and Faith depart:
Fraud enters, ignorant in no bad Art;
Force, Treason, and the wicked love of gayne.
Their sailes, those winds, which yet they knew not, strayne:
And ships, which long on lofty Mountaines stood,
Then plow'd th'unpractiz'd bosom of the Flood.
The Ground, as common earst as Light, or Aire,
(*h*) By limit-giving Geometry they share.
Nor with rich Earth's just nourishments content,
(*j*) For treasure they her secret entrailes rent;
The powerfull Evill, which all power invades,
By her well hid, and wrapt in (*k*) *Stygian* shades.

f. The Scripture expresseth plenty, and felicity, by a land overflowing with
milke and hony; borrowed from thence by the Poets. Ours here addeth *Nectar*
which signifies a preserver of eternall youth: expressing the long & flourishing
lives of men in that age.
    g. Ilex.—the leaves like those of Holly ever flourishing. The dwarfe kind of
this oke bears the Kerms, an excrescens upon the leafe.
    h. The Scripture informs us, that the earth was divided in the daies of *Phalec*,
hee therefore so called, which signifies division.
    j. Lynceus was said to be the first that sunke mines: and therefore fained to
penetrat the Earth with the sharpnes of his sight.
    k. Hell, so called of *Styx* (which signifies loathsome) an infernall River.

Curst Steele, more cursed Gold she now forth brought:
And bloody-handed Warre, who with both fought:
All live by spoyle. The Host his Guest betrayes;
Sons, Fathers-in-lawe: 'twixt Brethren love decays.
Wives husbands, Husbands wives attempt to kill:
And cruell Step-mothers pale poysons fill.
The Sonne his Fathers hastie death desires:
Foild Pietie, trod underfoot, expires.
(*l*) *Astraea*, last of all the heavenly birth,
Affrighted, leaves the blood-defiled Earth.

l. Iustice the daughter of *Iupiter* and *Themis*. Or of *Astraeus* (who first gave names to the starres, and thereupon called their father,) and *Hemera*; that is the Daughter of the Day; or Goddesse of civility, because Iustice maketh men civill

Translated by G. SANDYS (1632)

12

ECLOGUE II

(*Mantuan*)

Faustus has given his friend Fortunatus an account of the recent floods, and says that though they have abated, Padua is still inundated, and its cellars are open to plunder. The subject, after this topical proem, turns to love, and Fortunatus tells this tale of:

A Shepherd, whom thou knowst full wel, to make it playne
in sight
What force there rests in *Venus* flame, and shewe hir stately
might.
Amyntas poore (God wotte) and borne unluckie under signe,
Six calves of equall age possesst, and had as many kine.
Whome as he drave to pasture with a Bull that father was
To all the herd, it was his chance by *Coytus* to passe.
A place where *Myncius* with his cleare and silver chanell flowes,
And swiftly all the grassy soyle and meadowes overgoes.
A castell new with battled walls there faceth on the floode:
High raysed up that *Coyto* hight, and on the marishe stoode.
Here resting him by Rivers side where grew a goodly vine,
That with his boughs did shade the banks and waters passing
fine,

He stayde to catch the gliding fish with baited hook and line.
'Twas Harvest time, and scorching beams of scalding *Phoebus*
    rayes
Had singed the soyle; the Nightingale had laid aside her layes.
The ground was withered in such wyse as neither flocke could
    feede
Theron by day, nor deawe was left for Grassehoppers at neede,
By night to moist their crikyng chaps. Here whylst he spent
    the tyde
About the River, and this fonde and vayne devise applyde.
The Bull first vexed with the Waspe, and next with curres they
    say,
And last by filching Souldiers meane was quite convayde away,
Not to be found in field. Which when the Boy had under-
    stoode,
He gat hym to a Mountayne by and cried out a good
For Bull unhaply lost of late, and all the country sought
With greedy gazing eye. But when he sawe it booted nought
And that his payne could not prevaile, his bended Bowe he
    tooke,
And painted Quiver full of shafts, and for his beast gan looke
Through woods wher was no haunted path, through every
    flock and fold,
Through pastures eke to see where he his Bullocke might
    behold.
About *Benacus* bankes he went, and Mountes with Olive tree
Beset, and places where both Figge and Vine was greene to see.
At length a haughtie hill he hent, where did a Chappell stande
Of Sulphur, and from thence he cast his eies about the lande,
And over-viewde *Benacus* bounds, and all the country rounde,
To see where in that coast there were his Bullocke to be founde.
It was Sainct *Peters* day by course and custome of the yere;
The youth of every village by at afternoon was there:
And underneath a greenysh Elme that shadowed all the soyle,
At sounde of pleasant countrey pipe they dauncde and kept a
    coyle.

haunted, Frequented.

FAUSTUS

The country clownes cannot be tamde by any kinde of arte;
Unquiet they delight in sweate: when Priest hath done his parte,
And mornyng Prayers ended are, the Holy day (when all
Should cease from toyle) impacient they of rest and hunger, fall
To fillyng of their greedy mawes and tossyng off the cup:
And hye to daunce, as soone as mynstrell gyns to pype it up:
They treade it tricksie under tree; one skips as he were mad,
Another jumps as 'twere an Oxe unto the Aultar lad.
The sacred soyle (that synne it were to turne with toyling share,
And cut with crooked coulter) they can not endure to spare:
But friske theron like frantike fooles, unwieldy wights, God
    wot,
With leaden legs and heavy heels about the Churchyarde trot.
And all the day do crie and laugh, and lay their lips to pot.

FORTUNATUS

Thou dolt, why dost thou chat of this ? thy selfe a rustike
    borne?
The maners of the countrey Clownes and rustike rout doest
    scorne.
Thou dost thyself condemne withall, thou art thy proper foe.

FAUSTUS

Tushe, of *Amyntas* let us chat, let all these matters go.
I spake it but in sporte, my friend, I trust you take it so.

FORTUNATUS

He stayde, and leaning gaynst his staffe ymade of Acer tree,
Did stint from travaile till the heate might somwhat swaged
    bee.
O most unhappy haplesse youth, in shade a greater slash
Will seaze thy corps: shut up thine eyes, lest when *Diana* wash
Hir lovely limmes in silver streame thou naked her espie:
Or lend a listning eare unto the *Syrens* when they crie.
Thy lucke with *Narciss'* heavy love may well compared bee:
For whilst in Well he sought to slake his thirst, the more was
    hee
(Unlucky lad) with drought attachde: so whilst thou dost
    devise

Acer, Maple.

This outward heate to flee, an inwarde flame doth thee surprise.
Now much had better been (I pray) and happier for thee,
(Unlesse the fatall Gods would have thy destnie so to be)
To thy remainder flocke in fielde to have returned backe,
And kept thy kine, and let alone the Bull that was a lacke:
And taken in good part the loss of that one beast alone,
Than thus, in seeking nought to finde, thy selfe to have forgone.

FAUSTUS

Oh friende, who is not wise become when things are at the worst?
'Tis naught to give advise in fine that should bene had at furst.

FORTUNATUS

The counsell that comes after all thyngs are dispatcht at last,
Is like a showre of rayne that falls when sowing time is past.
Among the rest of all the rout a passing proper lasse,
A white haired trull of twenty yeares or neere aboute there was:
In stature passyng all the rest, a gallant Girle for hewe:
To be compared with Townish nymphs, so fair she was to viewe.
Hir forhead cloth with gold was purlde, a little here and theare:
With copper claspe about her necke a kerchiefe did she weare,
That reached to her breast and paps: the Wench about her wast,
A gallant gaudy ribande had that girte her body fast.
In Peticote of countrey stuffe, Mockadoe like, she goes:
'Twas plaited brave, and length was such it hung nie to her toes.
As soone as her the youth had spide, he perisht by and by:
By sight he sucked in the flame, and meane of wanton eye:
He swallowde up the blinding fyre, and in his belly placed
The coles that neither waves could quench nor rainie imber waste;
No, not inchantments, witches words, it cloong so close and fast.
Forgetful he of former flocke, and damage done with knaves,
Was all inraged with this flash; at night he nought but raves.
The season that for quiet sleepe by nature poynted was,
In bitter plaintes and cruell cries, this burning Boy did passe.
I sundry times for pities sake his growing flame to stay,

Mockadoe, Mohair.

And stop the frantike furie, would to hym full often say:
O lamentable lad, what God hath forcde thee thus to fare?
But sure it was no worke of Gods that bred this bitter care.
Nay rather 'twas the cruelst impe, and spitefulst fiende of hell,
Of those with *Lucifer* that from the skies to dungeon fell,
That nine dayes space were tumbling downe: I pray thee make
    me show
And call to mynde where ever yet thou any man dydst know
By foolish love advancde to wealth, or any office borne,
Or raisde by meanes therof his house, or stufft his barnes with
    corne?
Dydst ever knowe that hath therby enlargde his bounds,
Increaste his flocke, or for his herd ygotten fruitful grounds?
Among so many countreys tell me, if thou heardst of one;
At any tyme through all the earth I thinke was never none.
There are that to their bloudy boordes our crushed bodies
    beare,
And butcherlike, with greedy teeth, our rented corses teare.
There are, I say, whom spitefull fiends unto suche practise
    dryve:
Yet is there no such kynde of men so cruell here alyve:
No country is so barbarous, is none so savage sect,
As doth not hate the womans love and fansies fonde reject.
Thence brawles are bred, thence chidings come, thence broiling
    warre and strife;
Yea, often eke with sheading bloud, the cruell losse of life.
By meanes therof are Cities sackt, and Bulwarks beate to
    grounde:
Moreover Lawes and sacred Bookes in yron chaines ybounde
Forbid and give us charge to flee in any case this Love:
With words expressly *Cupid* they and all his toyes disprove.
Amyntas had no sooner heard the name of Lawes rehearst,
But answered (for in Citie he a Boy was fostred earst)
Thou goest about to far surmount, by giving this advise,
The *Catos* both, and to be thought both circumspect and wise.
This errour and this madnesse beares eche where a cruell swaye:
Man flattreth with him selfe, and would be counted crafty, aye
A creature able to forsee: yet many a snare and gin

And ditch that he him selfe hath delv'de the Miser falleth in.
He first was free, but to his necke him selfe did frame the yoke:
In servile chaine him selfe he bounde, and bands of freedome
    broke.
So weighty are those Lawes (my selfe have sene the Bookes ere
    this)
As neither predecessors, nor our selves can kepe, ywis:
Nor aftercommers shall observe the meanyng of the same.
Behold the foolish wit of man, that thinkes such feate to frame,
As to the heavens to aspire; and hopes at length to get
Among the glistring starres aloft a stately roome and seate.
Perhaps when life is lost, he shall unto a foule convarte,
And then his feathred soule with wyngs to welkin shall departe.
And then (quod I) what brawle is this? since God did so devise
The lawes, 'twere foul offence for man his statutes to despise.

                    FAUSTUS
    These are debates of great affaires, and weighty things indeed.
                    FORTUNATUS
    Wott'st thou what kind of man I was? though ragged in my
        weede,
And I a rustike now to see, then both in force and mynde
And lookes, I was a roysting lad; thou shouldst not lightly
    fynde
A shepeheard to be matchte with me.
                    FAUSTUS
                            And yet if bolte upright
Thou stalke with countnance cast aloft thou wilt appeare in
    sight,
A second *Marius* to be: let Barber shave thy face
With razer, and in countenance thou wilt matche with *Carbos*
    grace.
                    FORTUNATUS
    Amyntas would like aunswer make when I his follie blamde.
But to proceede: when God had man in perfect figure framde,
He did repine therat and thought the pleasures he allowde
Too passing were: and did restrayne our lust with law, and
    bowde
Our Rebell minds with new decrees: as Horsemen use to tie

Their jades with brakes about the jawes for fear they go awrie.
Herein *Love* maks me shew my minde, and fansie freely tell:
Who so debarres his wife to go, in common doth not well,
But envious may accompted be. But yet this spitefull hate
The cloake of honest custome doth in some respect abate.
For whilst each man unto himself (not forcing common good)
Reserv'd his private joyes, and to his marriage bargain stood.
A common custome is incroached that Honestie is hight,
Good faith, to make such peevish lawes 'twas mad and foolish
    spight.
A hatefull thing is Love (God wotte) and pleasure spitefull eke.
Then I no longer daring to the Youth athwarte to speake,
Shooke off the raging wanton Boy that seemde berefte of sense,
And on my former voyage I eftsoon departed thence.

FAUSTUS

Seest how this vile Affection fonde our inwarde eyes of mynd
Shutts up in such despiteous sorte, and makes us men so blinde,
As headlong we to errors runne and to deceiptfull snare:
Till tyme we bee in wilfull trappe and nipt with cutting care?

FORTUNATUS

Oh, dost thou see (frend *Faustus*) how the pitchy cloudes
    upon
Mount *Baldus* to a cluster goe, and joyne them selves in one?
It hayles; for feare our cattell bee dispersed, let's be gone.

Translated by GEORGE TURBERVILLE (1567)

13

SONNET

(*Sannazaro*)

To heare my Plaints faire River Christalline
Thou in a silent Slumber seemes to stay,
Delicious Flowrs, Lillie and Columbine,
Yee bowe your Heades when I my Woes display.
Forrests, in you the *Mirtle*, *Palme*, and *Bay*,
Have had compassion listning to my Grones,

The Winds with Sighes have solemniz'd my Mones
'Mong leaves, which whisper'd what they could not say.
The Caves, the Rockes, the Hills, the *Sylvans* Thrones
(As if even Pitie did in them appeare)
Have at my Sorrowes rent their ruthlesse Stones,
Each thing I finde hath sense except my Deare
  Who doth not thinke I love, or will not know
  My Griefe, perchance delighting in my Woe.
      Translated by SIR WM. DRUMMOND (1616)

14

From AMINTA—First Chorus, "O Bella Età de l'Oro"

(*Tasso*)

O happy Age of Gould; happy' houres;
Not for with milke the rivers ranne,
And hunny dropt from ev'ry tree;
Nor that the Earth bore fruits, and flowres,
Without the toyle or care of Man,
And Serpents were from poyson free;
Nor for th'Ayre (ever calme to see)
Had quite exil'de the lowring Night;
Whilst clad in an eternall Spring
(Nor fiery hott, or else freezing)
The cheekes of heav'n smil'de with clear light;
Nor that the wandring Pine of yore
Brought neither warres, nor wares from forraine shore;
 But therefore only happy Dayes,
Because that vaine and ydle name,
That couz'ning Idoll of unrest,
Whom the madd vulgar first did raize,
And call'd it Honour, whence it came
To tyrannize or'e ev'ry brest,
 Was not then suffred to molest
Poore lovers hearts with new debate;
More happy they, by these his hard

And cruell lawes, were not debarr'd
Their innate freedome; happy state;
The goulden lawes of Nature, they
Found in their brests; and them they did obey.
Amidd the silver streames and floures,
The winged *Genii* then would daunce,
Without their bowe, without their brande;
The Nymphes sate by their Paramours,
Whispring love-sports, and dalliance,
And ioyning lips, and hand to hand;
    The fairest Virgin in the land
Nor scornde, nor glor'yed to displaye
Her cheekes fresh roses to the eye,
Or ope her faire brests to the day,
(Which now adayes so vailed lye,)
But men and maydens spent free houres
In running Rivers, Lakes, or shady Bowres.
    Then *Honour*, thou didst first devize
To maske the face of Pleasure thus;
Barr water to the thirst of Love,
And lewdly didst instruct faire eyes
They should be nyce, and scrupulous,
And from the gazing world remoove
    Their beauties; thy hands new netts wove
T'intrap the wilde curles, faire dispred
To th'open ayre; thou mad'st the sweet
Delight of Love seeme thus unmeete;
And (teaching how to looke, speake, tread,)
By thy ill lawes this ill has left,
That what was first Loves gift, is now our theft.
    Nor ought thy mighty working brings,
But more annoyes, and woe to us;
But thou (of Nature and of Love
The Lord, and scourge of mighty Kings,)
Why do'st thou shrowde thy greatnesse thus
In our poore cells? hence, and remoove
Thy powre; and it display above.
    Disturbing great ones in their sleepe;

And let us meaner men alone
T'inioyne againe, (when thou art gone)
And lawes of our Forefathers keepe.
Live we in love, for our lives houres
Haste on to death, that all at length devoures.
    Love we while we may; the wayne
Of Heav'n can set, and rise againe;
But we (when once we looze this light)
Must yeeld us to a never ending Night.

Translated by HENRY REYNOLDS (1628)

15

From IL PASTOR FIDO, Act IV

(Guarini)

Fair Golden Age! when milk was th'onely food,
And cradle of the infant world the wood
(Rock'd by the windes); and th'untoucht flocks did bear
Their dear young for themselves! None yet did fear
The sword or poyson; no black thoughts begun
T'eclipse the light of the eternall Sun:
Nor wandring Pines unto a forreign shore
Or War, or Riches, (a worse mischief) bore.
That pompous sound, Idoll of vanity,
Made up of Title, Pride, and Flattery,
Which they call Honour whom Ambition blindes,
Was not as yet the Tyrant of our mindes.
But to buy reall goods with honest toil
Amongst the woods and flocks, to use no guile,
Was honour to those sober souls that knew
No happiness but what from vertue grew.
Then sports and carols amongst Brooks and Plains
Kindled a lawful flame in Nymphs and Swains.
Their hearts and tongues concurr'd, the kisse and joy
Which were most sweet, and yet which least did cloy
Hymen bestow'd on them. To one alone

The lively Roses of delight were blown;
The theevish Lover found them shut on triall,
And fenc'd with prickles of a sharp deniall.
Were it in Cave or Wood, or purling Spring,
Husband and Lover signifi'd one thing.
    Base present age, which dost with thy impure
Delights the beauty of the soul obscure:
Teaching to nurse a Dropsie in the veins:
Bridling the look, but giv'st desire the reins.
Thus, like a net that spread and cover'd lies
With leaves and tempting flowrs, thou dost disguise
With coy and holy arts a wanton heart;
Mak'st life a *Stage-play*, vertue but a *part*:
Nor think'st it any fault Love's sweets to steal,
So from the world thou canst the theft conceal.
    But thou that art the King of Kings, create
In us true honour: Vertue's all the state
Great souls should keep. Unto these cells return
Which were thy Court, but now thy absence mourn:
From their dead sleep with thy sharp goad awake
Them who, to follow their base wills, forsake
Thee, and the glory of the ancient world.
    Let's hope: our ills have truce till we are hurld
From that: Let's hope; the sun that's set may rise,
And with new light salute our longing eyes.

        GUARINI, *translated by* SIR RICHARD FANSHAWE (1647)

16

*HARPALUS complaynt on PHILLIDAES love bestowed on
CORIN, who loved her not, and denyed him that loved her*

    Phillida was a faire maide,
        as fresh as any flower:
    Whom *Harpalus* the Heards-man praide
        to be his Paramour.

Harpalus and eke *Corin*
   were Heards-men both yfere:
And *Phillida* could twist and spinne,
   and thereto sing full cleere.
But *Phillida* was all too coy,
   for *Harpalus* to winne:
For *Corin* was her onely joy,
   who forc'd her not a pinne.
How often would she flowers twine,
   how often Garlands make:
Of Cowslips and of Cullumbine,
   and all for *Corins* sake?
But *Corin* he had Hawkes to lure,
   and forced more the field:
Of Lovers law hee tooke no cure,
   for once hee was beguild.
Harpalus prevailed naught,
   his labour all was lost:
For he was furthest from her thought,
   and yet he lov'd her most.
Therefore woxe he both pale and leane,
   and dry as clod of clay:
His flesh it was consumed cleane,
   his colour gone away.
His beard it had not long beene shave,
   his haire hung all unkempt:
A man most fit even for the grave,
   whom spitefull Love had spent.
His eyes were red and all fore-watcht,
   his face besprent with teares:
It seem'd unhap had him long hatcht,
   in midst of his dispaires.
His cloathes were blacke and also bare,
   as one forlorne was hee:
Upon his head he alwayes ware
   a wreath of Willow-tree.

yfere, Together.   *fore-watcht*, Over-watched, sleepless.
                 hatcht, Lined.

His beasts he kept upon the hill,
    and he sate in the Dale:
And thus with sighs and sorrowes shrill,
    he gan to tell his tale.
Oh *Harpalus*, thus he would say,
    unhappiest under Sunne:
The cause of thine unhappy day
    by love was first begun.
For thou went'st first by sute to seeke
    a Tyger to make tame:
That sets not by thy love a Leeke,
    but makes thy griefe a game.
As easie were it to convert
    the frost into a flame:
As for to turne a froward hart
    whom thou so faine wouldst frame.
Corin, he liveth carelesse,
    he leapes among the leaves:
He eates the fruites of thy redresse,
    thou reap'st, he takes the sheaves.
My beasts a-while your foode refraine,
    and harke your Heard-mans sound:
Whom spightfull Love alas hath slaine,
    through-girt with many a wound.
Oh happy be ye beasts wild,
    that heere your Pasture takes:
I see that ye be not beguild,
    of these your faithfull makes.
The Hart he feedeth by the Hinde,
    the Bucke hard by the Doe:
The Turtle-Dove is not unkinde
    to him that loves her so.
The Ewe she hath by her the Ram,
    the young Cowe hath the Bull:
The Calfe with many a lusty Lamb,
    doo feede their hunger full.

through-girt, Pierced through.   *makes*, Mates.

But well-away that Nature wrought,
   thee *Phillida* so faire:
For I may say that I have bought
   thy beauty all too deere.
What reason is't that cruelty
   with beauty should have part?
Or else that such great tirannie
   should dwell in womans hart?
I see therefore to shape my death,
   she cruelly is prest:
To th'end that I may want my breath,
   my dayes beene at the best.
Oh *Cupid* graunt this my request,
   and doo not stop thine eares:
That she may feele within her brest,
   the paine of my despaires.
Of *Corin* that is carelesse,
   that she may crave her fee:
As I have done in great distresse,
   that lov'd her faithfully.
But since that I shall die her slave,
   her slave and eke her thrall:
Write you my friends upon my grave,
   this chaunce that is befall.
Heere lyeth unhappy *Harpalus*,
   by cruell Love now slaine:
Whom *Phillida* unjustly thus,
   hath murdred with disdaine.

ANONYMOUS, *attributed to the* EARL OF SURREY (1557)

17

From EGLOGA TERTIA

MENALCAS   CORIDON

MENALCAS

A pleasaunt place is here to talke: good *Coridon* begyn,
And let us knowe the Townes estate, that thou remaynest in.

CORIDON

The Townes estate? *Menalcas* oh thou makste my harte to
    grone,
For Vice hath every place posseste, and Vertue thence is flowne.
Pryde beares her selfe as Goddesse chiefe, and boastes above the
    Skye,
And Lowlynes an abiecte lyes, with Gentlenes her bye,
Wyt is not ioynde with Symplenes, as she was wont to be,
But sekes the ayde of Arrogance, and craftye Polycie.
Nobylitie begyns to fade, and Carters up do sprynge,
Than whiche, no greater plague can hap, nor more pernicious
    thynge.
Menalcas I have knowen my selfe, within this thyrtye yeare,
Of Lordes and Auncient Gentelmen a hundreth dwellynge
    theare,
Of whom we Shephardes had reliefe; such Gentlenes of mynde
Was placed in theyr noble Hartes, as none is nowe to fynde.
But Hawtynes and proude Disdayne hath nowe the chiefe
    Estate,
For syr Iohn Straw, and syr Iohn Cur, wyll not degenerate.
And yet, they dare account them selves to be of Noble bludde.
But Fisshe bred up in durtye Pooles wyll ever stynke of mudde.
I promysse thee, *Menalcas* here, I wolde not them envye
Yf any spot of Gentlenes in them I myght espye.
For yf theyr Natures gentell be, though byrth be never so base,
Of Gentelmen (for mete it is) they ought have name and place:
But when by byrth, they base are bred, and churlisshe harte
    retaine,
Though place of gentlemen thei have yet churles they do
    remayne.
A proverbe olde hath ofte ben hearde, and now full true is
    tryed:
An Ape, wyll ever be an Ape, thoughe purple garments hyde.
For seldom wyll the mastiff course the Hare or els the Deare:
But styll, accordynge to his kynde, wyll holde the hogge by
    th'eare.
Unfitte are dunghill knights to serve the towne, with Speare in
    fielde: *envye*, Complain of.

Nor strange it semes, (a sudain Chop) to leape from whyp to shielde.

The chiefest man in all our towne, that beares the greatest swaye,

Is *Coridon* (no kynne to me) a Neteherd th'other daye.

This *Coridon* come from the Carte, In honour chiefe doth sytte,

And governes us: because he heth a Crabbed, Clownish wytte.

Nowe see the Churlysh Crueltye that in hys harte remayns—

The selye Sheape that Shephards good have fosterd up wyth Paynes,

And browght awaye from Stynkyng dales on pleasant Hylles to feade,

O Cruell Clownish Coridon, O cursed Carlish Seade!

—The simple Shepe constrayned he theyr Pasture swete to leave,

And to theyr old corrupted Grasse enforceth them to cleave.

Such Shepe, as would not them obaye, but in theyr Pasture byde,

With cruell flames they did consume and vex on every syde.

And with the shepe the Shephardes good (O hatefull Hounds of Hell)

They did torment, and dryve them out, in places farre to dwell.

There dyed *Daphnis* for his Shepe, the chiefest of them all;

And fayre *Alexis* flamde in Fyre, who never perysshe shall.

O Shephards wayle, for *Daphnis* deth, *Alexis* hap lament,

And curse the force of cruell hartes, that them to death have sent.

I, synce I sawe suche synfull syghts, dyd never lyke the Towne,

But thought it best to take my sheepe and dwell upon the downe.

Wheras I lyve a pleasaunt lyfe, and free from cruell handes;

I wolde not leave the plesaunt fyelde for all the Townysh Landes.

For syth that Pryde is placed thus, and Vice set up so hye,

And Crueltie doth rage so sore, and men lyve all awrye,

Thynkste thou that God will long forbere his scourge and plague to sende

Nor strange, Perhaps "For strange."

To suche as hym do styll despyse, and never seke to mende?
Let them be sure he wyll revenge, when they thynke leaste
    upon.
But looke, a stormy showre doth ryse, whiche wyll fall heare
    anone;
Menalcas, best we nowe departe, my Cottage us shall keepe,
For there is rowme for thee and me, and eke for all our sheepe.
Some Chestnuts have I there in store, with Cheese and pleasaunt
    whaye;
God sends me Vittayles for my nede, and I synge Care awaye.

BARNABY GOOGE (1563)

18

THE SHEPHEARDES CALENDER

AUGUST

ÆGLOGA OCTAVA. ARGUMENT

In this Æglogue is set forth a delectable controversie, made in imitation of that
in Theocritus: whereto also Virgile fashioned his third and seventh Æglogue.
They choose for umpere of their strife, CUDDIE, a neatherds boye; who, having
ended their cause, reciteth also himselfe a proper song, whereof Colin, he sayth,
was Authour.

WILLIE   PERIGOT   CUDDIE

WILLIE

Tell me, Perigot, what shalbe the game,
  Wherefore with myne thou dare thy musick matche?
Or bene thy Bagpypes renne farre out of frame?
  Or hath the Crampe thy joynts benomd with ache?

PERIGOT

Ah! Willie, when the hart is ill assayde,
  How can Bagpipe or joynts be well apayd?

WILLIE

What the foule evill hath thee so bestadde?
  Whilom thou was peregall to the best,
And wont to make the jolly shepeheards gladde,
  With pyping and dauncing did passe the rest.

benomd, Benumbed.

PERIGOT

Ah! Willie, now I have learnd a newe daunce;
My old musick mard by a newe mischaunce.

WILLIE

Mischiefe mought to that mischaunce befall,
That so hath raft us of our meriment.
But reede me what payne doth thee so appall;
Or lovest thou, or bene thy younglings miswent?

PERIGOT

Love hath misled both my younglings and mee:
I pyne for payne, and they my payne to see.

WILLIE

Perdie, and wellawaye, ill may they thrive!
Never knew I lovers sheepe in good plight:
But, and if in rymes with me thou dare strive,
Such fond fantsies shall soone be put to flight

PERIGOT

That shall I doe, though mochell worse I fared:
Never shall be sayde that Perigot was dared.

WILLIE

Then loe, Perigot, the Pledge which I plight,
A mazer ywrought of the Maple warre,
Wherein is enchased many a fayre sight
Of Beres and Tygres, that maken fiers warre;
And over them spred a goodly wild vine,
Entrailed with a wanton Yvie twine.

Thereby is a Lambe in the Wolves jawes:
But see, how fast renneth the shepheard swayne
To save the innocent from the beastes pawes,
And here with his shepe-hooke hath him slayne,
Tell me, such a cup hast thou ever sene?
Well mought it beseme any harvest Queene.

PERIGOT

Thereto will I pawne yonder spotted Lambe,
Of all my flocke there nis sike another,

mochell, Much.   *mazer ywrought of the Maple warre*, Maple bowl.

For I brought him up without the Dambe:
   But Colin Clout rafte me of his brother,
That he purchast of me in the playne field:
Sore against my will was I forst to yield.

WILLIE

Sicker, make like account of his brother.
   But who shall judge the wager wonne or lost?

PERIGOT

That shall yonder heardgrome, and none other,
Which over the pousse hetheward doth post.

WILLIE

But, for the Sunnbeame so sore doth us beate,
Were not better to shunne the scortching heate?

PERIGOT

Well agreed, Willie: then, sitte thee downe, swayne:
   Sike a song never heardest thou but Colin sing.

CUDDIE

Gynne when ye lyst, ye jolly shepheards twayne:
   Sike a judge as Cuddie were for a king.

PERIGOT

'It fell upon a holy eve,

WILLIE

Hey, ho, hollidaye!

PERIGOT

When holy fathers wont to shrieve;

WILLIE

Now gynneth this roundelay.

PERIGOT

Sitting upon a hill so hye,

WILLIE

Hey, ho, the high hyll!

PERIGOT

The while my flocke did feede thereby;

WILLIE

The while the shepheard selfe did spill.

PERIGOT

I saw the bouncing Bellibone,

WILLIE

Hey, ho, the fayre flocke!

PERIGOT

For priefe thereof, my death shall weepe,

WILLIE

And mone with many a mocke.

PERIGOT

So learnd I love on a holye eve,

WILLIE

Hey, ho, holidaye!

PERIGOT

That ever since my hart did greve,

WILLIE

Now endeth our roundelay!'

CUDDIE

Sicker, sike a roundle never heard I none:
    Little lacketh Perigot of the best,
And Willie is not greatly overgone,
    So weren his under-songs well addrest.

WILLIE

Herdgrome, I fear me, thou have a squint eye:
Areede uprightly who has the victorye.

CUDDIE

Fayth of my soule, I deeme ech have gayned:
    For-thy let the Lambe be Willie his owne:
And for Perigot, so well hath hym payned,
    To him be the wroughten mazer alone.

PERIGOT

Perigot is well pleased with the doome:
Ne can Willie wite the witelesse herdgroome.

WILLIE

Never dempt more right of beautye, I weene,
The shepheard of Ida that judged beauties Queene.

CUDDIE

But tell me, shepherds, should it not yshend
    Your roundels fresh, to heare a doolefull verse

yshend, Disgrace.

WILLIE

Hey, ho, Bonibell!

PERIGOT

Tripping over the dale alone,

WILLIE

She can trippe it very well.

PERIGOT

Well decked in a frocke of gray,

WILLIE

Hey, ho, gray is greete!

PERIGOT

And in a Kirtle of greene saye,

WILLIE

The greene is for maydens meete.

PERIGOT

A chapelet on her head she wore,

WILLIE

Hey, ho, chapelet!

PERIGOT

Of sweete Violets therein was store,

WILLIE

She sweeter then the Violet.

PERIGOT

My sheepe did leave theyr wonted foc

WILLIE

Hey, ho, seely sheepe!

PERIGOT

And gazd on her as they were wood,

WILLIE

Woode as he that did them keepe.

PERIGOT

As the bonilasse passed bye,

WILLIE

Hey, ho, bonilasse!

PERIGOT

She rovde at me with glauncing eye,

greete, Mournful.

WILLIE
As cleare as the christall glasse;
PERIGOT
All as the Sunnye beame so bright,
WILLIE
Hey, ho, the Sunne-beame!
PERIGOT
Glaunceth from Phœbus face forthright,
WILLIE
So love into thy hart did streame:
PERIGOT
Or as the thonder cleaves the cloudes,
WILLIE
Hey, ho, the Thonder!
PERIGOT
Wherein the lightsome levin shroudes,
WILLIE
So cleaves thy soule asonder:
PERIGOT
Or as Dame Cynthias silver raye,
WILLIE
Hey, ho, the Moonelight!
PERIGOT
Upon the glyttering wave doth playe,
WILLIE
Such play is a pitteous plight.
PERIGOT
The glaunce into my heart did glide;
WILLIE
Hey, ho, the glyder!
PERIGOT
Therewith my soule was sharply gryde,
WILLIE
Such woundes soone wexen wider.
PERIGOT
Hasting to raunch the arrow out,
WILLIE
Hey, ho, Perigot!

PERIGOT
I left the head in my hart-roote,
WILLIE
It was a desperate shot.
PERIGOT
There itranckleth, ay more and more,
WILLIE
Hey, ho, the arrowe!
PERIGOT
Ne can I find salve for my sore:
WILLIE
Love is a curelesse sorrowe.
PERIGOT
And though my bale with death I bought,
WILLIE
Hey, ho, heavie cheere!
PERIGOT
Yet should thilk lasse not from my thought,
WILLIE
So you may buye golde to deere.
PERIGOT
But whether in paynefull love I pyne,
WILLIE
Hey, ho, pinching payne!
PERIGOT
Or thrive in welth, she shalbe mine,
WILLIE
But if thou can her obteine.
PERIGOT
And if for gracelesse greefe I dye,
WILLIE
Hey, ho, gracelesse griefe!
PERIGOT
Witnesse shee slewe me with her eye,
WILLIE
Let thy follye be the priefe.
PERIGOT
And you, that sawe it, simple shepe,

WILLIE

Hey, ho, Bonibell!

PERIGOT

Tripping over the dale alone,

WILLIE

She can trippe it very well.

PERIGOT

Well decked in a frocke of gray,

WILLIE

Hey, ho, gray is greete!

PERIGOT

And in a Kirtle of greene saye,

WILLIE

The greene is for maydens meete.

PERIGOT

A chapelet on her head she wore,

WILLIE

Hey, ho, chapelet!

PERIGOT

Of sweete Violets therein was store.

WILLIE

She sweeter then the Violet.

PERIGOT

My sheepe did leave theyr wonted foc

WILLIE

Hey, ho, seely sheepe!

PERIGOT

And gazd on her as they were wood,

WILLIE

Woode as he that did them keepe.

PERIGOT

As the bonilasse passed bye,

WILLIE

Hey, ho, bonilasse!

PERIGOT

She rovde at me with glauncing eye,

greete, Mournful.

Willie

As cleare as the christall glasse;

Perigot

All as the Sunnye beame so bright,

Willie

Hey, ho, the Sunne-beame!

Perigot

Glaunceth from Phœbus face forthright,

Willie

So love into thy hart did streame:

Perigot

Or as the thonder cleaves the cloudes,

Willie

Hey, ho, the Thonder!

Perigot

Wherein the lightsome levin shroudes,

Willie

So cleaves thy soule asonder:

Perigot

Or as Dame Cynthias silver raye,

Willie

Hey, ho, the Moonelight!

Perigot

Upon the glyttering wave doth playe,

Willie

Such play is a pitteous plight.

Perigot

The glaunce into my heart did glide;

Willie

Hey, ho, the glyder!

Perigot

Therewith my soule was sharply gryde,

Willie

Such woundes soone wexen wider.

Perigot

Hasting to raunch the arrow out,

Willie

Hey, ho, Perigot!

PERIGOT
I left the head in my hart-roote,
WILLIE
It was a desperate shot.
PERIGOT
There itranckleth, ay more and more,
WILLIE
Hey, ho, the arrowe!
PERIGOT
Ne can I find salve for my sore:
WILLIE
Love is a curelesse sorrowe.
PERIGOT
And though my bale with death I bought,
WILLIE
Hey, ho, heavie cheere!
PERIGOT
Yet should thilk lasse not from my thought,
WILLIE
So you may buye golde to deere.
PERIGOT
But whether in paynefull love I pyne,
WILLIE
Hey, ho, pinching payne!
PERIGOT
Or thrive in welth, she shalbe mine,
WILLIE
But if thou can her obteine.
PERIGOT
And if for gracelesse greefe I dye,
WILLIE
Hey, ho, gracelesse griefe!
PERIGOT
Witnesse shee slewe me with her eye,
WILLIE
Let thy follye be the priefe.
PERIGOT
And you, that sawe it, simple shepe,

WILLIE
Hey, ho, the fayre flocke!

PERIGOT
For priefe thereof, my death shall weepe,

WILLIE
And mone with many a mocke.

PERIGOT
So learnd I love on a holye eve,

WILLIE
Hey, ho, holidaye!

PERIGOT
That ever since my hart did greve,

WILLIE
Now endeth our roundelay!'

CUDDIE
Sicker, sike a roundle never heard I none:
 Little lacketh Perigot of the best,
And Willie is not greatly overgone,
 So weren his under-songs well addrest.

WILLIE
Herdgrome, I fear me, thou have a squint eye:
Areede uprightly who has the victorye.

CUDDIE
Fayth of my soule, I deeme ech have gayned:
 For-thy let the Lambe be Willie his owne:
And for Perigot, so well hath hym payned,
 To him be the wroughten mazer alone.

PERIGOT
Perigot is well pleased with the doome:
Ne can Willie wite the witelesse herdgroome.

WILLIE
Never dempt more right of beautye, I weene,
The shepheard of Ida that judged beauties Queene.

CUDDIE
But tell me, shepherds, should it not yshend
 Your roundels fresh, to heare a doolefull verse

yshend, Disgrace.

Of Rosalend (who knowes not Rosalend?)
    That Colin made? ylke can I you rehearse.
                    PERIGOT
Now say it, Cuddie, as thou art a ladde:
With mery thing its good to medle sadde.
                    WILLIE
Fayth of my soule, thou shalt ycrouned be
    In Colins stede, if thou this song areede;
For never thing on earth so pleaseth me
    As him to heare, or matter of his deede.
                    CUDDIE
Then listneth ech unto my heavy laye,
And tune your pypes as ruthful as ye may.

'Ye wastefull Woodes! beare witnesse of my woe,
Wherein my plaints did oftentimes resound:
Ye careless byrds are privie to my cryes,
Which in your songs were wont to make a part:
Thou, pleasaunt spring, hast luld me oft asleepe,
Whose streames my tricklinge teares did ofte augment.

'Resort of people doth my greefs augment,
The walled townes doe worke my greater woe;
The forest wide is fitter to resound
The hollow Echo of my carefull cryes:
I hate the house, since thence my love did part,
Whose waylefull want debarres myne eyes from sleepe.

'Let stremes of teares supply the place of sleepe;
Let all, that sweete is, voyd: and all that may augment
My doole, draw neare! More meete to wayle my woe
Bene the wild woodes, my sorowes to resound,
Then bedde, or bowre, both which I fill with cryes,
When I them see so waist, and fynd no part

'Of pleasure past. Here will I dwell apart
In gastfull grove therefore, till my last sleepe
Doe close mine eyes: so shall I not augment

With sight of such as chaunge my restlesse woe.
Helpe me, ye banefull byrds, whose shrieking sound
Ys signe of dreery death, my deadly cryes

'Most ruthfully to tune: And as my cryes
(Which of my woe cannot bewray least part)
You heare all night, when nature craveth sleepe,
Increase, so let your yrksome yells augment.
Thus all the night in plaints, the daye in woe,
I vowed have to wayst, till safe and sound

'She home returne, whose voyces silver sound
To cheerefull songs can chaunge my cherelesse cryes.
Hence with the Nightingale will I take part,
That blessed byrd, that spends her time of sleepe
In songs and plaintive pleas, the more t'augment
The memory of hys misdeede that bred her woe.

        And you that feele no woe,
           When as the sound
        Of these my nightly cryes
           Ye heare apart,
        Let breake your sounder sleepe,
           And pitie augment.'

PERIGOT

O Colin, Colin! the shepheards joye,
    How I admire ech turning of thy verse!
And Cuddie, fresh Cuddie, the liefest boye,
    How dolefully his doole thou didst rehearse!

CUDDIE

Then blowe your pypes, shepheards, til you be at home;
The night nigheth fast, yts time to be gone.

PERIGOT HIS EMBLEME
Vincenti gloria victi.

WILLIES EMBLEME
Vinto non vitto.

CUDDIES EMBLEME
Felice chi puo.

GLOSSE

Bestadde, disposed, ordered.
Peregall, equall.
Whilome, once.
Rafte, bereft, deprived.
Miswent, gon a straye.
Ill may, according to Virgile.
                          'Infelix o semper ovis pecus.'
   A mazer: So also do Theocritus and Virgile feigne pledges of their strife.
   Enchased, engraved. Such pretie descriptions every where useth Theocritus
to bring in his Idyllia. For which speciall cause, indede, he by that name termeth
his Æglogues; for Idyllion in Greeke signifieth the shape or picture of any
thynge, his booke is ful. And not, as I have heard some fondly guesse, that they
wherof be called not Idyllia, but Hædilia, of the Goteheards in them.
   Entrailed, wrought betwene.
   Harvest Queene, The manner of country folke in harvest tyme.
   Pousse, Pease.
   It fell upon: Perigot maketh all his song in prayse of his love, to whom Willy
answereth every underverse. By Perigot who is meant, I can not uprightly say:
but if it be who is supposed, his love, shee deserveth no lesse prayse then he
giveth her.
   Greete, weeping and complaint.
   Chaplet, a kinde of Garlond lyke a crowne.
   Leven, Lightning.
   Cynthia, was sayd to be the Moone.
   Gryde, perced.
   But if, not unlesse.
   Squint eye, partiall judgement.
   Ech have, so saith Virgile,
                          'Et vitula tu dignus, et hic,' &c.
So by enterchaunge of gyfts Cuddie pleaseth both partes.
   Doome, judgement.
   Dempt, for deemed, judged.
   Wite the witelesse, blame the blamelesse.
   The shepherd of Ida, was sayd to be Paris.
   Beauties Queene, Venus, to whome Paris adjudged the golden Apple, as the
pryce of her beautie.

EMBLEME

   The meaning hereof is very ambiguous: for Perigot by his poesie claiming the
conquest, and Willie not yeelding, Cuddie the arbiter of theyr cause, and Patron
of his own, semeth to chalenge it, as his dew, saying, that he is happy which can,
so abruptly ending: but hee meaneth eyther him that can win the beste, or
moderate him selfe being best, and leave of with the best

EDMUND SPENSER (1579)

19

THE SHEPHEARDES CALENDER
OCTOBER

ÆGLOGA DECIMA. ARGUMENT

In CUDDIE is set out the perfecte paterne of a Poete, whiche, finding no maintenaunce of his state and studies, complayneth of the contempte of Poetrie, and the causes thereof: Specially having bene in all ages, and even amongst the most barbarous, alwayes of singular accoumpt and honor, and being indede so worthy and commendable an arte; or rather no arte, but a divine gift and heavenly instinct not to bee gotten by laboure and learning, but adorned with both; and poured into the witte by a certain 'Ενθουσιασμὸς and celestiall inspiration, as the Author hereof els where at large discourseth in his booke called *The English Poete*, which booke being lately come to my hands, I mynde also by Gods grace, upon further advisement, to publish.

PIERCE   CUDDIE

PIERS

Cuddie, for shame! hold up thy heavye head,
And let us cast with what delight to chace,
And weary thys long lingring Phœbus race.
Whilome thou wont the shepheards laddes to leade
In rymes, in ridles, and in bydding base;
Now they in thee, and thou in sleepe art dead.

CUDDIE

Piers, I have pyped erst so long with payne,
That all mine Oten reedes bene rent and wore,
And my poore Muse hath spent her spared store,
Yet little good hath got, and much lesse gayne.
Such pleasaunce makes the Grashopper so poore,
And ligge so layd, when Winter doth her straine.

The dapper ditties, that I wont devise
To feede youthes fancie, and the flocking fry,
Delighten much; what I the bett for-thy?
They han the pleasure, I a sclender prise;
I beate the bush, the byrds to them doe flye:
What good thereof toCuddie can arise?

PIERS

Cuddie, the prayse is better then the price,
The glory eke much greater then the gayne:
O! what an honor is it, to restraine
The lust of lawlesse youth with good advice,
Or pricke them forth with pleasaunce of thy vaine,
Whereto thou list their trayned willes entice.

Soone as thou gynst to sette thy notes in frame,
O, how the rurall routes to thee doe cleave!
Seemeth thou dost their soule of sence bereave;
All as the shepheard that did fetch his dame
From Plutoes balefull bowrie withouten leave,
His musicks might the hellish hound did tame.

CUDDIE

So praysen babes the Peacoks spotted traine,
And wondren at bright Argus blazing eye;
But who rewards him ere the more for-thy,
Or feedes him once the fuller by a graine?
Sike prayse is smoke, that sheddeth in the skye;
Sike words bene wynd, and wasten soone in vayne.

PIERS

Abandon, then, the base and viler clowne;
Lyft up thy selfe out of the lowly dust,
And sing of bloody Mars, of wars, of giusts;
Turne thee to those that weld the awful crowne,
To doubted Knights, whose woundlesse armour rusts,
And helmes unbruzed wexen dayly browne.

There may thy Muse display her fluttryng wing,
And stretch her selfe at large from East to West;
Whither thou list in fayre Elisa rest,
Or, if thee please in bigger notes to sing,
Advaunce the worthy whome shee loveth best,
That first the white beare to the stake did bring.

And, when the stubborne stroke of stronger stounds
Has somewhat slackt the tenor of thy string,
Of love and lustihead tho mayst thou sing,
And carroll lowde, and leade the Myllers rownde,
All were Elisa one of thilke same ring;
So mought our Cuddies name to heaven sownde.

CUDDIE

Indeede the Romish Tityrus, I heare,
Through his Mecænas left his Oaten reede,
Whereon he earst had taught his flocks to feede,
And laboured lands to yield the timely eare,
And eft did sing of warres and deadly drede,
So as the Heavens did quake his verse to here.

But ah! Mecænas is yclad in claye,
And great Augustus long ygoe is dead,
And all the worthies liggen wrapt in leade,
That matter made for Poets on to play:
For ever, who in derring-doe were dreade,
The loftie verse of hem was loved aye.

But after vertue gan for age to stoope,
And mightie manhode brought a bedde of ease,
The vaunting Poets found nought worth a pease
To put in preace among the learned troupe:
Tho gan the streames of flowing wittes to cease,
And sonne-bright honour pend in shamefull coupe.

And if that any buddes of Poesie,
Yet of the old stocke, gan to shoote agayne,
Or it mens follies mote be forst to fayne,
And rolle with rest in rymes of rybaudrye;
Or, as it sprong, it wither must agayne:
Tom Piper makes us better melodie.

PIERS

O pierlesse Poesye! where is then thy place?
If nor in Princes pallace thou doe sitt,

(And yet is Princes pallace the most fitt,)
Ne brest of baser birth doth thee embrace,
Then make thee winges of thine aspyring wit,
And, whence thou camst, flye backe to heaven apace.

CUDDIE

Ah, Percy! it is all to weake and wanne,
So high to sore and make so large a flight;
Her peeced pyneons bene not so in plight:
For Colin fittes such famous flight to scanne;
He, were he not with love so ill bedight,
Would mount as high, and sing as soote as Swanne.

PIERS

Ah, fon! for love does teach him climbe so hie,
And lyftes him up out of the loathsome myre:
Such immortal mirrhor, as he doth admire,
Would rayse ones mynd above the starry skie,
And cause a caytive corage to aspire;
For lofty love doth loath a lowly eye.

CUDDIE

All otherwise the state of Poet stands;
For lordly love is such a Tyranne fell,
That where he rules all power he doth expell;
The vaunted verse a vacant head demaundes,
Ne wont with crabbed care the Muses dwell:
Unwisely weaves, that takes two webbes in hand.

Who ever casts to compasse weightye prise,
And thinkes to throwe out thondring words of threate,
Let powre in lavish cups and thriftie bitts of meate,
For Bacchus fruite is frend to Phœbus wise;
And, when with Wine the braine begins to sweate,
The nombers flowe as fast as spring doth ryse.

Thou kenst not, Percie, howe the ryme should rage,
O! if my temples were distaind with wine,
And girt in girlonds of wild Yvie twine,

peeced, Imperfect.

How I could reare the Muse on stately stage,
And teache her tread aloft in buskin fine,
With queint Bellona in her equipage!

But ah! my corage cooles ere it be warme:
For-thy content us in thys humble shade,
Where no such troublous tydes han us assayde;
Here we our slender pypes may safely charme.
                    PIERS
And, when my Gotes shall han their bellies layd,
Cuddie shall have a Kidde to store his farme.
                              EDMUND SPENSER (1579)

20

THE SHEPHEARDES CALENDER
NOVEMBER

ÆGLOGA UNDECIMA. ARGUMENT

In this xi. Æglogue hee bewayleth the death of some mayden of greate bloud,
whom he calleth Dido. The personage is secrete, and to me altogether unknowne,
albe of him selfe I often required the same. This Æglogue is made in imitation of
Marot his song, which he made upon the death of Loys the Frenche Queene; but
farre passing his reache, and in myne opinion all other the Eglogues of this booke.

THENOT   COLIN
                    THENOT
Colin, my deare, when shall it please thee sing,
As thou were wont, songs of some jouisaunce?
Thy Muse to long slombreth in sorrowing,
Lulled a sleepe through loves misgovernaunce.
Now somewhat sing, whose endles sovenaunce
Emong the shepeheards swaines may aye remaine,
Whether thee list thy loved lasse advaunce,
Or honor Pan with hymnes of higher vaine.
                    COLIN
Thenot, now nis the time of merimake,
Nor Pan to herye, nor with love to playe;

Sike myrth in May is meetest for to make,
Or summer shade, under the cocked hay.
But nowe sadde Winter welked hath the day,
And Phœbus, weary of his yerely taske,
Ystabled hath his steedes in lowlye laye,
And taken up his ynne in Fishes haske.
Thilke sollein season sadder plight doth aske,
And loatheth sike delightes as thou doest prayse:
The mornefull Muse in myrth now list ne maske,
As shee was wont in youngth and sommer dayes;
But if thou algate lust light virelayes,
And looser songs of love to underfong,
Who but thy selfe deserves sike Poetes prayse?
Relieve thy Oaten pypes that sleepen long.

THENOT

The Nightingale is sovereigne of song,
Before him fits the Titmose silent bee;
And I, unfitte to thrust in skilful thronge,
Should Colin make judge of my fooleree:
Nay, better learne of hem that learned bee,
And han be watered at the Muses well;
The kindelye dewe drops from the higher tree,
And wets the little plants that lowly dwell.
But if sadde winters wrathe, and season chill,
Accorde not with thy Muses meriment,
To sadder times thou mayst attune thy quill,
And sing of sorrowe and deathes dreeriment;
For deade is Dido, dead, alas! and drent;
Dido! the greate Shepehearde his daughter sheene.
The fayrest May she was that ever went,
Her like shee has not left behinde I weene:
And, if thou wilt bewayle my wofull tene,
I shall thee give yond Cosset for thy payne;
And, if thy rymes as rownde and rufull bene
As those that did thy Rosalind complayne,
Much greater gyfts for guerdon thou shalt gayne,
Then Kidde or Cosset, which I thee bynempt.

sollein, Sad.   *underfong*, Undertake.   *drent*, Drowned.   *Then*, Than.

Then up, I say, thou jolly shepeheard swayne,
Let not my small demaund be so contempt.

COLIN

Thenot, to that I choose thou doest me tempt;
But ah! to well I wote my humble vaine,
And howe my rimes bene rugged and unkempt;
Yet, as I conne, my conning I will strayne.

'Up, then, Melpomene! the mournefulst Muse of nyne,
Such cause of mourning never hadst afore;
Up, grieslie ghostes! and up my rufull ryme!
Matter of myrth now shalt thou have no more;
For dead she is, that myrth thee made of yore.
Dido, my deare, alas! is dead,
Dead, and lyeth wrapt in lead.
O heavie herse!
Let streaming teares be poured out in store;
O carefull verse!

'Shepheards, that by your flocks on Kentish downes abyde,
Waile ye this wofull waste of Natures warke;
Waile we the wight whose presence was our pryde;
Waile we the wight whose absence is our carke;
The sonne of all the world is dimme and darke:
The earth now lacks her wonted light,
And all we dwell in deadly night.
O heavie herse!
Breake we our pypes, that shrild as lowde as Larke;
O carefull verse!

'Why doe we longer live, (ah! why live we so long?)
Whose better dayes death hath shut up in woe?
The fayrest floure our gyrlond all emong
Is faded quite, and into dust ygoe.
Sing now, ye shepheards daughters, sing no moe
The songs that Colin made you in her praise,
But into weeping turne your wanton layes.
O heavie herse!
Nowe is time to dye: Nay, time was long ygoe:
O carefull verse!

'Whence is it, that the flouret of the field doth fade,
And lyeth buryed long in Winters bale;
Yet, soone as spring his mantle hath displayde,
It floureth fresh, as it should never fayle?
But thing on earth that is of most availe,
    As vertues braunch and beauties budde,
    Reliven not for any good.
    O heavie herse!
The braunch once dead, the budde eke needes must quaile;
    O carefull verse!

'She, while she was, (that was, a woful word to sayne!)
For beauties prayse and plesaunce had no peere;
So well she couth the shepherds entertayne
With cakes and cracknells, and such country chere:
Ne would she scorne the simple shepheards swaine;
    For she would cal him often heame,
    And give him curds and clouted Creame.
    O heavie herse!
Als Colin Cloute she would not once disdayne;
    O carefull verse!

'But nowe sike happy cheere is turnd to heavie chaunce,
Such pleasaunce now displast by dolors dint:
All musick sleepes, where death doth leade the daunce,
And shepherds wonted solace is extinct.
The blew in black, the greene in gray is tinct;
    The gaudie girlonds deck her grave,
    The faded flowres her corse embrave.
    O heavie herse!
Morne nowe, my Muse, now morne with teares besprint;
    O carefull verse!

'O thou greate shepheard, Lobbin, how great is thy griefe!
Where bene the nosegayes that she dight for thee?
The coloured chaplets wrought with a chiefe.
The knotted rush-ringes, and gilte Rosemaree?
For shee deemed nothing too deere for thee.

Ah! they bene all yclad in clay;
One bitter blast blewe all away.
  O heavie herse!
Thereof nought remaynes but the memoree;
  O carefull verse!

'Ay me! that dreerie Death should strike so mortall stroke,
That can undoe Dame Natures kindly course;
The faded lockes fall from the loftie oke,
The flouds do gaspe, for dryed is theyr sourse,
And flouds of teares flowe in theyr stead perforse:
  The mantled medowes mourne,
  Theyr sondry colours tourne.
  O heavie herse!
The heavens doe melt in teares without remorse;
  O carefull verse!

'The feeble flocks in field refuse their former foode,
And hang theyr heads as they would learne to weepe;
The beastes in forest wayle as they were woode,
Except the Wolves, that chase the wandring sheepe,
Now she is gone that safely did hem keepe:
  The Turtle on the bared braunch
  Laments the wound that death did launch.
  O heavie herse!
And Philomele her song with teares doth steepe;
  O carefull verse!

'The water Nymphs, that wont with her to sing and
    daunce,
And for her girlond Olive braunches beare,
Nowe balefull boughes of Cypres doen advaunce;
The Muses, that were wont greene bayes to weare,
Now bringen bitter Eldre braunches seare;
  The fatall sisters eke repent
  Her vitall threde so soone was spent.
  O heavie herse!

woode, Mad.

Morne now, my Muse, now morne with heavy cheare,
   O carefull verse!

'O! trustlesse state of earthly things, and slipper hope
Of mortal men, that swincke and sweate for nought,
And, shooting wide, doe misse the marked scope;
Now have I learnd (a lesson derely bought)
That nys on earth assuraunce to be sought;
   For what might be in earthlie mould,
   That did her buried body hould.
   O heavie herse!
Yet saw I on the beare when it was brought;
   O carefull verse!

'But maugre death, and dreaded sisters deadly spight,
And gates of hel, and fyrie furies forse,
She hath the bonds broke of eternall night,
Her soule unbodied of the burdenous corpse
Why then weepes Lobbin so without remorse?
   O Lobb! thy losse no longer lament;
   Dido nis dead, but into heaven hent.
   O happye herse!
Cease now, my Muse, now cease thy sorrowes sourse;
   O joyfull verse!

'Why wayle we then? why weary we the Gods with
     playnts,
As if some evil were to her betight?
She raignes a goddesse now emong the saintes,
That whilome was the saynt of shepheards light,
And is enstalled nowe in heavens hight.
   I see thee, blessed soule, I see
   Walke in Elisian fieldes so free.
   O happy herse!
Might I once come to thee, (O that I might!)
   O joyfull verse!

slipper, Slippery

'Unwise and wretched men, to weete whats good or ill,
We deeme of Death as doome of ill desert;
But knewe we, fooles, what it us bringes until,
Dye would we dayly, once it to expert!
No daunger there the shepheard can astert;
    Fayre fieldes and pleasaunt layes there bene;
    The fieldes ay fresh, the grasse ay greene.
    O happy herse!
Make hast, ye shepheards, thether to revert:
    O joyfull verse!

'Dido is gone afore; (whose turne shall be the next?)
There lives shee with the blessed Gods in blisse,
There drincks she Nectar with Ambrosia mixt,
And joyes enjoyes that mortall men doe misse.
The honor now of highest gods she is,
    That whilome was poore shepheards pryde,
    While here on earth she did abyde.
    O happy herse!
Ceasse now, my song, my woe now wasted is;
    O joyfull verse!'

THENOT

Ay, francke shepheard, how bene thy verses meint
With doleful pleasaunce, so as I ne wotte
Whether rejoyce or weepe for great constrainte.
Thyne be the cossette, well hast thow it gotte.
Up, Colin up! ynough thou morned hast;
Now gynnes to mizzle, hye we homeward fast.

COLINS EMBLEME
La mort ny mord.

GLOSSE

Jouisaunce, myrth.
Sovenaunce, remembrance.
Herie, honour.
    Welked, shortned or empayred. As the Moone being in the waine is sayde of Lidgate to welk.
    In lowly lay, according to the season of the moneth November, when the sonne draweth low in the South toward his Tropick or returne.

In fishes haske, the sonne reigneth, that is, in the signe Pisces all November: a haske is a wicker pad, wherein they use to cary fish.

Virelaies, a light kind of song.

Bee watred, for it is a saying of Poetes, that they have dronk of the Muses well Castalias, whereof was before sufficiently sayd.

Dreriment, dreery and heavy cheere.

The great shepheard, is some man of high degree, and not, as some vainely suppose, God Pan. The person both of the shepheard and of Dido is unknowen, and closely buried in the Authors conceipt. But out of doubt I am, that it is not Rosalind, as some imagin: for he speaketh soone after of her also.

Shene, fayre and shining.

May, for mayde.

Tene, sorrow.

Guerdon, reward.

Bynempt, bequethed.

Cosset, a lambe brought up without the dam.

Unkempt. Incompti. Not comed, that is, rude and unhansome.

 EDMUND SPENSER (1579)

21

ASTROPHEL

A PASTORALL ELEGIE,

UPON THE DEATH OF THE MOST NOBLE AND VALOROUS KNIGHT,
SIR PHILIP SIDNEY.

DEDICATED TO THE MOST BEAUTIFULL AND VERTUOUS LADIE,
THE COUNTESS OF ESSEX.

Shepheards, that wont, on pipes of oaten reed,
Oft times to plaine your loves concealed smart;
And with your piteous layes have learnd to breed
Compassion in a countrey lasses hart
Hearken, ye gentle shepheards, to my song,
And place my dolefull plaint your plaints emong.

To you alone I sing this mournfull verse,
The mournfulst verse that ever man heard tell:
To you whose softened hearts it may empierse
With dolours dart for death of Astrophel.
To you I sing and to none other wight,
For well I wot my rymes bene rudely dight.

Yet as they been, if any nycer wit
Shall hap to heare, or covet them to read:
Thinke he, that such are for such ones most fit,
Made not to please the living but the dead.
And if in him found pity ever place,
Let him be moov'd to pity such a case.

ASTROPHEL

A gentle shepheard borne in Arcady,
Of gentlest race that ever shepheard bore,
About the grassie bancks of Hæmony
Did keepe his sheep, his litle stock and store:
Full carefully he kept them day and night,
In fairest fields; and Astrophel he hight.

Young Astrophel, the pride of shepheards praise,
Young Astrophel, the rusticke lasses love:
Far passing all the pastors of his daies,
In all that seemly shepheard might behove.
In one thing onely fayling of the best,
That he was not so happie as the rest.

For from the time that first the Nymph his mother
Him forth did bring, and taught her lambs to feed;
A sclender swaine, excelling far each other,
In comely shape, like her that did him breed,
He grew up fast in goodnesse and in grace,
And doubly faire wox both in mynd and face.

Which daily more and more he did augment,
With gentle usuage and demeanure myld:
That all mens harts with secret ravishment
He stole away, and weetingly beguyld.
Ne spight it selfe, that all good things doth spill,
Found ought in him, that she could say was ill.

His sports were faire, his joyance innocent,
Sweet without sowre, and honny without gall:

And he himselfe seemed made for meriment,
Merily masking both in bowre and hall.
There was no pleasure nor delightfull play,
When Astrophel so ever was away.

For he could pipe, and daunce, and caroll sweet,
Emongst the shepheards in their shearing feast;
As Somers larke that with her song doth greet
The dawning day forth comming from the East.
And layes of love he also could compose:
Thrise happie she, whom he to praise did chose.

Full many Maydens often did him woo,
Them to vouchsafe emongst his rimes to name,
Or make for them as he was wont to doo
For her that did his heart with love inflame.
For which they promised to dight for him
Gay chapelets of flowers and gyrlonds trim.

And many a Nymph both of the wood and brooke,
Soone as his oaten pipe began to shrill,
Both christall wells and shadie groves forsooke,
To heare the charmes of his enchanting skill;
And brought him presents, flowers if it were prime,
Or mellow fruit if it were harvest time.

But he for none of them did care a whit,
Yet woodgods for them often sighed sore:
Ne for their gifts unworthie of his wit,
Yet not unworthie of the countries store.
For one alone he cared, for one he sigh't,
His lifes desire, and his deare loves delight.

Stella the faire, the fairest star in skie,
As faire as Venus or the fairest faire,
(A fairer star saw never living eie,)
Shot her sharp pointed beames through purest aire,
Her he did love, her he alone did honor,
His thoughts, his rimes, his songs were all upon her.

To her he vowd the service of his daies,
On her he spent the riches of his wit:
For her he made hymnes of immortall praise,
Of onely her he sung, he thought, he writ.
Her, and but her, of love he worthie deemed;
For all the rest but litle he esteemed.

Ne her with ydle words alone he wowed,
And verses vaine, (yet verses are not vaine,)
But with brave deeds to her sole service vowed,
And bold atchievements her did entertaine.
For both in deeds and words he nourtred was,
Both wise and hardie, (too hardie, alas!)

In wrestling nimble, and in renning swift,
In shooting steddie, and in swimming strong:
Well made to strike, to throw, to leape, to lift,
And all the sports that shepheards are emong.
In every one he vanquisht every one,
He vanquisht all, and vanquisht was of none.

Besides, in hunting such felicitie,
Or rather infelicitie, he found,
That every field and forest far away
He sought, where salvage beasts do most abound.
No beast so salvage but he could it kill;
No chace so hard, but he therein had skill.

Such skill, matcht with such courage as he had,
Did prick him foorth with proud desire of praise
To seek abroad, of daunger nought ydrad,
His mistresse name, and his owne fame to raise.
What needeth perill to be sought abroad,
Since round about us it doth make aboad!

It fortuned as he that perilous game
In forreine soyle pursued far away,
Into a forest wide and waste he came,

Where store he heard to be of salvage pray.
So wide a forest and so waste as this,
Nor famous Ardeyn, nor fowle Arlo, is.

There his welwoven toyles, and subtil traines,
He laid the brutish nation to enwrap:
So well he wrought with practise and with paines,
That he of them great troups did soone entrap.
Full happie man (misweening much) was hee,
So rich a spoile within his power to see.

Eftsoones, all heedlesse of his dearest hale,
Full greedily into the heard he thrust,
To slaughter them, and worke their finall bale,
Least that his toyle should of their troups be brust.
Wide wounds emongst them many one he made,
Now with his sharp bore-spear, now with his blade.

His care was all how he them all might kill,
That none might scape, (so partiall unto none:)
Ill mynd so much to mynd anothers ill,
As to become unmyndfull of his owne.
But pardon that unto the cruell skies,
That from himselfe to them withdrew his eies.

So as he rag'd emongst that beastly rout,
A cruell beast of most accursed brood
Upon him turnd, (despeyre makes cowards stout,)
And, with fell tooth accustomed to blood,
Launched his thigh with so mischievous might,
That it both bone and muscles ryved quight.

So deadly was the dint and deep the wound,
And so huge streames of blood thereout did flow,
That he endured not the direfull stound,
But on the cold deare earth himselfe did throw;
The whiles the captive heard his nets did rend,
And, having none to let, to wood did wend.

Ah! where were ye this while his shepheard peares,
To whom alive was nought so deare as hee:
And ye fayre Mayds, the matches of his yeares,
Which in his grace did boast you most to bee!
Ah! where were ye, when he of you had need,
To stop his wound that wondrously did bleed!

Ah! wretched boy, the shape of dreryhead,
And sad ensample of mans suddein end:
Full litle faileth but thou shalt be dead,
Unpitied, unplaynd, of foe or frend:
Whilest none is nigh, thine eylids up to close,
And kisse thy lips like faded leaves of rose.

A sort of shepheards, sewing of the chace,
As they the forest raunged on a day,
By fate or fortune came unto the place,
Where as the lucklesse boy yet bleeding lay;
Yet bleeding lay, and yet would still have bled,
Had not good hap those shepheards thether led.

They stopt his wound, (too late to stop it was!)
And in their armes then softly did him reare:
Tho (as he wild) unto his loved lasse,
His dearest love, him dolefully did beare.
The dolefulst beare that ever man did see,
Was Astrophel, but dearest unto mee!

She, when she saw her love in such a plight,
With crudled blood and filthie gore deformed,
That wont to be with flowers and gyrlonds dight,
And her deare favours dearly well adorned;
Her face, the fairest face that eye mote see,
She likewise did deforme, like him to bee.

Her yellow locks that shone so bright and long,
As Sunny beames in fairest somers day,
She fiersly tore, and with outragious wrong

From her red cheeks the roses rent away;
And her faire brest, the threasury of joy,
She spoyld thereof, and filled with annoy.

His palled face, impictured with death,
She bathed oft with teares, and dried oft:
And with sweet kisses suckt the wasting breath
Out of his lips like lilies pale and soft:
And ofte she cald to him, who answerd nought,
But onely by his lookes did tell his thought.

The rest of her impatient regret,
And piteous mone the which she for him made,
No toong can tell, nor any forth can set,
But he whose heart like sorrow did invade.
At last, when paine his vitall powres had spent,
His wasted life her wearie lodge forwent.

Which when she saw, she staied not a whit,
But after him did make untimely haste;
Forth-with her ghost out of her corps did flit,
And followed her make like turtle chaste,
To prove that death their hearts cannot divide,
Which living were in love so firmly tide.

The gods, which all things see, this same beheld,
And, pittying this paire of lovers trew,
Transformed them, there lying on the field,
Into one flowre that is both red and blew;
It first growes red, and then to blew doth fade,
Like Astrophel, which thereinto was made.

And in the midst thereof a star appeares,
As fairly formd as any star in skyes;
Resembling Stella in her freshest yeares,
Forth darting beames of beautie from her eyes:
And all the day it standeth full of deow,
Which is the teares, that from her eyes did flow.

That hearbe of some Starlight is cald by name,
Of others Penthia, though not so well:
But thou, where ever thou doest finde the same,
From this day forth do call it Astrophel:
And, when so ever thou it up doest take,
Do pluck it softly for that shepheards sake.

Hereof when tydings far abroad did passe,
The shepheards all which loved him full deare,
And sure full deare of all he loved was,
Did thether flock to see what they did heare;
And when that pitteous spectacle they vewed,
The same with bitter teares they all bedewed.

And every one did make exceeding mone,
With inward anguish and great griefe opprest:
And every one did weep and waile, and mone,
And meanes deviz'd to shew his sorrow best.
That from that houre, since first on grassie greene
Shepheards kept sheep, was not like mourning seen.

EDMUND SPENSER (1595)

22

THE FAERIE QUEENE, BOOK VI

Canto IX

Calidore hostes with Meliboe,
And loves fayre Pastorell:
Coridon envies him, yet he
For ill rewards him well.

I

Now turne againe my teme, thou jolly swayne,
Backe to the furrow which I lately left.
I lately left a furrow, one or twayne,
Unplough'd, the which my coulter hath not cleft;
Yet seem'd the soyle both fayre and frutefull eft,

As I it past: that were too great a shame,
That so rich frute should be from us bereft;
Besides the great dishonour and defame,
Which should befall to Calidores immortall name.

II

Great travell hath the gentle Calidore
And toyle endured, sith I left him last
Sewing the Blatant Beast; which I forbore
To finish then, for other present hast.
Full many pathes and perils he hath past,
Through hils, through dales, through forests, and through
    plaines,
In that same quest which fortune on him cast,
Which he atchieved to his owne great gaines,
Reaping eternall glorie of his restlesse paines.

III

So sharply he the Monster did pursew,
That day nor night he suffred him to rest,
Ne rested he himselfe, but natures dew,
For dread of daunger not to be redrest,
If he for slouth forslackt so famous quest.
Him first from court he to the citties coursed,
And from the citties to the townes him prest,
And from the townes into the countrie forsed,
And from the country back to private farmes he scorsed.

IV

From thence into the open fields he fled,
Whereas the Heardes were keeping of their neat,
And shepherds singing to their flockes (that fed)
Layes of sweete love and youthes delightfull heat:
Him thether eke, for all his fearefull threat,
He followed fast, and chaced him so nie,
That to the folds, where sheepe at night doe seat,
And to the litle cots, where shepherds lie
In winters wrathfull time, he forced him to flie.

Sewing, Following.   *scorsed*, Pursued.

V

There on a day, as he pursew'd the chace,
He chaunst to spy a sort of shepheard groomes,
Playing on pipes and caroling apace,
The whyles their beasts there in the budded broomes
Beside them fed, and nipt the tender bloomes;
For other worldly wealth they cared nought.
To whom Sir Calidore yet sweating comes,
And them to tell him courteously besought,
If such a beast they saw, which he had thether brought.

VI

They answer'd him that no such beast they saw,
Nor any wicked feend that mote offend
Their happie flockes, nor daunger to them draw;
But if that such there were (as none they kend)
They prayd high God them farre from them to send.
Then one of them, him seeing so to sweat,
After his rusticke wise, that well he weend,
Offred him drinke to quench his thirstie heat,
And, if he hungry were, him offred eke to eat.

VII

The knight was nothing nice, where was no need,
And tooke their gentle offer: so adowne
They prayd him sit, and gave him for to feed
Such homely what as serves the simple clowne,
That doth despise the dainties of the towne.
Tho, having fed his fill, he there besyde
Saw a faire damzell, which did weare a crowne
Of sundry flowres with silken ribbands tyde,
Yclad in home-made greene that her owne hands had dyde.

VIII

Upon a litle hillocke she was placed
Higher then all the rest, and round about
Environ'd with a girland, goodly graced,
Of lovely lasses; and them all without

The lustie shepheard swaynes sate in a rout,
The which did pipe and sing her prayses dew,
And oft rejoyce, and oft for wonder shout,
As if some miracle of heavenly hew
Were downe to them descended in that earthly vew.

IX
And soothly sure she was full fayre of face,
And perfectly well shapt in every lim,
Which she did more augment with modest grace
And comely carriage of her count'nance trim,
That all the rest like lesser lamps did dim:
Who, her admiring as some heavenly wight,
Did for their soveraine goddesse her esteeme,
And, caroling her name both day and night,
The fayrest Pastorella her by name did hight.

X
Ne was there heard, ne was there shepheards swayne,
But her did honour; and eke many a one
Burnt in her love, and with sweet pleasing payne
Full many a night for her did sigh and grone:
But most of all the shepheard Coridon
For her did languish, and his deare life spend;
Yet neither she for him nor other none
Did care a whit, ne any liking lend:
Though meane her lot, yet higher did her mind ascend.

XI
Her whyles Sir Calidore there vewed well,
And markt her rare demeanure, which him seemed
So farre the meane of shepheards to excell,
As that he in his mind her worthy deemed
To be a Princes Paragone esteemed,
He was unwares surprisd in subtile bands
Of the blynd boy; ne thence could be redeemed
By any skill out of his cruell hands;
Caught like the bird which gazing still on others stands.

XII

So stood he still long gazing thereupon,
Ne any will had thence to move away,
Although his quest were farre afore him gon:
But after he had fed, yet did he stay
And sate there still, untill the flying day
Was farre forth spent, discoursing diversly
Of sundry things as fell, to worke delay;
And evermore his speach he did apply
To th' heards, but meant them to the damzels fantazy.

XII

By this the moystie night approching fast
Her deawy humour gan on th' earth to shed,
That warn'd the shepheards to their homes to hast
Their tender flocks, now being fully fed,
For feare of wetting them before their bed.
Then came to them a good old aged syre,
Whose silver lockes bedeckt his beard and hed,
With shepheards hooke in hand, and fit attyre,
That wild the damzell rise; the day did now expyre.

XIV

He was, to weet, by common voice esteemed
The father of the fayrest Pastorell,
And of her selfe in very deede so deemed;
Yet was not so; but, as old stories tell,
Found her by fortune, which to him befell,
In th' open fields an Infant left alone;
And, taking up, brought home and noursed well
As his owne chyld; for other he had none;
That she in tract of time accompted was his owne.

XV

She at his bidding meekely did arise,
And streight unto her litle flocke did fare:
Then all the rest about her rose likewise,
And each his sundrie sheepe with severall care

Gathered together, and them homeward bare:
Whylest everie one with helping hands did strive,
Amongst themselves, and did their labours share,
To helpe faire Pastorella home to drive
Her fleecie flocke; but Coridon most helpe did give.

XVI

But Melibœe (so hight that good old man)
Now seeing Calidore left all alone,
And night arrived hard at hand, began
Him to invite unto his simple home:
Which though it were a cottage clad with lome,
And all things therein meane, yet better so
To lodge then in the salvage fields to rome.
The knight full gladly soone agreed thereto,
(Being his harts owne wish,) and home with him did go.

XVII

There he was welcom'd of that honest syre
And of his aged Beldame homely well;
Who him besought himselfe to disattyre,
And rest himselfe till supper time befell;
By which home came the fayrest Pastorell,
After her flocke she in their fold had tyde:
And supper readie dight they to it fell
With small adoe, and nature satisfyde,
The which doth litle crave contented to abyde.

XVIII

Tho when they had their hunger slaked well,
And the fayre mayd the table ta'ne away,
The gentle knight, as he that did excell
In courtesie and well could doe and say,
For so great kindnesse as he found that day
Gan greatly thanke his host and his good wife;
And drawing thence his speach another way,
Gan highly to commend the happie life
Which Shepheards lead, without debate or bitter strife.

XIX

'How much' (sayd he) 'more happie is the state
In which ye, father, here doe dwell at ease,
Leading a life so free and fortunate
From all the tempests of these worldly seas,
Which tosse the rest in daungerous disease;
Where warres, and wreckes, and wicked enmitie
Doe them afflict, which no man can appease;
That certes I your happinesse envie,
And wish my lot were plast in such felicitie.'

XX

'Surely, my sonne,' (then answer'd he againe)
'If happie, then it is in this intent,
That having small yet doe I not complaine
Of want, ne wish for more it to augment,
But doe my selfe with that I have content;
So taught of nature, which doth litle need
Of forreine helpes to lifes due nourishment:
The fields my food, my flocke my rayment breed;
No better doe I weare, no better doe I feed.

XXI

'Therefore I doe not any one envy,
Nor am envyde of any one therefore:
They, that have much, feare much to loose thereby,
And store of cares doth follow riches store.
The litle that I have growes dayly more
Without my care, but onely to attend it;
My lambes doe every yeare increase their score,
And my flockes father daily doth amend it.
What have I, but to praise th' Almighty that doth send it!

XXII

'To them that list the worlds gay showes I leave,
And to great ones such follies doe forgive;
Which oft through pride do their owne perill weave,
And through ambition downe themselves doe drive

To sad decay, that might contented live.
Me no such cares nor combrous thoughts offend,
Ne once my minds unmoved quiet grieve;
But all the night in silver sleepe I spend,
And all the day to what I list I doe attend.

XXIII
'Sometimes I hunt the Fox, the vowed foe
Unto my Lambes, and him dislodge away;
Sometime the fawne I practise from the Doe,
Or from the Goat her kidde, how to convay:
Another while I baytes and nets display
The birds to catch, or fishes to beguyle;
And when I wearie am, I downe doe lay
My limbes in every shade to rest from toyle,
And drinke of every brooke when thirst my throte doth boyle.

XXIV
'The time was once, in my first prime of yeares,
When pride of youth forth pricked my desire,
That I disdain'd amongst mine equall peares
To follow sheepe and shepheards base attire:
For further fortune then I would inquire;
And, leaving home, to roiall court I sought,
Where I did sell my selfe for yearely hire,
And in the Princes gardin daily wrought:
There I beheld such vainenesse as I never thought.

XXV
'With sight whereof soone cloyd, and long deluded
With idle hopes which them doe entertaine,
After I had ten yeares my selfe excluded
From native home, and spent my youth in vaine,
I gan my follies to my selfe to plaine,
And this sweet peace, whose lacke did then appeare:
Tho, backe returning to my sheepe againe,
I from thenceforth have learn'd to love more deare
This lowly quiet life which I inherite here.'

XXVI

Whylest thus he talkt, the knight with greedy eare
Hong still upon his melting mouth attent;
Whose sensefull words empierst his hart so neare,
That he was rapt with double ravishment,
Both of his speach, that wrought him great content,
And also of the object of his vew,
On which his hungry eye was always bent;
That twixt his pleasing tongue, and her faire hew,
He lost himselfe, and like one halfe entraunced grew.

XXVII

Yet to occasion meanes to worke his mind,
And to insinuate his harts desire,
He thus replyde: 'Now surely, syre, I find,
That all this worlds gay showes, which we admire,
Be but vaine shadowes to this safe retyre
Of life, which here in lowlinesse ye lead,
Fearelesse of foes, or fortunes wrackfull yre
Which tosseth states, and under foot doth tread
The mightie ones, affrayd of every chaunges dread.

XXVIII

'That even I, which daily doe behold
The glorie of the great mongst whom I won,
And now have prov'd what happinesse ye hold
In this small plot of your dominion,
Now loath great Lordship and ambition;
And wish th' heavens so much had graced mee,
As graunt me live in like condition;
Or that my fortunes might transposed bee
From pitch of higher place unto this low degree.'

XXIX

'In vaine' (said then old Meliboe) 'doe men
The heavens of their fortunes fault accuse,
Sith they know best what is the best for them;
For they to each such fortune doe diffuse,

As they doe know each can most aptly use:
For not that which men covet most is best,
Nor that thing worst which men do most refuse;
But fittest is, that all contented rest
With that they hold: each hath his fortune in his brest.

XXX
'It is the mynd that maketh good or ill,
That maketh wretch or happie, rich or poore;
For some, that hath abundance at his will,
Hath not enough, but wants in greatest store,
And other, that hath litle, askes no more,
But in that litle is both rich and wise;
For wisedome is most riches: fooles therefore
They are which fortunes doe by vowes devize,
Sith each unto himselfe his life may fortunize.'

XXXI
'Since then in each mans self' (said Calidore)
'It is to fashion his owne lyfes estate,
Give leave awhyle, good father, in this shore
To rest my barcke, which hath bene beaten late
With stormes of fortune and tempestuous fate
In seas of troubles and of toylesome paine;
That, whether quite from them for to retrate
I shall resolve, or backe to turne againe,
I may here with your selfe some small repose obtaine.

XXXII
'Not that the burden of so bold a guest
Shall chargefull be, or chaunge to you at all;
For your meane food shall be my daily feast,
And this your cabin both my bowre and hall:
Besides, for recompence hereof I shall
You well reward, and golden guerdon give,
That may perhaps you better much withall,
And in this quiet make you safer live.'
So forth he drew much gold, and toward him it drive.

XXXIII

But the good man, nought tempted with the offer
Of his rich mould, did thrust it farre away,
And thus bespake: 'Sir knight, your bounteous proffer
Be farre fro me, to whom ye ill display
That mucky masse, the cause of mens decay,
That mote empaire my peace with daungers dread;
But, if ye algates covet to assay
This simple sort of life that shepheards lead,
Be it your owne: our rudenesse to your selfe aread.'

XXXIV

So there that night Sir Calidore did dwell,
And long while after, whilest him list remaine,
Dayly beholding the faire Pastorell,
And feeding on the bayt of his owne bane:
During which time he did her entertaine
With all kind courtesies he could invent;
And every day, her companie to gaine,
When to the field she went he with her went:
So for to quench his fire he did it more augment.

XXXV

But she that never had acquainted beene
With such queint usage, fit for Queenes and Kings,
Ne ever had such knightly service seene,
But, being bred under base shepheards wings,
Had ever learn'd to love the lowly things,
Did litle whit regard his courteous guize,
But cared more for Colins carolings
Then all that he could doe, or ever devize:
His layes, his loves, his lookes, she did them all despize.

XXXVI

Which Calidore perceiving, thought it best
To chaunge the manner of his loftie looke;
And doffing his bright armes himselfe addrest
In shepheards weed; and in his hand he tooke,

Instead of steele-head speare, a shepheards hooke;
That who had seene him then, would have bethought
On Phrygian Paris by Plexippus brooke,
When he the love of fayre Oenone sought,
What time the golden apple was unto him brought.

XXXVII

So being clad unto the fields he went
With the faire Pastorella every day,
And kept her sheepe with diligent attent,
Watching to drive the ravenous Wolfe away,
The whylest at pleasure she mote sport and play;
And every evening helping them to fold:
And otherwhiles, for need, he did assay
In his strong hand their rugged teats to hold,
And out of them to presse the milke: love so much could.

XXXVIII

Which seeing Coridon, who her likewise
Long time had lov'd, and hop'd her love to gaine,
He much was troubled at that straungers guize,
And many gealous thoughts conceiv'd in vaine,
That this of all his labour and long paine
Should reap the harvest ere it ripened were:
That made him scoule, and pout, and oft complaine
Of Pastorell to all the shepheards there,
That she did love a stranger swayne then him more dere.

XXXIX

And ever, when he came in companie
Where Calidore was present, he would loure
And byte his lip, and even for gealousie
Was readie oft his owne heart to devoure,
Impatient of any paramoure:
Who, on the other side, did seeme so farre
From malicing, or grudging his good houre,
That all he could he graced him with her,
Ne ever shewed signe of rancour or of jarre.

XL

And oft, when Coridon unto her brought
Or litle sparrowes stolen from their nest,
Or wanton squirrels in the woods farre sought,
Or other daintie thing for her addrest,
He would commend his guift, and make the best;
Yet she no whit his presents did regard,
Ne him could find to fancie in her brest:
This new-come shepheard had his market mard.
Old love is litle worth when new is more prefard.

XLI

One day, when as the shepheard swaynes together
Were met to make their sports and merrie glee,
As they were wont in faire sunshynie weather,
The whiles their flockes in shadowes shrouded bee,
They fell to daunce: then did they all agree
That Colin Clout should pipe, as one most fit;
And Calidore should lead the ring, as hee
That most in Pastorellaes grace did sit:
Therat frown'd Coridon, and his lip closely bit.

XLII

But Calidore, of courteous inclination,
Tooke Coridon and set him in his place,
That he should lead the daunce, as was his fashion;
For Coridon could daunce, and trimly trace:
And when as Pastorella, him to grace,
Her flowry garlond tooke from her owne head,
And plast on his, he did it soone displace,
And did it put on Coridons instead:
Then Coridon woxe frollicke, that earst seemed dead.

XLIII

Another time, when as they did dispose
To practise games and maisteries to try,
They for their Judge did Pastorella chose;
A garland was the meed of victory:
There Coridon forth stepping openly

Did chalenge Calidore to wrestling game;
For he, through long and perfect industry,
Therein well practisd was, and in the same
Thought sure t' avenge his grudge, and worke his foe great
    shame.

XLIV

But Calidore he greatly did mistake,
For he was strong and mightily stiffe pight,
That with one fall his necke he almost brake;
And had he not upon him fallen light,
His dearest joynt he sure had broken quight.
Then was the oaken crowne by Pastorell
Given to Calidore as his due right;
But he, that did in courtesie excell,
Gave it to Coridon, and said he wonne it well.

XLV

Thus did the gentle knight himselfe abeare
Amongst that rusticke rout in all his deeds,
That even they, the which his rivals were,
Could not maligne him, but commend him needs;
For courtesie amongst the rudest breeds
Good will and favour. So it surely wrought
With this faire Mayd, and in her mynde the seeds
Of perfect love did sow, that last forth brought
The fruite of joy and blisse, though long time dearely bought.

XLVI

Thus Calidore continu'd there long time
To winne the love of the faire Pastorell,
Which having got, he used without crime
Or blamefull blot; but menaged so well,
That he, of all the rest which there did dwell,
Was favoured and to her grace commended.
But what straunge fortunes unto him befell,
Ere he attain'd the point by him intended,
Shall more conveniently in other place be ended.
                    EDMUND SPENSER (1595)

23

DORUS HIS COMPARISONS

My Sheepe are thoughts, which I both guide & serve,
Their pasture is faire hils of fruitlesse love:
On barren sweetes they feede, and feeding sterve,
I waile their lot, but will not other prove.
My Sheepe-hooke is wanne hope, which all upholds:
My weedes, desires, cut out in endlesse folds.
What wooll my Sheepe shall beare, while thus they live
In you it is, you must the judgement give.

Sir Philip Sidney (1590)

sterve, Die.
wanne hope, Wanne hope conceals a pun. Wanhope is the old word for the deadly
    sin of *Accidia* or despair.
weedes, Garments.

24

SESTINA

Strephon   Klaius

Strephon

You Gote-heard Gods, that love the grassie mountaines,
You Nimphes that haunt the springs in pleasant vallies,
You Satyrs joyde with free and quiet forrests,
Vouchsafe your silent eares to playning musique,
Which to my woes gives still an early morning:
And drawes the dolor on till wery evening.

Klaius

O *Mercurie*, foregoer to the evening,
O heavenlie huntresse of the savage mountaines,
O lovelie starre, entitled of the morning,
Which that my voice doth fill these wofull vallies,
Vouchsafe your silent eares to plaining musique,
Which oft hath *Echo* tir'd in secrete forrests.

Strephon

I that was once free-burgess of the forrests,
Where shade from Sunne, and sports I sought at evening,
I that was once esteem'd for pleasant musique,
Am banisht now among the monstrous mountaines
Of huge despaire, and foule afflictions vallies,
Am growne a shrich-owle to my selfe each morning.

Klaius

I that was once delighted every morning,
Hunting the wild inhabiters of forrests,
I that was once the musique of these vallies,
So darkened am, that all my day is evening,
Hart-broken so, that mole-hills seem high mountaines,
And fill the vales with cries in steed of musique.

Strephon

Long since alas, my deadly Swannish musique
Hath made it selfe a crier of the morning,
And hath with wailing strength clim'd highest mountaines:
Long since my thoughts more desert be than forrests:
Long since I see my joyes come to their evening,
And state thrown downe to over-trodden vallies.

Klaius

Long since the happie dwellers of these vallies,
Have praide me leave my strange exclaiming musique,
Which troubles their dayes worke, and joyes of evening:
Long since I hate the night, more hate the morning:
Long since my thoughts chase me like beasts in forrests,
And make me wish myself layd under mountaines.

Strephon

Me seemes I see the high and stately mountaines,
Transforme themselves to lowe dejected vallies:
Me seemes I heare in these ill-changed forrests,
The Nightingales doo learne of Owles their musique:
Me seemes I feele the comfort of the morning
Turnde to the mortall serene of an evening.

Klaius

Me seemes I see a filthie clowdie evening,
As soone as Sunne begins to clime the mountaines:

Me seemes I feele a noisome scent, the morning
When I doo smell the flowers of these vallies:
Me seemes I heare, when I doo heare sweete musique,
The dreadfull cries of murdred men in forrests.

STREPHON

I wish to fire the trees of all these forrests;
I give the Sunne a last farewell each evening;
I curse the fidling finders out of musique:
With envie I doo hate the loftie mountaines;
And with despite despise the humble vallies:
I doo detest night, evening, day, and morning.

KLAIUS

Curse to my selfe my prayer is, the morning:
My fire is more than can be made with forrests;
My state more base, than are the basest vallies;
I wish no evenings more to see, each evening;
Shamed I have my selfe in sight of mountaines,
And stoppe mine eares, lest I growe mad with Musicke.

STREPHON

For she, whose parts maintainde a perfect musique,
Whose beautie shin'de more than the blushing morning,
Who much did pass in state the stately mountaines,
In straightnes past the Cedars of the forrests,
Hath cast me wretch into eternall evening
By taking her two Sunnes from these darke vallies.

KLAIUS

For she, to whom compar'd, the Alpes are vallies,
She, whose least word brings from the spheares their musique,
At whose approach the Sunne rose in the evening,
Who, where she went, bare in her forehead morning,
Is gone, is gone from these our spoyled forrests,
Turning to desarts our best pastur'de mountaines.

STREPHON, KLAIUS

These mountaines witness shall, so shall these vallies,
These forrests eke, made wretched by our musique,
Our morning hymne is this, and song at evening.

SIR PHILIP SIDNEY (1590)

25

THE SHEPHEARD TO HIS CHOSEN NIMPH

Onely joy, now heere you are,
Fit to heare and ease my care:
Let my whispring voyce obtaine
Sweet reward for sharpest paine.
    Take me to thee, and thee to me,
    No, no, no, no, my Deere, let be.

Night hath clos'd all in her cloke,
Twinkling starres Love-thoughts provoke,
Daunger hence good care dooth keepe,
Jealousie it selfe doth sleepe.
    Take me to thee, and thee to me:
    No, no, no, no, my Deere, let be.

Better place no wit can finde,
Cupids yoake to loose or binde,
These sweet flowers on fine bed too,
Us in their best language woo,
    Take me to thee, and thee to me:
    No, no, no, no, my Deere, let be.

This small light the Moone bestowes,
Serves thy beames but to enclose,
So to raise my hap more hie,
Feare not else, none can us spie.
    Take me to thee, and thee to me;
    No, no, no, no, my Deare, let be.

That you heard was but a Mouse,
Dumbe sleepe holdeth all the house,
Yet a-sleepe me thinks they say,
Young folkes, take time while you may.
    Take me to thee, and thee to me:
    No, no, no, no, my Deere, let be.

Niggard Time threats, if we misse
This large offer of our blisse,
Long stay, ere he graunt the same,
Sweet then, while each thing dooth frame,
   Take me to thee, and thee to me:
   No, no, no, no, my Deere, let be.

Your faire Mother is a bed,
Candles out, and Curtaines spred;
She thinks you doo Letters write;
Write, but let me first indite.
   Take me to thee, and thee to me:
   No, no, no, no, my Deere, let be.

Sweete, alas, why faine you thus?
Concord better fitteth us.
Leave to *Mars* the force of hands;
Your power in your beauty stands.
   Take me to thee, and thee to me:
   No, no, no, no, my Deere, let be.

Woe to me, and you doe sweare
Me to hate, but I forbeare,
Cursed be my destinies all,
That brought me to so high a fall.
   Soone with my death I will please thee:
   No, no, no, no, my Deere, let be.

                 SIR PHILIP SIDNEY (1591)

26

ASTROPHELL TO HIS STELLA

In a Grove most rich of shade,
Where Birds wanton musique made,
May, then young, his pyed weedes showing,
New perfum'd, with flowers fresh growing,

Astrophell with *Stella* sweete,
Did for mutuall comfort meete,
Both within them-selves oppressed,
But each in the other blessed.
   Him great harmes had taught much care,
Her faire necke a foule yoake bare:
But her sight his cares did banish,
In his sight her yoake did vanish.
Wept they had, alas the while,
But now teares them-selves did smile,
While their eyes by Love directed,
Enterchangeably reflected.
   Sigh they did, but now betwixt,
Sighs of woes, were glad sighs mixt,
With armes crost, yet testifying
Restlesse rest, and living dying.
Their eares hungry of each word,
Which the deare tongue would afford,
But their tongues restrain'd from walking,
Till their harts had ended talking.
   But when their tongues could not speake,
Love it selfe did silence breake,
Love did set his lips a-sunder,
Thus to speake in love and wonder.
Stella, Soveraigne of my joy,
Faire triumpher of annoy,
Stella, starre of heavenly fire,
Stella, Loadstarre of desire.
   Stella, in whose shining eyes,
Are the lights of *Cupids* skies,
Whose beames where they once are darted,
Love there-with is strait imparted.
Stella, whose voyce when it speakes,
Sences all asunder breakes.
Stella, whose voyce when it singeth,
Angels to acquaintance bringeth.
   Stella, in whose body is
Writ each Character of blisse,

Whose face all, all beauty passeth,
Save thy minde, which it surpasseth.
Graunt, o graunt: but speech alas
Failes me, fearing on to passe.
Graunt, O me, what am I saying?
But no fault there is in praying.
    Graunt (O deere) on knees I pray,
(Knees on ground he then did stay)
That not I, but since I love you,
Time and place for me may move you.
Never season was more fit,
Never roome more apt for it.
Smiling ayre alowes my reason.
The birds sing, now use the season.
    This small winde, which so sweete is,
See how it the leaves doth kisse,
Each tree in his best attyring
Sence of love to love inspiring.
Love makes earth the water drinke,
Love to earth makes water sinke:
And if dumbe things be so wittie,
Shall a heavenly grace want pittie?
    There his hands in their speech, faine
Would have made tongues language plaine.
But her hands, his hands repelling:
Gave repulse, all grace excelling.
Then she spake; her speech was such,
As not eares, but hart did touch:
While such wise she love denied,
As yet love she signified.
    Astrophell, she said, my Love,
Cease in these effects to prove.
Now be still, yet still beleeve me,
Thy greefe more then death dooth greeve me.
If that any thought in me,
Can tast comfort but of thee,
Let me feede with hellish anguish,
Joylesse, helplesse, endlesse languish.

If those eyes you praised, be
Halfe so deere as you to me:
Let me home returne starke blinded
Of those eyes, and blinder minded.
If to secret of my hart
I doe any wish impart:
Where thou art not formost placed;
Be both wish and I defaced.

If more may be said, I say
All my blisse on thee I lay.
If thou love, my love content thee,
For all love, all faith is meant thee.
Trust me, while I thee denie,
In my selfe the smart I trie.
Tirant honour dooth thus use thee,
Stellaes selfe might not refuse thee.

Therefore (deere) this no more move,
Least, though I leave not thy love,
Which too deepe in me is framed:
I should blush when thou art named.
There-with-all, away she went,
Leaving him to passion rent:
With what she had done and spoken,
That there-with my Song is broken.

SIR PHILIP SIDNEY (1598)

27

*ESPILUS AND THERION, THEIR CONTENTION IN
SONG FOR THE MAY-LADIE*

ESPILUS

Tune up my voyce, a higher note I yeeld,
To high conceit, the Song must needs be hie:
More high than stars, more firme than flintie field
Are all my thoughts, in which I live and die.
Sweet soule to whom I vowed am a slave;
Let not wild woods so great a treasure have.

THERION

The highest note comes oft from basest minde,
As shallow Brookes doe yeeld the greatest sound:
Seeke other thoughts thy life or death to finde,
Thy starres be falne, plowed is thy flinty ground.
  Sweet soule, let not a wretch that serveth sheep
  Among his Flock so sweet a treasure keep.

ESPILUS

Two thousand Sheepe I have as white as milke,
Though not so white as is thy lovely face:
The pasture rich, the wooll as soft as silke,
All this I give, let me possesse thy grace.
  But still take heed, least thou thy selfe submit:
  To one that hath no wealth, and wants his wit.

THERION

Two thousand Deere in wildest woods I have,
Them can I take, but you I cannot hold:
He is not poore who can his freedome save,
Bound but to you, no wealth but you I would.
  But take this beast, if beasts you feare to misse:
  For of his beasts the greatest beast he is.

Both kneeling to her Majestie.

ESPILUS

Judge you, to whom all beauties force is lent:

THERION

Judge you of love, to whom all love is bent.

*This Song was sung before the Queenes most
excellent Majestie, in Wansted Garden: as a
contention betweene a Forrester and a Shepheard
for the May-Ladie.*
                    SIR PHILIP SIDNEY (1598)

28

DISPRAYSE OF A COURTLY LIFE

Walking in bright *Phoebus* blaze
Where with heate opprest I was,
I got to a shady wood,
Where greene leaves did newly bud.
And of grasse was plenty dwelling,
Deckt with pyde flowers sweetely smelling.

In this wood a man I met,
On lamenting wholy set:
Rewing change of wonted state,
Whence he was transformed late,
Once to Shepheards God retayning,
Now in servile Court remayning.

There he wandring malecontent,
Up and downe perplexed went,
Daring not to tell to mee,
Spake unto a senceless tree,
One among the rest electing
These same words, or this effecting:

My old mates I grieve to see,
Voyde of me in field to bee,
Where we once our lovely sheepe,
Lovingly like friends did keepe,
Oft each others friendship proving,
Never striving, but in loving.

But may Love abiding bee
In poore shepheards base degree?
It belongs to such alone
To whom arte of Love is knowne:
Seely shepheards are not witting
What in art of Love is fitting.

Nay, what neede the Arte to those,
To whom we our love disclose?
It is to be used then,
When we doe but flatter men:
Friendship true in hart assured,
Is by natures giftes procured.

Therefore shepheardes wanting skill,
Can Loves duties best fulfill:
Since they know not how to faine,
Nor with Love to cloake Disdaine,
Like the wiser sorte, whose learning,
Hides their inward will of harming.

Well was I, while undershade
Oten Reedes me musicke made,
Striving with my Mates in Song,
Mixing mirth our Songs among,
Greater was that shepheards treasure,
Then this false, fine, Courtly pleasure.

Where, how many Creatures be,
So many pufft in minde I see,
Like to *Junoes* birdes of pride,
Scarce each other can abide,
Friends like to blacke Swannes appearing,
Sooner these than those in hearing.

Therefore Pan, if thou mayst be
Made to listen unto me,
Grant, I say (if seely man
May make treaty to god *Pan*)
That I, without thy denying,
May be still to thee relying.

Only for my two loves sake,   *Sir Edward Dyer and*
In whose love I pleasure take,   *Master Fulke Greville*
Only two do me delight

With their ever-pleasing sight,
Of all men to thee retaining,
Grant me with those two remaining.

So shall I to thee alwayes,
With my reedes, sound mighty praise;
And first Lambe that shall befall,
Yearely decke thine Altar shall:
If it please thee be reflected,
And I from thee not rejected.

So I left him in that place,
Taking pitty on his case,
Learning this among the rest,
That the meane estate is best,
Better filled with contenting,
Voyde of wishing and repenting.

SIR PHILIP SIDNEY (1611)

29

A DIALOGUE

*betweene two shepheards, Thenot, and Piers, in praise of Astrea, made by
the excellent Lady, the Lady Mary Countesse of Pembrook, at the Queenes
Majesties being at her house at Anno* 15—

THENOT
I Sing divine ASTREAS praise,
O Muses! help my wittes to raise,
And heave my Verses higher.

PIERS
Thou needst the truth, but plainly tell,
Which much I doubt thou canst not well,
Thou art so oft a lier.

THENOT

If in my Song no more I show,
Than Heav'n, and Earth, and Sea do know,
Then truely I have spoken.

PIERS

Sufficeth not no more to name,
But being no lesse, the like, the fame,
Else lawes of truth be broken.

THENOT

Then say, she is so good, so faire,
With all the earth she may compare,
Not *Momus* selfe denying.

PIERS

Compare may thinke where likenesse holds,
Nought like to her the earth enfoldes,
I lookt to finde you lying.

THENOT

ASTREA sees with Wisedoms sight,
Astrea workes by Vertues might,
And joyntly both do stay in her.

PIERS

Nay take from them, her hand, her minde,
The one is lame, the other blinde,
Shall still your lying staine her?

THENOT

Soone as ASTREA shewes her face,
Strait every ill avoides the place,
And every good aboundeth.

PIERS

Nay long before her face doth showe,
The last doth come, the first doth goe,
How lowde this lie resoundeth!

THENOT

ASTREA is our chiefest joy,
Our chiefest guarde against annoy,
Our chiefest wealth, our treasure.

PIERS

Where chiefest are, there others bee,
To us none else but only shee;
When wilt thou speake in measure?

THENOT

ASTREA may be justly sayd,
A field in flowry Roabe arrayd,
In Season freshly springing.

PIERS

That Spring indures but shortest time,
This never leaves *Astreas* clime,
Thou liest, instead of singing.

THENOT

As heavenly light that guides the day,
Right so doth thine each lovely Ray,
That from *Astrea* flyeth.

PIERS

Nay, darknes oft that light enclowdes
Astreas beames no darknes shrowdes
How lowdly *Thenot* lyeth!

THENOT

ASTREA rightly terme I may,
A manly Palme, a Maiden Bay,
Her verdure never dying.

PIERS

Palme oft is crooked, Bay is lowe,
Shee still upright, still high doth growe,
Good *Thenot* leave thy lying.

THENOT
Then *Piers*, of friendship tell me why,
My meaning true, my words should ly,
And strive in vaine to raise her.

PIERS
Words from conceit do only rise,
Above conceit her honour flies;
But silence, nought can praise her.
MARY, COUNTESS OF PEMBROKE (1611)

30

THE PASSIONATE SHEPHEARD TO HIS LOVE

Come live with me, and be my Love,
And we will all the pleasures prove,
That Vallies, Groves, hills and fields,
Woods, or steepie mountaines yeeldes.

And we will sit upon the Rockes,
Seeing the Shepheards feede their Flockes,
By shallow Rivers, to whose falls,
Melodious birds sing Madrigalls.

And I will make thee beds of Roses,
And a thousand fragrant poesies,
A cap of flowers, and a kirtle,
Imbroydered all with leaves of Mirtle.

A gowne made of the finest wooll,
Which from our pretty Lambs we pull,
Faire lined slippers for the cold:
With buckles of the purest gold.

A belt of straw, and Ivie buds,
With Corall clasps and Amber studs,
And if these pleasures may thee move,
Come live with me, and be my Love.

The Shepheard Swaines shall dance and sing,
For thy delight each May-morning,
If these delights thy minde may move;
Then live with me and be my Love.

CHRISTOPHER MARLOWE (1599)

31

THE NIMPHS REPLY TO THE SHEEPHEARD

If all the world and love were young,
And truth in every Shepheards tongue,
These pretty pleasures might me move,
To live with thee, and be thy Love.

Time drives the Flockes from field to fold,
When Rivers rage, and Rockes grow cold,
And *Philomell* becommeth dombe,
The rest complaines of cares to come.

The flowers doe fade, and wanton fields,
To wayward Winter reckoning yeelds,
A hony tongue, a heart of gall,
Is fancies spring, but sorrowes fall.

Thy gownes, thy shooes, thy beds of Roses,
Thy cap, thy kirtle, and thy posies,
Soone breake, soone wither, soone forgotten:
In folly ripe, in reason rotten.

Thy belts of straw and Ivie buds,
Thy Corall claspes and Amber studs,
All these in me no meanes can move,
To come to thee, and be thy Love.

But could youth last, and love still breede,
Had joyes no date, nor age no neede,
Then these delights my minde might move,
To live with thee, and be thy Love.

SIR W. RALEIGH (1599)

32

THE SHEPHEARDS DESCRIPTION OF LOVE

MELIBEUS
Shepheard, what's Love, I pray thee tell?

FAUSTUS
It is that Fountaine, and that Well,
Where pleasure and repentance dwell.
It is perhaps that sauncing bell,
    That toules all into heaven or hell,
    And this is Love as I heard tell.

MELIBEUS
Yet what is Love, I pre-thee say?

FAUSTUS
It is a worke on holy-day,
It is December match'd with May,
When lustie-bloods in fresh aray
    Heare ten months after of the play.
    And this is Love, as I heare say.

MELIBEUS
Yet what is Love, good Shepheard saine?

prooves, Tries it.

FAUSTUS

It is a Sun-shine mixt with raine,
It is a tooth-ach, or like paine,
It is a game where none dooth gaine,
    The Lasse saith no, and would full faine:
    And this is Love, as I heare saine.

MELIBEUS

Yet Shepheard, what is Love, I pray?

FAUSTUS

It is a yea, it is a nay,
A pretty kind of sporting fray;
It is a thing will soone away.
    Then *Nimphs* take vantage while ye may:
    And this is love, as I heare say.

MELIBEUS

Yet what is love, good Shepheard show?

FAUSTUS

A thing that creepes, it cannot goe,
A prize that passeth to and fro,
A thing for one, a thing for moe,
    And he that prooves shall finde it so;
    And Shepheard this is love I trow.

        ANONYMOUS (SIR W. RALEIGH?) (1600)

saucing bell, Sanctus bell.

33

MADRIGAL

What are my Sheepe, without their wonted food?
What is my life, except I gaine my Love?
My Sheepe consume, and faint for want of blood;
My life is lost unlesse I Grace approve.
    No flower that saplesse thrives,
    No Turtle without pheare.

pheare, Mate.

The day without the Sunne doth lower for woe,
Then woe mine eyes, unlesse they beauty see;
My Sonne *Samelaes* eyes, by whom I know
Wherein delight consists, where pleasures be.
   Nought more the heart revives,
   Than to embrace his Deere.

The starres from earthly humours gaine their light;
Our humours by their light possesse their power:
Samelaes eyes fed by my weeping sight,
Infuse my paines or joyes, by smile or lower.
   So wends the source of love,
   It feedes, it failes, it ends.

Kind lookes, cleare to your Joy, behold her eyes,
Admire her heart, desire to tast her kisses:
In them the heaven of joy and solace lyes;
Without them, every hope his succour misses.
   Oh how I live to prove
   Whereto this solace tends?

ROBERT GREENE

34

THE SHEPHEARDS SORROW, BEING
DISDAINED IN LOVE

Muses, help me; sorrow swarmeth,
   Eyes are fraught with Seas of languish:
Haplesse hope my solace harmeth,
   Mindes repast is bitter anguish.

Eye of day regarded never,
   Certaine trust in world untrustie:
Flattering hope beguileth ever,
   Wearie old, and wanton lustie.

Dawne of day beholds enthroned
    Fortunes darling proud and dreadlesse:
Darksome night dooth heare him moaned,
    Who before was rich and needlesse.

Rob the Spheare of lines united,
    Make a suddaine voide in nature:
Force the day to be benighted,
    Reave the cause of time and creature,

Ere the world will cease to varie;
    This I weepe for, this I sorrow:
Muses, if you please to tarie,
    Further helpe I meane to borrow;

Courted once by Fortunes favour,
    Compast now with Envies curses:
All my thoughts of sorrowes savour,
    Hopes runne fleeting like the Sourses.

Aye me, wanton scorne hath maimed
    All the joyes my hart enjoyed:
Thoughts their thinking have disclaimed,
    Hate my hopes have quite annoyed.

Scant regard my weale hath scanted,
    Looking coy, hath forc'd my lowring:
Nothing lik'd, where nothing wanted,
    Weds mine eyes to ceaselesse showring.

Former love was once admired,
    Present favour is estraunged:
Loath'd the pleasure long desired,
    Thus both men and thoughts are changed.

Lovely Swaine with luckie speeding,
    Once, but now no more so friended:
You my Flocks have had in feeding,
    From the morne, till day was ended.

Sourses, Fountains.

Drink and fodder, foode and folding,
 Had my Lambs and Ewes together:
I with them was still beholding,
 Both in warmth and Winter weather.

Now they languish, since refused,
 Ewes and Lambes are pain'd with pining:
I with Ewes and Lambs confused,
 All unto our deaths declining.

Silence, leave thy Cave obscured,
 Daigne a dolefull Swaine to tender:
Though disdaines I have endured,
 Yet I am no deepe offender.

Phillips Sonne can with his finger
 Hide his scarre, it is so little:
Little sinne a day to linger,
 Wise men wander in a tittle.

Trifles yet my Swaine have turned,
 Though my Sunne he never showeth:
Though I weepe, I am not mourned,
 Though I want, no pittie groweth.

Yet for pittie, love my Muses,
 Gentle silence be their cover:
They must leave their wonted uses,
 Since I leave to be a Lover.

They shall live with thee enclosed,
 I will loath my Pen and Paper:
Art shall never be supposed,
 Sloth shall quench the watching Taper.

Kisse them silence, kisse them kindly,
 Though I leave them, yet I love them:
Though my wit have led them blindly,
 Yet a Swaine did once approve them.

I will travaile soiles removed,
   Night and morning never merrie:
Thou shalt harbour that I loved,
   I will love that makes me wearie.

If perchaunce the Shepheard strayeth,
   In thy walkes and shades unhaunted:
Tell the teene my hart betrayeth,
   How neglect my joyes have daunted.

THOMAS LODGE (1593)

soiles removed, Remote countries.

35

IDEA THE SHEPHEARDS GARLAND
FASHIONED IN NINE EGLOGS

The Eighth Eglog

MOTTO

Good *Gorbo* of the golden world
   and *Saturns* raigne doth tell
And afterward doth make reporte
   of bonnie *Dowsabell*.

Shepheard, why creepe we in this lowly vaine,
   as though our muse no store at all affords,
Whilst others vaunt it with the frolicke swayne,
   and strut the stage with reperfumed wordes?

See how these yonkers rave it out in rime,
   who make a traffique of their rarest wits,
And in *Bellonas* buskin tread it fine,
   like *Bacchus* priests raging in franticke fits.

yonkers, Young men.

Those mirtle Groves decay'd, done growe againe,
    their rootes refresht with *Heliconas* spring,
Whose pleasant shade invites the homely swayne,
    to sit him downe and heare the Muses sing.

Then if thy Muse hath spent her wonted zeale,
    with Ivie twist thy temples shall be crownd,
Or if she dares hoyse up top-gallant sayle,
    amongst the rest, then may she be renownd.

Gorbo

My boy, these yonkers reachen after fame,
    and so done presse into the learned troupe,
With filed quill to glorifie their name,
    which otherwise were pend in shamefull coupe.

But this hie object hath abjected me,
    and I must pipe amongst the lowly sorte,
Those little heard-groomes who admir'd to see,
    when I by Moone-shine made the fayries sporte.

Who dares describe the toyles of *Hercules*,
    and puts his hand to fames eternall penne,
Must invocate the soule of *Hercules*,
    attended with the troupes of conquered men.

Who writes of thrice renowned *Theseus*,
    a monster-tamers rare description,
Trophies the jawes of uglie *Cerberus*,
    and paynts out *Styx*, and fiery *Acheron*.

My Muse may not affect night-charming spels,
    whose force effects th'*Olympicke* vault to quake,
Nor calls those grysly Goblins from their Cels,
    the ever-damned frye of *Limbo* lake.

boyse, Hoist.

And who erects the brave *Pyramides*,
   of Monarches or renowned warriours,
Neede bath his quill for such attempts as these,
   in flowing streames of learned *Maros* showres.

For when the great worlds conquerer began,
   to prove his helmet and his habergeon,
The sweat that from the Poets-God *Orpheus* ran,
   foretold his Prophets had to play upon.

When Pens and Launces sawe the *Olympiad* prize,
   those charriot triumphes with the Lawrell crowne,
Then gan the worthies glorie first to rise,
   and plumes were vayled to the purple gowne.

The gravest Censor, sagest Senator,
   with wings of Justice and Religion,
Mounted the top of *Nimrods* statelie Tower,
   soring unto that hie celestiall throne:

Where blessed Angels in their heavenly queares,
   chaunt Anthemes with shrill *Syren* harmonie,
Tun'd to the sound of those aye-crouding sphears,
   which herien their makers eternitie.

Those who foretell the times of unborne men,
   and future things in foretime augured,
Have slumbred in that spell-gods darkest den,
   which first inspir'd his prophesying head.

Sooth-saying *Sibels* sleepen long agone,
   we have their reede, but few have conned their Arte;
Welch-wisard *Merlyn*, cleveth to a stone,
   no Oracle more wonders may impart.

herien, Praise.

The Infant age could deftly caroll love,
    till greedy thirst of that ambitious honor
Drew Poets pen, from his sweete lasses glove,
    to chaunt of slaughtering broiles & bloody horror.

Then *Joves* love-theft was privily descri'd,
    how he playd false in *Amphitrios* bed;
And how *Apollo* in the mount of *Ide*,
    gave *Oenon* phisick for her maydenhead.

The tender grasse was then the softest bed,
    the pleasant'st shades were deem'd the statelyest hals;
No belly-god with *Bacchus* banqueted,
    nor paynted ragges then covered rotten wals.

Then simple love with simple vertue way'd;
    flowers the favours which true fayth revayled,
Kindnes with kindnes was againe repay'd,
    with sweetest kisses covenants were sealed.

Then beauties selfe with her self beautified,
    scornd payntings pergit, and the borrowed hayre,
Nor monstrous formes deformities did hide,
    nor foule was vernisht with compounded fayre.

The purest fleece then covered purest skin,
    for pride as then with *Lucifer* remaynd:
Deformed fashions now were to begin,
    nor clothes were yet with poison'd liquor staynd.

But when the bowels of the earth were sought,
    and men her golden intrayles did espie,
This mischiefe then into the world was brought,
    this fram'd the mint which coynd our miserie.

pergit, Paint.

Then lofty *Pines* were by ambition hewne,
    and men sea-monsters swamme the brackish flood,
In waynscot tubs, to seeke out worlds unknowne,
    for certain ill to leave assured good.

The starteling steede is manag'd from the field,
    and serves a subject to the riders lawes;
He whom the churlish bit did never weeld,
    now feels the courb controll his angrie jawes.

The hammering *Vulcane* spent his wasting fire,
    till he the use of tempred mettals found,
His anvile wrought the steeled cotes attire,
    and forged tooles to carve the foe-mans wound.

The Citie builder then intrencht his towres,
    and wald his wealth within the fenced towne,
Which afterward in bloudy stormy stours,
    kindled that flame which burnt his Bulwarks downe.

And thus began th'*Exordium* of our woes,
    the fatall dumbe shewe of our miserie:
Here sprang the tree on which our mischiefe growes,
    the drery suject of worlds tragedie.

Motto

Well, shepheard, well, the golden age is gone,
    wishes may not revoke that which is past:
It were no wit to make two griefes of one;
    our proverb sayth, Nothing can alwayes last.

Listen to me my lovely shepheards joye,
    and thou shalt heare with mirth and mickle glee,
A pretie Tale, which when I was a boy,
    my toothles Grandame oft hath tolde to me.

Gorbo

Shepheard say on, so may we passe the time;
There is no doubt it is some worthy ryme.

Motto

Farre in the countrey of *Arden*,
There wond a knight hight *Cassemen*,
   as bolde as *Isenbras*:
Fell was he and eger bent,
In battell and in Tournament,
   as was the good sir *Topas*.
He had, as antique stories tell,
A daughter cleaped *Dowsabell*,
   a mayden fayre and free:
And for she was her fathers heire,
Full well she was ycond the leyre,
   of mickle curtesie.
The silke wel couth she twist and twine,
And make the fine Marchpine,
   and with the needle werke;
And she couth helpe the priest to say
His Mattens on a holyday,
   and sing a Psalme in Kirke.
She ware a frock of frolicke greene,
Might well beseeme a mayden Queene,
   which seemly was to see.
A hood to that so neat and fine,
In colour like the colombine,
   ywrought full featuously.
Her feature all as fresh above
As is the grasse that growes by Dove,
   as lyth as lasse of Kent:
Her skin as soft as Lemster wooll,
As white as snow on peakish hull,
   or Swanne that swims in Trent.

cleaped, Called.   *ycond the leyre*, She understood the lore.
Marchpine, Marzipan (sweet biscuit).   *featuously*, Skilfully.
hull, Hill.

This mayden in a morne betime,
Went forth when May was in her prime,
    to get sweet Cetywall,
The hony-suckle, the Harlocke,
The Lilly and the Lady-smocke,
    to deck her summer hall.
Thus as she wandred here and there,
Ypicking of the bloomed Breere,
    she chanced to espie
A shepeard sitting on a bancke,
Like *Chanteclere* he crowed crancke,
    and pyp'd with merrie glee:
He leard his sheepe as he him list,
When he would whistle in his fist,
    to feede about him rounde:
Whilst he full many a caroll sung,
Untill the fields and medowes rung,
    and that the woods did sound.
In favour this same shepheards swayne
Was like the bedlam *Tamburlayne*,
    which helde prowd Kings in awe:
But meeke he was as Lamb mought be,
Ylike that gentle *Abel* he,
    whom his lewd brother slaw.
This shepheard ware a sheepe gray cloke,
Which was of the finest loke,
    that could be cut with sheere;
His mittens were of Bauzens skinne,
His cockers were of Cordiwin,
    his hood of Meniveere.
His aule and lingell in a thong,
His tar-boxe on his broad belt hong,
    his breech of Coyntrie blew;
Full crispe and curled were his lockes,

Cetywall, Valerian.   *Harlocke*, Charlock.
crancke, Cheerfully (Spenserian).   *Bauzens*, Badger's.
Cordiwin, Leather.   *Meniveere*, White fur.   *lingell*, Thread.
Coyntrie, Coventry (this is the conventional pastoral dress).

His browes as white as *Albion* rocks,
   so like a lover true.
And pyping still he spent the day,
So mery as the Popingay:
   which liked *Dowsabell*.
That would she ought or would she nought,
This lad would never from her thought;
   She in love-longing fell.
At length she tucked up her frocke,
White as the Lilly was her smocke,
   she drew the shepheard nie;
But then the shepheard pyp'd a good,
That all his sheepe forsooke their foode,
   to heare his melodie.
Thy sheepe, *quoth she*, cannot be leane,
That have a jolly shepheards swayne,
   the which can pype so well.
Yea, but, *sayth he*, their shepheard may,
If pyping thus he pine away,
   in love of *Dowsabell*.
Of love, fond boy, take thou no keepe,
Quoth she, looke well unto thy sheepe,
   lest they should hap to stray.
Quoth he, so had I done full well,
Had I not seene fayre *Dowsabell*
   come forth to gather Maye.
With that she gan to vayle her head,
Her cheekes were like the Roses red,
   but not a word she sayd.
With that the shepheard gan to frowne,
He threw his pretie pypes adowne,
   and on the ground him layd.
Sayth she, I may not stay till night,
And leave my summer hall undight,
   and all for long of thee.
My Coate, *sayth he*, nor yet my foulde,
Shall neither sheepe nor shepheard hould,

     foulde, Fold.

except thou favour me.
Sayth she, yet lever I were dead,
Then I should lose my maydenhead,
    and all for love of men:
Sayth he, yet are you too unkind,
If in your heart you cannot finde
    to love us now and then:
And I to thee will be as kinde
As *Colin* was to *Rosalinde*
    of curtesie the flower.
Then will I be as true, *quoth she*,
As ever mayden yet might be,
    unto her Paramour.
With that she bent her snow-white knee,
Downe by the shepheard kneeled shee,
    and him she sweetely kist.
With that the shepheard whoop'd for joy,
Quoth he, ther's never shepheards boy
    that ever was so blist.

Gorbo

Now by my sheep-hooke here's a tale alone,
    learne me the same and I will give thee hier,
This were as good as curds for our *Jone*,
    When at a night we sitten by the fire.

Motto

Why, gentle hodge, I will not sticke for that,
    When we two meeten here another day;
But see whilst we have set us downe to chat,
    Yon tikes of mine begin to steale away.

And if thou wilt but come unto our greene
    On Lammas day when as we have our feast,
Thou shalt sit next unto our summer Queene,
    And thou shalt be the onely welcome guest.

                   MICHAEL DRAYTON (1593)

    lever, Rather.   *blist*, Blessed.

36

From *ENDIMION AND PHOEBE*

In this faire Region on a goodly Plaine,
Stretching her bounds unto the bordring Maine,
The Mountaine *Latmus* over-lookes the Sea,
Smiling to see the Ocean billowes play:
Latmus where young *Endimion* usd to keepe
His fairest flock of silver-fleeced sheepe.
To whom *Silvanus* often would resort,
At barly-brake to see the Satyres sport;
And when rude *Pan* his Tabret list to sound,
To see the faire Nymphes foote it in a round,
Under the trees which on this Mountaine grew;
As yet the like *Arabia* never knew;
For all the pleasures Nature could devise
Within this plot she did imparadize;
And great *Diana* of her speciall grace
With *Vestall* rytes had hallowed all the place.
Upon this Mount there stood a stately Grove,
Whose reaching armes, to clip the Welkin strove;
Of tufted Cedars, and the branching Pine,
Whose bushy tops themselves doe so intwine,
As seem'd when Nature first this work begun,
Shee then conspir'd against the piercing Sun;
Under whose covert (thus divinely made)
Phoebus green Laurell florisht in the shade;
Faire *Venus* Mirtile, *Mars* his warlike Fyrre,
Minervas Olive, and the weeping Myrhe,
The patient Palme, which thrives in spite of hate,
The Poplar, to *Alcides* consecrate;
Which Nature in such order had disposed,
And there-withall these goodly walkes inclosed,
As serv'd for hangings and rich Tapestry,
To beautifie this stately Gallery;

Imbraudring these in curious trailes along,
The clustred Grapes, the golden Citrons hung,
More glorious than the precious fruite were these,
Kept by the Dragon in *Hesperides*;
Or gorgious Arras in rich colours wrought,
With silk from *Affrick*, or from *Indie* brought.
Out of thys soyle sweet bubling Fountains crept,
As though for joy the sencelesse stones had wept;
With straying channels dauncing sundry wayes,
With often turnes, like to a curious Maze;
Which breaking forth, the tender grasse bedewed;
Whose silver sand with orient Pearle was strewed,
Shadowed with Roses and sweet Eglantine,
Dipping theyr sprayes into this christalline;
From which the byrds the purple berries pruned,
And to theyr loves their small recorders tuned.
The Nightingale, woods Herauld of the Spring,
The whistling Woosell, Mavis carroling,
Tuning theyr trebles to the waters fall,
Which made the musique more angelicall;
Whilst gentle *Zephyre* murmuring among,
Kept time, and bare the burthen of the song.
About whose brims, refresht with dainty showers,
Grew Amaranthus, and sweet Gilliflowers;
The Marigold, *Phoebus* beloved friend;
The Moly, which from sorcery doth defend;
Violet, Carnation, Balme and Cassia,
Ideas Primrose, coronet of May.
    Above this Grove a gentle fair ascent,
Which by degrees of Milk-white Marble went:
Upon the top, a Paradise was found,
With which, Nature this miracle had crownd;
Empaled with Rocks of rarest precious stone,
Which like the flames of *Aetna* brightly shone,
And serv'd as Lanthornes furnished with light,
To guide the wandring passengers by night:

Imbraudring, Embroidering.
recorders, Voices (the word is generally used of birdsong).

For which fayre *Phoebe* sliding from her Sphere,
Used oft times to come and sport her there,
And from the Azure starry-painted Sky
Embalmed the bancks with precious lunary,
That now her *Menalus* she quite forsooke,
And unto *Latmus* wholy her betooke,
And in this place her pleasure us'd to take,
And all was for her sweet *Endimions* sake.
Endimion, the lovely Shepheards boy,
Endimion, great *Phoebes* onely joy;
Endimion, in whose pure-shining eyes,
The naked Fairies daunst the heydegies.
The shag-haird Satyrs Mountain-climing race
Have been made tame by gazing in his face.
For this boyes love, the water-Nymphs have wept,
Stealing oft times to kisse him whilst he slept,
And tasting once the Nectar of his breath,
Surfet with sweet, and languish unto death;
And *Jove* oft-times bent to lascivious sport,
And comming where *Endimion* did resort,
Hath courted him, inflamed with desire,
Thinking some Nymph was cloth'd in boyes attire.
And often-times the simple rural Swaines,
Beholding him in crossing o'er the Plaines,
Imagined, *Apollo* from above
Put on this shape, to win some Maidens love.
This Shepheard, *Phoebe* ever did behold,
Whose love already had her thoughts controld.
From *Latmus* top (her stately throne) she rose,
And to *Endimion* downe beneath she goes.
Her brothers beames now had shee layd aside,
Her horned cressent, and her full-fac'd pride;
For had shee come adorned with her light,
No mortall eye could have endur'd the sight;
But like a Nymph, crown'd with a flowrie twine,
And not like *Phoebe*, as herself divine.

MICHAEL DRAYTON (1595)

heydegies, Country-dances (Spenserian).

37

EGLOGUE INTITULED CUDDY

A Litle Heard-groome (for he was no bett')
   When course of yeere return'd the pleasant spring,
At break of day without-en further lett
   Cast with himselfe his flocke afield to bring,
And for they had so long beene pent with paine,
At sight of Sun they seem'd to live againe.

Such was the flocke all bent to brouse and play,
   But nothing such their Maister was to see.
Downe hung his drooping head like rainy day,
   His cheeks with teares like springs bedeawed bee.
His wringed hand such silent mone did make.
Well might you guesse he was with love y'take.

Tho while his flocke went feeding on the greene,
   And wantonly for joy of Summer plaid,
All in despight as if he n'ould be seene
   He cast himselfe to ground full ill appayd.
Should seeme their pleasance made him more complaine
For joy in sight not felt, is double paine.

Unhappy Boy why liv'st thou still, quoth he,
   And hast thy deadly wound so long ago?
What hope of after hap sustayneth thee?
   As if there might be found some ease of wo.
Nay better dye ten thousand times then live,
Since every houre new cause of death doth give.

The joyfull Sunne, whom clowdy Winters spight,
   Had shut from us in watry fishes haske,
Returnes againe to lend the world his light,
   And red as Rose begins his yeerely taske.

n'ould, Would not.   *ill appayd*, Melancholy.
hap, Good fortune.   *haske*. See Notes.

His fiery steeds the steepy welkin beate,
And both the hornes of clyming Bull do heate.

But ah no Sun of grace aspires to mee,
   Close hid she lies, from whom I should have light,
The clowds of black disdaine so foggy bee,
   That blind I ly (poore boy) bereft of sight:
And yet *I* see the Sun I seeke to find,
And yet the more I see, the more am blind.

Thrice happy ground, whom spoyld with winters rage,
   The heat of pleasant spring renewes againe:
Unhappy I, whom in my spring of age,
   The frost of cold Despaire hath well-nigh slayne.
How shall *I* bide your stormy Winters smart,
When spring it selfe hath frorne my bloodlesse hart?

I see the beawty of thy flowers renew,
   Thy mantle greene with sundry collours spread,
Thou seest in me a change of former hew,
   Palenesse for white, blacknes for lively red.
What hope of Harvest fruit, or Summer flowres,
Since that my Spring is drownd with teares like showres.

And last of all, but liev'st of all to mee,
   Thou leany flock, that didst of late lament,
And witnesse wast for shepheards all to see,
   (Thy knees so weake, thy fleece so rough and rent)
That thou with paine didst pine away unfed,
All for thy Maister was with love misled.

Thou 'ginst at earst forget thy former state,
   And range amid the busks thy selfe to feede,
Faire fall thee little flocke both rathe and late,
   (Was never Lovers sheepe, that well did speede)
Thou free, *I* bound, thou glad, I pinde in payne,
I strive to dye, and thou to live full faine.

     frorne, Frozen ('Doric').   *rathe*, Soon.   *pinde*, Pined.

Wo worth the stund, wherein I tooke delight,
　　To frame the shifting of my nimble feete,
To cheerefull sound of Pipe in Moon-shine night,
　　Such pleasance past at earst now makes me greet.
I ween'd by Night have shun'd the parching ray,
But night it selfe was twice more hott then day.

Then first of all (and all too soone for me)
　　I saw thilk Lasse (nay grav'd her in my brest)
Her christall eyes more bright then Moone to see,
　　Her eies, her eies, that have robd me of rest,
On them I gaz'd, then saw I to my cost,
Through too much sight mine onely sight is lost.

Where beene the dapper Ditties that I dight,
　　And Roundelaies, and Virelayes so soot?
Whilome with Collins selfe compare I might
　　For other Swaine, to strive was little boote,
Such skill I had in making all above
But all to little skill to conquer Love.

What helps it me to have my piping prayz'd,
　　Of all save her, whom I would only please?
Nought care I, though my fame to sky be rayz'd
　　For pleasant song that brings my heart no ease.
Wherfore both Pipe and Song I all forsweare,
And former pleasance wilfully forbeare.

With that he cast his looke to Welkin high,
　　And saw the doubled shadowes flit away:
And as he glaunst halfe in despight awry,
　　He spide the shepheards starre shut in the Day;
Then rose, and homeward with his flock him went,
Whose voice did helpe their Maisters case lament.
　　　　　　　　　　　　　　　ANONYMOUS (1602)

stund, Time.　　　　soot, Sweet.　　　　boote, Use.

38

PHILLIDA AND CORIDON

In the merry month of May,
In a morne by breake of day,
Forth I walked by the Wood-side,
When as May was in his pride:
There I spied all alone,
Phillida and *Coridon*.
Much a-doo there was, God wot,
He would love, and she would not.
She said never man was true,
He said, none was false to you.
He said, he had lov'd her long,
She said, Love should have no wrong.
Coridon would kisse her then,
She said, Maides must kisse no men,
Till they did for good and all.
Then she made the Shepheard call
All the heavens to witnesse truth:
Never lov'd a truer Youth.
Thus with many a pretty oath,
Yea and nay, and faith and troath,
Such as silly Shepheards use,
When they will not Love abuse;
Love, which had beene long deluded,
Was with kisses sweet concluded.
And *Phillida* with garlands gay
Was made the Lady of the May.

NICHOLAS BRETON (1591)

39

A SOLEMN LONG ENDURING PASSION

Wearie thoughts doe waite upon me,
Greefe hath too much over-gone me,
Time doth howerly over-toyle me,
While deepe sorrowes seeke to spoile me,
Wit and sences all amazed,
In their Graces over-gazed:
In exceeding torments tell me,
Never such a death befell mee. . . .
Let mee thinke no more on thee,
Thou hast too much wounded me. . . .
Petrarche, in his thoughts divine,
Tasso in his highest line,
Ariostos best invention,
Dantes best obscur'd intention,
Ovid in his sweetest vaine,
Pastor Fidos purest straine,
With the finest Poets wit,
That of wonders ever writ,
Wee they all but now alive,
And would for the Garland strive,
In the gratious praise of love,
Heere they might their passions proove,
On such excellences grownded,
That their wittes would be confounded. . . .
I have neither Plummes nor Cherries,
Nuts, nor Aples, nor Straw-berries;
Pins nor Laces, Pointes nor gloves,
Nor a payre of painted Doves;
Shuttle-Cocke nor trundle-ball,
To present thy love withal:
But a heart, as true and kinde
As an honest faithfull minde
Can devise for to invent,

To thy patience I present.
At thy fairest feete it lies:
Blesse it with thy blessed eyes:
Take it up into thy handes,
At whose onely grace it standes.
To be comforted for ever
Or to looke for comfort never.
Oh it is a strange affect
That my fancie doth effect!
I am caught and can not start:
Wit and reason, eye and heart,
All are witnesses to mee,
Love hath sworne me slave to thee.
Let me then be but thy slave,
And no further favour crave:
Send mee foorth to tende thy flocke,
On the highest Mountaine rocke,
Or commaund me but to goe
To the valley grownd belowe:
All shall be alike to me,
Where it please thee I shall bee;
Let my fate be what thou wilt,
Save my life, or see it spilt:
Keepe me fasting on thy Mountaine,
Charge me not come near thy Fountaine.
In the Stormes and bitter blastes,
Where the skie all overcasts:
In the coldest frost and snowe
That the earth did ever knowe,
Let me sit and bite my thumbes
Where I see no comfort comes:
All the sorrowes I can proove
Cannot put me from my love.
Tell me that thou art content
To behold me passion-rente,
That thou know'st I deerely love thee,
Yet withall it cannot moove thee;
That thy pride doth growe so great,

Nothing can thy grace intreate,
That thou wilt so cruell bee
As to kill my love and mee,
That thou wilt no food reserve,
But my flockes and I shall sterve.
Be thy rage yet nere so great,
When my little Lambes doe bleate,
To behold their Shepheard die;
Then will truth her passion trie,
How a Hart it selfe hath spent
With concealing of content.

NICHOLAS BRETON (1604)

40

THE SHEPHEARDS SONG: A CAROLL OR HIMNE FOR CHRISTMAS

Sweet Musicke, sweeter farre
Then any song is sweet:
Sweet Musicke heavenly rare,
Mine eares (O peeres) doth greete.
You gentle Flocks, whos fleeces pearl'd with dewe,
Resemble heaven, whom golden drops make bright,
Listen, O listen, now, O not to you
Our pipes make sport to shorten weary night.
But voices most divine,
Make blisfull Harmonie:
Voyces that seem to shine,
For what else cleares the skie?
Tunes we can heare, but not the Singers see;
The tunes divine, and so the Singers be.

Loe how the firmament,
Within an azure fold
The flock of starres hath pent,
That we might them behold.
Yet from their beames proceedeth not this light.
Nor can their Christals such reflection give:
What then doth make the Element so bright?
The heavens are come downe upon earth to live.
But harken to the song,
Glory to glories king:
And peace all men among,
These Queristers doe sing.
Angels they are, as also (Shepheards) hee,
Whom in our feare we doe admire to see.

Let not amazement blinde
Your soules (said he) annoy:
To you and all mankinde
My message bringeth joy.
For loe the worlds great Shepheard now is borne
A blessed Babe, and Infant full of power!
After long night, up-risen is the morne,
Renowning *Bethlem* in the Saviour.
Sprung is the perfect day,
By Prophets seene a farre:
Sprung is the mirthfull May,
Which Winter cannot marre.
In *Davids* Citie doth this Sunne appeare:
Clouded in flesh, yet Shepheards sit we here.

E.B. [Edmund Bolton?]

41

From THE SECOND DAYES LAMENTATION OF
    THE AFFECTIONATE SHEPHEARD

Next Morning when the golden Sunne was risen,
    And new had bid good morrow to the Mountaines;
When Night her silver light had lockt in prison,
    Which gave a glimmering on the christall fountaines:
Then ended sleepe: and then my cares began,
Ev'n with the uprising of the silver Swan.

O glorious Sunne quoth I, (viewing the Sunne)
    That lightenst everie thing but me alone:
Why is my Summer season almost done?
    My Spring-time past, and Ages Autumne gone?
My Harvest's come, and yet I reapt no corne:
My love is great, and yet I am forlorne.

Witness these watrie eyes my sad lament
    (Receaving cisternes of my ceaseles teares),
Witness my bleeding hart my soules intent,
    Witnes the weight distressed *Daphnis* beares:
Sweet Love, come ease me of thy burthens paine;
Or els I die, or else my hart is slaine.

And thou Love-scorning Boy, cruell, unkinde;
    Oh let me once againe intreat some pittie:
May be thou wilt relent thy marble minde,
    And lend thine eares unto my dolefull Dittie:
Oh pittie him, that pittie craves so sweetly;
Or else thou shalt be never named meekly.

If thou wilt love me, thou shalt be my Boy,
    My sweet Delight, the Comfort of my minde,
My love, my dove, my Sollace, and my Joy:
    But if I can no grace nor mercie finde,
Ile goe to *Caucasus* to ease my smart,
And let a Vulture gnaw upon my hart.

Yet if thou wilt but show me one kinde looke
    (A small reward for my so great affection)
Ile grave thy name in Beauties golden Booke,
    And shrowd thee under *Hellicons* protection;
Making the Muses chaunt thy lovely prayse:
(For they delight in Shepheards lowly layes.)

And when th'art wearie of thy keeping Sheepe
    Upon a lovely Downe, (to please thy minde)
Ile give thee fine ruffe-footed Doves to keepe,
    And pretie Pidgeons of another kinde:
A Robbin-red-brest shall thy Minstrell bee,
Chirping thee sweet and pleasant Melodie.

Or if thou wilt goe shoote at little Birds
    With bow and boult (the Thrustle-cocke and Sparrow)
Such as our Countrey hedges can afford's;
    I have a fine bowe, and an yvorie arrow:
And if thou misse, yet meate thou shalt not lacke,
Ile hang a bag and bottle at thy backe.

Wilt thou set springes in a frostie Night,
    To catch the long-billd Woodcocke and the Snype?
(By the bright glimmering of the Starrie light)
    The Partridge, Phaesant, or the greedie Grype?
Ile lend thee lyme-twigs, and fine sparrow calls,
Wherewith the Fowler silly Birds inthralls.

Or in a mystie morning if thou wilt
    Make pit-falls for the Larke and Pheldifare;
Thy prop and sweake shall be both over-gilt;
    With *Cyparissus* selfe thou shalt compare
For gins and wiles, the Oozels to beguile;
Whilst thou under a bush shalt sit and smile.

afford's, Afford us.   *Pheldifare,* Fieldfare.
prop and sweake, Part of fowler's trap.

Or with Hare-pypes (set in a muset hole)
    Wilt thou deceave the deep-earth-delving Coney?
Or wilt thou in a yellow Boxen bole,
    Taste with a woodden splent the sweet lythe honey?
Clusters of crimson Grapes Ile pull thee downe;
And with Vine-leaves make thee a lovely Crowne.

Or wilt thou drinke a cup of new-made Wine
    Froathing at top, mixt with a dish of Creame;
And Straw-berries, or Bil-berries in their prime,
    Bath'd in a melting Sugar-Candie streame:
Bunnell and Perry I have for thee alone
When Vynes are dead, and all the Grapes are gone.

I have a pleasant noted Nightingale,
    That sings as sweetly as the silver Swan,
Kept in a cage of bone as white as Whale,
    Which I with singing of *Philemon* won:
Her shalt thou have, and all I have beside;
If thou wilt be my Boy, or else my Bride.

Then will I lay out all my Lardarie
    (Of Cheese, of Cracknells, Curds and Clowted-creame)
Before thy malcontent ill-pleasing eye:
    But why doo I of such great follies dreame?
Alas, he will not see my simple Coate;
For all my speckled Lambe, nor milk-white Goate.

Against my Birth-day thou shalt be my guest:
    Weele have Greene-cheeses and fine Silly-bubs;
And thou shalt be the chiefe of all my feast.
    And I will give thee two fine pretie Cubs,
With two young Whelps, to make thee sport withall,
A golden Racket, and a Tennis-ball.

Hare-pypes, Traps.
muset, Shrew.   *Bunnell*, A drink made from apples and pears.
    Coate, Sheepcote.

A gilded Nutmeg, and a race of Ginger,
   A silken Girdle, and a drawn -worke Band,
Cuffs for thy wrists, a gold Ring for thy finger,
   And sweet Rose-water for thy Lilly-white hand,
A Purse of silke, bespangd with spots of gold,
As brave a one as ere thou didst behold.

A pair of Knives, a greene Hat and a Feather,
   New Gloves to put upon thy milk-white hand
Ile give thee, for to keep thee from the weather;
   With Phoenix feathers shall thy Face be fanned,
Cooling those Cheekes, that being cool'd wax red
Like Lillyes in a bed of Roses shed.

RICHARD BARNEFIELD (1594)

42

From THE SHEPHEARDS CONTENT

He sits all Day lowd-piping on a Hill,
   The whilst his flocke about him daunce apace,
His hart with joy, his eares with Musique fill:
   Anon a bleating Wether beares the Bass,
   A Lambe the Treble; and to his disgrace
Another answers like a middle Meane:
Thus every one to beare a Part are faine.

Like a great King he rules a little Land,
   Still making Statutes, and ordayning Lawes;
Which if they breake, he beates them with his Wand:
   He doth defend them from the greedy Jawes
   Of rav'ning Wolves, and Lyons bloudy Pawes.
His Field, his Realme; his Subjects are his Sheepe;
Which he doth still in due obedience keepe.

First he ordaines by Act of Parlament,
    (Holden by custome in each Country Towne),
That if a sheepe (with any bad intent)
    Presume to breake the neighbour Hedges downe,
    Or haunt strange Pastures that be not his owne,
He shall be pounded for his lustines,
Untill his Master finde out some redres.

.   .   .   .   .

Thus doth he keepe them still in awfull feare,
    And yet allowes them liberty inough;
So dear to him their welfare doth appeare,
    That when their fleeces gin to waxen rough,
    He combs and trims them with a Rampicke bough,
Washing them in the streames of silver *Ladon*,
To cleanse their skinnes from all corruption.

Another while he wooes his Country Wench,
    (With Chaplets crownd, and gaudy girlonds dight)
Whose burning Lust her modest eye doth quench,
    Standing amazed at her heavenly sight,
    (Beauty doth ravish Sense with sweet Delight)
Clearing *Arcadia* with a smoothed Browe
When Sun-bright smiles melts flakes of driven snowe.

Thus doth he frollicke it each day by day,
    And when Night comes drawes homeward to his Coate,
Singing a Jigge or merry Roundelay;
    (For who sings commonly so merry a Noate,
    As he that cannot chop or change a groate?)
And in the winter Nights (his chiefe desire)
He turns a Crabbe or Cracknell in the fire.

pounded, Impounded.   *Rampicke bough*, Spiky branch.
Crabbe, Small apple.   *Cracknell*, Biscuit.

He leads his Wench a Country Horn-pipe Round,
    About a May-pole on a Holy-day;
Kissing his lovely Lasse (with Garlands Crownd)
    With whoopping heigh-ho singing Care away;
    Thus doth he passe the merry month of May:
And all th'yere after in delight and joy,
(Scorning a King) he cares for no annoy.

What though with simple cheere he homely fares?
    He lives content, a King can doo no more;
Nay not so much, for Kings have manie cares:
    But he hath none; except it be that sore
    Which yong and old, which vexeth rich and poore,
The pangs of Love. O! who can vanquish Love?
That conquers Kingdomes, and the Gods above?

Deepe-wounding Arrow, hart-consuming Fire;
    Ruler of Reason, slave to tyrant Beautie;
Monarch of harts, Fuell of fond desire,
    Prentice to Folly, foe to feigned Duetie;
    Pledge of true Zeale, Affections moietie;
If thou kilst where thou wilt, and whom it list thee,
Alas, how can a silly Soule resist thee?

By thee great *Collin* lost his libertie,
    By thee sweet *Astrophel* forwent his joy;
By thee *Amyntas* wept incessantly,
    By thee good *Rowland* liv'd in great annoy;
    O cruell, peevish, vile, blind-seeing Boy:
How canst thou hit their harts, and yet not see?
(If thou be blinde, as thou art faind to be).

A Shepheard loves no ill, but onely thee;
    He hath no care, but onely by thy causing;
Why doost thou shoot thy cruell shafts at mee?
    Give me some respite, some short time of pausing:
    Still my sweet Love with bitter lucke th'art sawcing:
Oh, if thou hast a minde to shew thy might,
Kill mightie Kings, and not a wretched wight.

.   .   .   .   .

How happie were a harmles Shepheards life,
  If he had never knowen what Love did meane;
But now fond Love in every place is rife,
    Staining the purest Soule with spots uncleane,
    Making thicke purses, thin: and fat bodies, leane:
Love is a fiend, a fire, a heaven, a hell;
Where pleasure, paine, and sad repentance dwell.

.   .   .   .   .

Thus have I showed in my Countrey veine
  The sweet Content that Shepheards still injoy;
The mickle pleasure, and the little paine
    That ever doth awayte the Shepheards Boy:
    His hart is never troubled with annoy.
He is a King, for he commands his Sheepe;
He knowes no woe, for he doth seldome weepe.

He is a Courtier, for he courts his Love:
  He is a Scholler, for he sings sweet Ditties:
He is a Souldier, for he wounds doth prove;
    He is the fame of Townes, the shame of Citties;
    He scornes false Fortune, but true Vertue pitties.
He is a Gentleman, because his nature
Is kinde and affable to everie Creature.

Who would not then a simple Shepheard bee,
  Rather than be a mightie Monarch made?
Since he injoyes such perfect libertie,
    As never can decay, nor never fade:
    He seldome sits in dolefull Cypresse shade,
But lives in hope, in joy, in peace, in blisse:
Joying all joy with this content of his.
                              RICHARD BARNEFIELD (1594)

prove, Experience.

43

"FIELDS WERE OVER-SPREAD WITH FLOWERS"

Fields were over-spread with flowers,
Fairest choise of *Floraes* treasure:
Shepheards there had shadie Bowers,
Where they oft repos'd with pleasure.
   Meadowes flourish'd fresh and gay,
   Where the wanton Heards did play.

Springs more cleare then Christall streames,
Seated were the Groves among:
Thus nor *Titans* scorching beames,
Nor earths drouth could Shepheards wrong.
   Fair *Pomonaes* fruitfull pride
   Did the budding braunches hide.

Flocks of sheepe fed on the Plaines,
Harmelesse sheepe that roamd at large:
Here and there sate pensive Swaines,
Wayting on their wandring charge.
   Pensive while their Lasses smil'd:
   Lasses which had them beguil'd.

Hills with trees were richly dight,
Vallies stor'd with *Vestaes* wealth:
Both did harbour sweet delight,
Nought was there to hinder health.
   Thus did Heaven grace the soyle,
   Not deform'd with work-mens toile.

Purest plot of earthly mold
Might that Land be justly named;
Art by Nature was controld,
Art which no such pleasures framed.
   Fayrer place was never seene,
   Fittest place for Beauties Queene.

                              J.M. (1600)

44

TO AMARILLIS

Though *Amarillis* daunce in greene,
  Like Fairie Queene,
  And sing full cleere,
  With smiling cheere.
Yet since her eyes make hart so sore,
  hey hoe, chill love no more.

My Sheepe are lost for want of foode
  And I so wood
  That all the day
I sit and watch a Heard-mayde gay
Who laughs to see me sigh so sore:
  hey hoe, chill love no more.

Her loving lookes, her beautie bright,
  Is such delight,
  That all in vaine
I love to like, and loose my gaine,
For her that thanks me not therefore,
  hey hoe, chill love no more.

Ah wanton eyes, my friendly foes,
  And cause of woes,
  Your sweet desire
Breedes flames of Ice, and freeze in fire.
You scorne to see me weepe so sore:
  hey hoe, chill love no more.

Love ye who list, I force him not,
  Sith God it wot
  The more I waile:
The lesse my sighs and teares prevaile.
What shall I doo, but say therefore,
  hey hoe, chill love no more?

WILLIAM BYRD (1588)

chill, I will (rustic).

45

A SONG, IN PRAISE OF A BEGGERS LIFE

Bright shines the Sun, play Beggers play,
Here's scraps enough to serve to day.
What noyse of Viols is so sweete,
As when our merry clappers ring?
What mirth doth want where Beggers meete?
A Beggers life is for a King.
Eate, drinke, and play, sleepe when wee list,
Go where wee will, so stocks be missed.
Bright shines, &c.

The world is ours, and ours alone,
For wee alone have world at will,
Wee purchase not, all is our owne,
Both fields and streetes wee Beggers fill.
Nor care to get, nor feare to keepe,
Did ever breake a Beggers sleepe.
Bright shines, &c.

A hundred head of blacke and white,
Upon our downes securely feede,
If any dare his master bite,
He dies therefore as sure as Creede.
Thus Beggers Lord it as they please,
And none but Beggers live at ease.
Bright shines, &c.

ANONYMOUS (1611)

46

"*I CARE NOT FOR THESE LADIES*"

I care not for these Ladies
   That must be woode and praide;
Give me kind Amarillis,
   The wanton countrey maide.
Nature art disdaineth,
Her beauty is her owne;
   Her when we court and kisse,
   She cries, forsooth, let go.
   But when we come where comfort is,
   She never will say no.

If I love Amarillis,
   She gives me fruit and flowers,
But if we love these Ladies,
   We must give golden showers,
Give them gold that sell love;
Give me the Nutbrowne lasse,
   Who when we court and kiss,
   She cries, forsooth, let go.
   But when we come where comfort is,
   She never will say no.

These Ladies must have pillowes,
   And beds by strangers wrought;
Give me a Bower of willowes,
   Of mosse and leaves unbought.
And fresh Amarillis,
With milk and honie fed,
   Who, when we court and kiss,
   She cries, forsooth, let go.
   But when we come where comfort is,
   She never will say no.

                THOMAS CAMPION (1601)

47

"*JACK AND JONE THEY THINKE NO ILL*"

Jacke and Jone they thinke no ill,
But loving live, and merry still,
Doe their weeke dayes worke, and pray
Devoutly on the holy day:
Skip and trip it on the greene,
And help to chuse the Summer Queen:
Lash out, at a Country Feast,
Their silver penny with the best.

Well can they judge of nappy Ale,
And tell at large a Winter tale;
Climbe up to the Apple loft,
And turne the Crabs till they be soft.
Tib is all the fathers joy,
And little *Tom* the mothers boy.
All their pleasure is content;
And care, to pay their yearely rent.

Jone can call by name her Cowes,
And decke her windowes with greene boughs;
Shee can wreathes and tuttyes make,
And trim with plums a Bridall Cake.
Jacke knowes what brings gaine or losse;
And his long Flaile can stoutly tosse:
Make the hedge, while others breake,
And ever thinkes what he doth speake.

Now, you Courtly Dames and Knights,
That study onely strange delights;
Though you scorne the home-spun gray,
And revell in your rich array:

Though your tongues dissemble deepe,
And can your heads from danger keepe;
Yet, for all your pompe and traine,
Securer lives the silly Swaine.

THOMAS CAMPION (1613)

48

PASTORAL MORNING HYMN

Sing his praises that doth keep
    Our Flocks from harm;
Pan the Father of our Sheep,
    And arm in arm
Tread we softly in a round,
Whilest the hollow neighbouring ground
Fills the Musick with her sound.

Pan, O great God *Pan*, to thee
    Thus do we sing:
Thou that keep'st us chaste and free
    As the young spring,
Ever be thy honour spoke,
From that place the morn is broke,
To that place Day doth unyoke.

JOHN FLETCHER, *The Faithful Shepherdess* (1609?), I, i

49

PASTORAL EVENING HYMN

Shepherds all, and maidens fair,
Fold your flocks up, for the Air
'Gins to thicken, and the sun
Already his great course hath run.

See the dew-drops how they kiss
Every little flower that is;
Hanging on their velvet heads,
Like a rope of crystal beads;
See the heavy clouds low falling,
And bright Hesperus down calling
The dead Night from under ground;
At whose rising, mists unsound,
Damps and vapours fly apace,
Hovering o're the wanton face
Of these pastures, where they come,
Striking dead both bud and bloom:
Therefore from such danger lock
Every one his loved flock;
And let your Dogs lye loose without,
Lest the Wolf come as a scout
From the mountain, and e're day,
Bear a Lamb or Kid away;
Or the crafty theevish Fox
Break upon your simple flocks.
To secure your selves from these,
Be not too secure in ease;
Let one eye his watches keep,
Whilst the t'other eye doth sleep;
So you shall good Shepherds prove,
And for ever hold the love
Of our great god. Sweetest slumbers
And soft silence, fall in numbers
On your eyelids! So farewel:
Thus I end my evening's knel.

JOHN FLETCHER, *The Faithful Shepherdess* (1609?), II, i

50

PASTORAL REVEILLE

Shepherds, rise, and shake off sleep!
See, the blushing Morn doth peep
Through the windows, whilst the Sun
To the mountain-tops is run,
Gilding all the Vales below
With his rising flames, which grow
Greater by his climbing still.
Up, ye lazie grooms, and fill
Bagg and Bottle for the field!
Clasp your cloaks fast, lest they yield
To the bitter North-East wind.
Call the Maidens up, and find
Who lay longest, that she may
Go without a friend all day;
Then reward your Dogs, and pray
Pan to keep you from decay;
So unfold, and then away.

JOHN FLETCHER, *The Faithful Shepherdess* (1609?), V, i

51

THE CITIZEN ON THE COUNTRYMAN

1 CITIZEN: Lord how fine the fields be, what sweet living 'tis in the Country!

2 CITIZEN: Ay, poor souls, God help 'em; they live as contentedly as one of us.

1 CITIZEN: My husband's cousin would have had me gone into the Country last year; wert thou ever there?

2 CITIZEN: Ay, poor souls, I was amongst 'em once.

1 Citizen:	And what kind of creatures are they, for love of God?
2 Citizen:	Very good people, God help 'em.
1 Citizen:	Wilt thou go down with me this Summer when I am brought to bed?
2 Citizen:	Alas, it is no place for us.
1 Citizen:	Why, pray thee?
2 Citizen:	Why, you can have nothing there, there's no body cryes brooms.
1 Citizen:	No?
2 Citizen:	No truly, nor milk.
1 Citizen:	Nor milk! How do they?
2 Citizen:	They are fain to milk themselves i' th' Country.
1 Citizen:	Good Lord! But the people there, I think, will be very dutiful to one of us.
2 Citizen:	Ay, God knows will they, and yet they do not greatly care for our husbands.
1 Citizen:	Do they not? Alas! I'good faith I cannot blame them: for we do not greatly care for them ourselves.

BEAUMONT AND FLETCHER,

A King and No King (1619), Act II

52

ART AND NATURE

PERDITA

Sir, welcome:
It is my Fathers will, I should take on mee
The Hostesseship o' th' day: you're welcome, sir.
Give me those Flowres there, *Dorcas.* Reverend Sirs,
For you there's Rosemary and Rue, these keepe
Seeming and savour all the Winter long:
Grace and Remembrance be to you both,
And welcome to our Shearing.

POLIXENES

Shepherdesse,
(A faire one are you) well you fit our ages
With flowres of Winter.

PERDITA

Sir, the yeare growing ancient,
Not yet on summers death, nor on the birth
Of trembling winter, the fayrest flowres o' th' season
Are our Carnations, and streak'd Gilly-vors
(Which some call Natures bastards) of that kind
Our rusticke Gardens barren, and I care not
To get slips of them.

POLIXENES

Wherefore (gentle Maiden)
Do you neglect them?

PERDITA

For I have heard it said,
There is an Art, which in their pideness shares
With great creating-Nature.

POLIXENES

Say there be:
Yet Nature is made better by no meane
But Nature makes that Meane; so over that Art,
(Which you say adds to Nature) is an Art
That Nature makes: you see (sweet Maid) we marry
A gentler Scion to the wildest Stocke,
And make conceive a barke of baser kinde
By bud of Nobler race: this is an Art
Which do's mend Nature, change it rather, but
The Art it selfe, is Nature.

PERDITA

So it is.

POLIXENES

Then make your Garden rich in Gilly'vors,
And do not call them bastards.

PERDITA

Ile not put
The Dibble in earth, to set one slip of them:
No more than were I painted, I would wish
This youth should say 'twere well.

The Winter's Tale, IV, iii, 70–102

53

From "THE SAD SHEPHERD"

Act I, Scene iv. Robin-hood, "the chiefe Wood-man," Clarion, "the Rich Shepherd," Friar Tuck, "The Chaplaine and Steward," Lionell, "The Courteous Shepherd."

ROBIN-HOOD

Now that the shearing of your sheepe is done,
And the wash'd Flocks are lighted of their wooll,
The smoother Ewes are ready to receive
The mounting Rams againe; and both doe feed,
As either promist to increase your breed
At eaning time; and bring you lusty twins.
Why should, or you, or wee so much forget
The season in our selves: as not to make
Use of our youth, and spirits, to awake
The nimble Horne-pipe, and the Timburine,
And mixe our Songs, and Dances in the Wood,
And each of us cut downe a Triumph-bough?
Such are the Rites, the youthfull *June* allow.

CLARION

They were, gay *Robin*, but the sowrer sort
Of Shepherds now disclaime in all such sport:
And say, our Flocks, the while, are poorely fed,
When with such vanities the Swaines are led.

Tuck

Would they, wise *Clarion*, were not hurried more
With Covetise and Rage, when to their store
They adde the poore mans Eaneling, and dare sell
Both Fleece, and Carkasse, not gi'ing him the Fell.
When to one Goat, they reach that prickly weed,
Which maketh all the rest forbeare to feed;
Or strew *Tods*' haires, or with their tailes doe sweepe
The dewy grasse, to d'off the simpler sheepe;
Or digge deepe pits, their Neighbours Neat to vexe,
To drowne the Calves, and crack the Heifers necks.
Or with pretence of chasing thence the Brock,
Send in a curre to worrie the whole Flock.

Lionell

O Friar, those are faults that are not seene,
Ours open, and of worst example beene.
They call ours, *Pagan* pastimes, that infect
Our blood with ease, our youth with all neglect,
Our tongues with wantonnesse, our thoughts with lust;
And what they censure ill, all others must.

Robin-hood

I do not know, what their sharpe sight may see
Of late, but I should thinke it still might be
(As 'twas) a happy age, when on the Plaines,
The Wood-men met the Damsells, and the Swaines
The Neat'ards, Plow-men, and the Pipers loud,
And each did dance, some to the Kit, or Crowd,
Some to the Bag-pipe, some the Tabret mov'd,
And all did either love, or were belov'd.

Lionell

The dextrous Shepherd then would try his sling,
Then dart his Hooke at Daysies, then would sing,
Sometimes would wrastle.

CLARION
Ay, and with a Lasse:
And give her a new garment on the grasse;
After a course at Barley-breake, or Base.

LIONELL
And all these deeds were seene without offence,
Or the least hazard o' their innocence.

ROBIN-HOOD
Those charitable times had no mistrust.
Shepherds knew how to love, and not to lust.

BEN JONSON (1640)

54

PANS ANNIVERSARIE

NYMPH I
Thus, thus, begin the yearly rites
Are due to PAN on these bright nights;
His Morne now riseth, and invites
To sports, to dances, and delights:
All envious, and Prophane away,
This is the Shepherds Holy-day.

NYMPH II
Strew, strew, the glad and smiling ground
With every flower, yet not confound
The Prime-rose drop, the Springs owne spouse,
Bright Dayes-eyes, and the lips of Cowes,
The Garden-star, the Queene of May,
The Rose, to crowne the Holy-day.

NYMPH III
Drop, drop you Violets, change your hues,
Now red, now pale, as Lovers use,
And in your death goe out as well,

As when you liv'd unto the smell:
That from your odour all may say,
This is the Shepherds Holy-day.

BEN JONSON (1640)

55

SONG OF PASSERAT

AMINTAS   DAPHNÈ

DAPHNÈ

Shephard loveth thow me vell?

AMINTAS

So vel that I cannot tell.

DAPHNÈ

Like to vhat, good shephard, say?

AMINTAS

Like to thee, faire cruell May.

DAPHNÈ

Ah! how strange thy vords I find!
But yet satisfie my mind;
Shephard vithout flatterie,
Beares thow any love to me,
Like to vhat, good shephard, say?

AMINTAS

Like to thee, faire cruell May.

DAPHNÈ

Better answer had it beene
To say, I love thee as mine eyne.

AMINTAS

Voe is me, I love them not,
For be them love entress got
At the time they did behold
Thy sveet face & haire of gold.

May, Maid   *entress*, Entrance

DAPHNÈ
Like to vhat, good shephard, say?

AMINTAS
Like to thee, faire cruelle May.

DAPHNÈ
But, deare shephard, speake more plaine,
And I sal not aske againe;
For to end this gentle strife,
Doth thow love me as thy life?

AMINTAS
No, for it doth eb and flow
Vith contrare tides of grief & voe;
And now I through loves strange force
A man am not, but a dead corse.

DAPHNÈ
Like to vhat, good shephard, say?

AMINTAS
Like to thee, faire cruell May.

DAPHNÈ
This 'like to thee' O leave, I pray,
And as my selfe, good shephard, say.

AMINTAS
Alas! I do not love my selff,
For I me split on beuties shelf.

DAPHNÈ
Like to vhat, good shephard, say?

AMINTAS
Like to thee, faire cruell May.
Translated by SIR WILLIAM DRUMMOND (1711)

56

From THE SHEPHEARD'S HUNTING

Now to chant it were but reason;
Song and Musicke are in season.
Now in this sweet jolly tide,
Is the earth in all her pride:
The fair Lady of the *May*,
Trimm'd up in her best array,
Hath invited all the Swains
With the Lasses of the Plains,
To attend upon her sport
At the places of resort.
Corridon with his bold Rout
Hath already beene about
For the elder Shepheards dole,
And fetch'd in the *Summer-Pole*:
While the rest have built a *Bower*
To defend them from a shower,
Seil'd so close, with boughes all greene,
Tytan cannot pry betweene.
Now the *Dayrie Wenches* dreame
Of their Strawberries and Creame,
And each doth her selfe advance
To be taken in to dance;
Every one that knowes to sing,
Fits him for his Carolling;
So doe those that hope for meede,
Either by the Pipe or Reede:
And though I am kept away,
I do heare, this very day,
Many learned Groomes doe wend
For the Garlands to contend,
Which a Nimph that hight *Desart*,
Long a stranger in this part,

With her owne faire hand hath wrought;
A rare worke, they say, past thought,
As appeareth by the name,
For she calles them *Wreathes of fame.*
She hath set in their due place
Ev'ry flower that may grace;
And among a thousand moe,
Whereof some but serve for show,
She hath wove in *Daphne's* tree,
That they may not blasted bee.
Which with *Time* she edg'd about,
Lest the worke should ravell out.
And that it migh wither never,
Intermixt it with *Live-ever.*
These are to be shar'd among
Those that do excell for song:
Or their passions can rehearse
In the smooth'st and sweetest verse.
Then for those among the rest
That can play and pipe the best,
There's a kidling with the Damme,
A fat Wether, and a Lambe.
And for those that leapen farre,
Wrastle, run, and throw the barre,
There's appointed guerdons too:
He that best the first can doe
Shall, for his reward, be paid
With a *Sheepe-hooke*, faire inlaid
With fine bone, of a strange beast
That men bring from out the west:
For the next, a *Scrip* of red,
Tassel'd with fine coloured thred:
There's prepared for their meed
That in running make most speed,
Or the cunning measures foot,
Cups of turned *Maple-roote*,
Whereupon the skilfull man
Hath ingrav'd the *Loves* of *Pan*;

And the last hath for his due
A fine Napking wrought with blew.

GEORGE WITHER (1615), ECL. iv, 67–138

57

A CHRISTMAS CARROLL

So, now is come our joyfulst *Feast*;
    Let ever man be jolly.
Each Roome, with Yvie leaves is drest,
    And every Post, with Holly.
Though some Churles at our mirth repine,
Round your forheads Garlands twine,
Drowne sorrow in a Cup of Wine.
And let us all be merry.

Now, all our Neighbours Chimneys smoke,
    And *Christmas* blocks are burning;
Their Ovens, they with bakt-meats choke,
    And all their Spits are turning.
Without the doore, let sorrow lie:
And, if for cold, it hap to die,
Weele bury't in a *Christmas* Pye.
And evermore be merry.

Now, every *Lad* is wondrous trim,
    And no man minds his Labour.
Our Lasses have provided them,
    A Bag-pipe, and a Tabor.
Young men, and Mayds, and Girles & Boyes,
Give life, to one anothers Joyes:
And, you anon shall by their noyse,
Perceive that they are merry.

Ranke Misers now, doe sparing shun:
   Their Hall of Musicke soundeth:
And, Dogs, thence with whole shoulders run,
   So, all things there aboundeth.
The Countrey-folke, themselves advance;
For *Crowdy-Mutton's* come out of *France*:
And *Jack* shall pipe, and *Jyll* shall dance,
And all the Towne be merry.

Ned Swash hath fetcht his Bands from Pawne,
   And all his best Apparell.
Brisk *Nell* hath brought a Ruffe of Lawne,
   With droppings of the Barrell.
And those that hardly all the yeare
Had Bread to eat, or Raggs to weare,
Will have both Clothes, and daintie fare:
And all the day be merry.

Now poore men to the *Justices*,
   With Capons make their arrants,
And if they hap to faile of these,
   They plague them with their Warrants.
But now they feed them with good cheere,
And what they want, they take in Beere:
For, Christmas *comes but once a yeare*:
And then they shall be merry.

Good *Farmers*, in the Country, nurse
   The poore, that else were undone.
Some *Land*-lords spend their money worse
   On Lust, and Pride at *London*.
There, the Roysters they doe play;
Drabb and Dice their Lands away,
Which may be ours, another day:
And therefore lets be merry.

Crowdy-Mutton's, Not explained: possibly a fiddler ('crowder'), as Halliwell
  suggests; but that leaves much to the imagination.
               arrants, Errands.

The Clyent now his suit forbeares,
    The Prisoners heart is eased,
The Debtor drinks away his cares,
    And, for the time is pleased.
Though others Purses be more fat,
Why should we pine or grieve at that?
Hang sorrow, care will kill a Cat.
And therefore lets be merry.

Harke, how the *Wagges*, abroade doe call
    Each other foorth to rambling.
Anon, you'll see them in the Hall,
    For Nutts, and Apples scambling.
Harke, how the Roofes with laughters sound
Anon they'l thinke the house goes round:
For, they the Sellars depth have found.
And there they will be merry.

The *Wenches* with their *Wassell-Bowles*,
    About the Streets are singing:
The *Boyes* are come to catch the *Owles*,
    The *Wild-mare*, in is bringing.
Our *Kitchin-Boy* hath broke his Boxe,
And, to the dealing of the Oxe,
Our honest neighbours come by flocks,
And here they will be merry.

Now *Kings* and *Queenes*, poore Sheep-cotes have,
    And mate with every body:
The honest, now, may play the *knave*,
    And wise men play at *Noddy*.
Some Youths will now a *Mumming* goe;
Some others play at *Rowland-hoe*,
And, twenty other Gameboyes moe:
Because they will be merry.

Gameboyes, Gambols.

Then wherefore in these merry daies,
    Should we I pray, be duller?
No; let us sing some *Roundelayes*,
    To make our mirth the fuller.
And, whilest thus inspir'd we sing,
Let all the Streets with ecchoes ring:
Woods, and Hills, and every thing,
Beare witnesse we are merry.

GEORGE WITHER (1622)

58

ALETHEIA ARISES FROM THE CORPSE OF FIDA'S HIND

As that *Arabian* bird (whom all admire)
Her exequies prepar'd and funerall fire,
Burnt in a flame conceived from the Sunne,
And nourished with slips of *Cynamon*,
Out of her ashes hath a second birth,
And flies abroad, a wonderment on earth:
So from the ruines of this mangled Creature
Arose so faire and so divine a feature,
That *Envy* for her heart would doate upon her;
Heaven could not chuse but be enamour'd on her:
Were I a *Starre*, and shee a second *Spheare*,
Ide leave the other, and be fixed there.
Had faire *Arachne* wrought this Maidens haire,
When she with *Pallas* did for skill compare,
Minerva's worke had never been esteemd,
But this had been more rare and highly deemd;
Yet gladly now she would reverse her doome,
Weaving this haire within a Spiders Loome.

Upon her forehead, as in glory, sate
Mercy and Majesty, for wondring at,
As pure and simple as *Albania*'s snow,
Or milke-white Swannes which stem the streames of *Poe*:
Like to some goodly foreland, bearing out
Her haire, the tufts which fring'd the shoare about.
And lest the man which sought these coasts might slip,
Her eyes like Starres did serve to guide the ship.
Upon her front (heavens fairest *Promontory*)
Delineated was th'Authentique Story
Of those Elect, whose sheepe at first began
To nibble by the springs of *Canaan*:
Out of whose sacred loyns (brought by the stem
Of that sweet Singer of *Jerusalem*)
Came the best Shepheard ever flockes did keepe,
Who yeelded up his life to save his sheepe.
   O thou Eterne! by whom all beings move,
Giving the Springs beneath, and Springs above;
Whose finger doth this *Universe* sustaine,
Bringing the former and the latter rain;
Who dost with plenty Meades and Pastures fill,
By drops distil'd like dew on *Hermon* Hill:
Pardon a silly Swaine who (farr unable
In that which is so rare, so admirable)
Dares on an Oaten-pipe thus meanely sing
Her praise immense, worthy a silver string.
And thou which through the Desart and the Deepe
Didst lead thy Chosen like a flocke of sheepe;
As sometime by a Starre thou guided'st them,
Which fed upon the plaines of *Bethlehem*;
So by thy sacred spirit direct my quill,
When I shall sing ought of thy *Holy Hill*,
That times to come, when they my rimes rehearse,
May wonder at me, and admire my Verse:
For who but one rapt in Celestiall fire;
Can by his Muse to such a pitch aspire,
That from aloft he might behold and tell
Her worth, whereon an iron Pen might dwell?

When she was borne, *Nature* in sporte began
To learne the cunning of an *Artizan*,
And did Vermilion with a white compose,
To mocke herselfe and paint a damaske Rose.
But scorning *Nature* unto *Art* should seeke,
She spilt her colours on this Maidens cheeke.
Her mouth the gate from whence all goodnesse came,
Of power to give the dead a living name.
Her words embalmed in so sweet a breath,
That made them triumph both on Time and Death;
Whose fragrant sweets, since the *Chameleon* knew,
And tasted of, he to this humor grew,
Left other Elements, held this so rare,
That since, he never feedes on ought but Ayre.
    WILLIAM BROWNE, *Britannias Pastorals* (1613), I, 4, 155–224

59

MARINA READS A SHEPHERD'S LAMENT

Long on the shore distrest *Marina* lay:
For he that ope's the pleasant sweets of *May*,
Beyond the *Noonstead* so farre drove his teame,
That Harvest folkes, with curds and clouted creame,
With cheese and butter, cakes, and oates ynow,
That are the *Yeomans*, from the yoke or Cowe,
On sheaves of corne were at their noonshuns close,
Whilst by them merrily the *Bagpipe* goes:
Ere from her hand she lifted up her head,
Where all the *Graces* then inhabited.
When casting round her over-drowned eyes,
(So have I seen a Gemme of mickle price
Roll in a *Scallop-shell* with water fild)
She, on a marble rocke at hand behild,
In Characters deepe cut with Iron stroke,
A Shepheards moane, which, read by her, thus spoke:

Glide soft, ye silver Floods,
And every Spring:
Within the shady Woods
Let no Bird sing!
Nor from the Grove a *Turtle-Dove*
Be seene to couple with her love;
But silence on each Dale and Mountaine dwell,
Whilst *Willy* bids his friend and joy *Farewell*.

But (of greet *Thetis* trayne)
Ye *Mermaides* faire,
That on the shores doe plaine
Your Sea-greene haire,
As ye in tramels knit your locks,
Weep yee; and so enforce the rocks
In heavy murmures through the broade shores tell
How *Willy* bade his friend and joy *Farewell*.

Cease, cease, yee murdring winds,
To move a wave;
But if with troubled minds
You seeke his grave;
Know 'tis as various as your selves,
Now in the deepe, then on the shelves,
His coffin toss'd by fish and surges fell,
Whilst *Willy* weeps and bids all joy *Farewell*.

Had her *Arion* like
Beene judg'd to drowne,
He on his lute could strike
So rare a sowne,
A thousand *Dolphins* would have come
And jointly strive to bring him home.
But he on Shipboard dyde, by sicknesse fell,
Since when his *Willy* bade all joy *Farewell*.

Great *Neptune*, hear a Swaine!
His Coffin take,
And with a golden chaine
(For pittie) make
It fast unto a rock neere land!
Where ev'ry calmy morne Ile stand,
And ere one sheepe out of my fold I tell,
Sad *Willy's* Pipe shall bid his friend *Farewell*.
WILLIAM BROWNE, *Britannias Pastorals* (1616), II, 1, 225–280

60

From the *PISCATORIE ECLOGUES*

CHROMIS
Ah wretched swains, that live in fishers trade;
  With inward griefs, and outward wants distressed;
While every day doth more your sorrow lade;
  By others scorn'd, and by yourselves oppressed!
  The great the greater serve, the lesser these:
  And all their art is how to rise and please.

THELGON
Those fisher-swains, from whom our trade doth flow,
  That by the King of seas their skill were taught;
As they their boats on *Jordan* wave did row,
  And catching fish, were by a Fisher caught;
  (Ah blessed chance! much better was the trade,
  That being fishers, thus were fishes made.)

Those happy swains, in outward shew unblest,
  Were scourg'd, were scorn'd, yet was this losse their gain;
By land, by sea, in life, in death, distrest;
  But now with King of seas securely reigne:
  For that short wo in this base earthly dwelling,
  Enjoying joy all excellence excelling.

Then do not thou, my boy, cast down thy minde,
  But seek to please with all thy busie care
The King of seas; so shalt thou surely finde
  Rest, quiet, joy, in all this troublous fare.
  Let not thy net, thy hook, thy singing cease:
  And pray these tempests may be turn'd to peace.

Oh Prince of waters, Soveraigne of seas,
  Whom storms & calms, whom windes and waves obey;
If ever that great Fisher did thee please,
  Chide thou the windes, and furious waves allay:
  So on thy shore the fisher-boys shall sing
  Sweet songs of peace to our sweet peaces king

IV, 27–31

DAPHNIS

Thrice happy swains! thrice happy shepherds fate!

THOMALIN

Ah blessed life! ah blessed fishers state!
Your pipes asswage your love; your nets maintain you.

DAPHNIS

Your lambkins clothe you warm; your flocks sustain you:
You fear no stormy seas, nor tempests roaring.

THOMALIN

You sit not rots or burning starres deploring:
In calms you fish; in roughs use songs and dances.

DAPHNIS

More do you fear your Loves sweet-bitter glances,
Than certain fate, or fortune ever changing.

THOMALIN

Ah that the life in seas so safely ranging,
Should with loves weeping eye be sunk, and drown'd!

DAPHNIS

The shepherds life *Phoebus* a shepherd crown'd,
His snowy flocks by stately *Peneus* leading.

THOMALIN

What herb was that, on which old *Glaucus* feeding,
Grows never old, but now the gods augmenteth?

DAPHNIS

Delia herself her vigour hard relenteth:
To play with shepherds boy she's not ashamed.

THOMALIN

Venus, of frothy seas thou first was framed;
The waves thy cradle: now *Love's Queen* art named.

VII, 32

PHINEAS FLETCHER (1633)

61

From L'ALLEGRO

Hard by, a Cottage chimney smokes,
From betwixt two aged Okes,
Where *Corydon* and *Thyrsis* met,
Are at their savory dinner set
Of Hearbs, and other Country Messes,
Which the neat-handed *Phillis* dresses;
And then in haste her Bowre she leaves,
With *Thestylis* to bind the Sheaves;
Or if the earlier season lead
To the tann'd Haycock in the Mead.
Some times with secure delight
The up-land Hamlets will invite,
When the merry Bells ring round,
And the jocund rebecks sound
To many a youth, and many a maid,
Dancing in the Chequer'd shade;

And young and old com forth to play
On a Sunshine Holyday,
Till the live-long day-light fail,
Then to the Spicy Nut-brown Ale,
With stories told of many a feat,
How *Faery Mab* the junkets ate,
She was pincht and pull'd, she sed,
And he by Friars Lanthorn led;
Tells how the drudging *Goblin* swet,
To ern his Cream-bowle duly set,
When in one night, ere glimps of morn,
His shadowy Flale hath threshed the Corn
That ten day-labourers could not end,
Then lies him down the Lubbar Fend,
And, stretch'd out all the Chimney's length,
Basks at the fire his hairy strength;
And Cropful out of doors he flings,
Ere the first Cock his Mattin rings.

JOHN MILTON

62

Two Songs from ARCADES

O're the smooth enameld green
Where no print of step hath been,
   Follow me as I sing,
   And touch the warbled string.
Under the shady roof
Of branching Elm Star-proof,
   Follow me,
I will bring you where she sits
Clad in splendor as befits
   Her deity.
Such a rural Queen
All *Arcadia* hath not seen.

Nymphs and Shepherds dance no more
    By sandy *Ladons* Lillied banks.
On old *Lycaeus* or *Cyllene* hoar,
    Trip no more in twilight ranks,
Though *Erymanth* your loss deplore,
    A better soyl shall give ye thanks.
From the stony *Maenalus*,
Bring your Flocks, and live with us,
Here ye shall have greater grace,
To serve the Lady of this place.
    Though *Syrinx* your *Pans* Mistres were,
Yet *Syrinx* well might wait on her.
    Such a rural Queen
All *Arcadia* hath not seen.

JOHN MILTON

63

From COMUS

COMUS
    O foolishnes of men! that lend their ears
To those budge doctors of the Stoick fur,
And fetch their precepts from the Cynick tub,
Praising the lean and sallow Abstinence.
Wherefore did Nature powre her bounties forth,
With such a full and unwithdrawing hand,
Covering the earth with odours, fruits, and flocks,
Thronging the Seas with spawn innumerable,
But all to please, and sate the curious taste?
And set to work millions of spinning Worms,
That in their green shops weave the smooth-hair'd silk
To deck her Sons; and that no corner might

Be vacant of her plenty, in her own loyns
She hutch'd the all-worshipp'd ore, and precious gems,
To store her children with: if all the world
Should in a pet of temperance feed on Pulse,
Drink the clear stream, and nothing wear but Frieze,
Th' all-giver would be unthank't, would be unprais'd,
Not half his riches known, and yet despis'd;
And we should serve him as a grudging master,
As a penurious niggard of his wealth;
And live like Natures bastards, not her sons,
Who would be quite surcharged with her own weight,
And strangled with her waste fertility;
Th' earth cumber'd, and the wing'd air dark't with plumes,
The herds would over-multitude their Lords,
The sea o'erfraught would swell, and th' unsought diamonds
Would so emblaze the forhead of the Deep,
And so bestudd with Stars, that they below
Would grow inur'd to light, and com at last
To gaze upon the Sun with shameless brows.
List, Lady, be not coy, and be not cozen'd
With that same vaunted name Virginity.
Beauty is Natures coyn, must not be hoorded,
But must be current, and the good thereof
Consists in mutual and partak'n bliss,
Unsavoury in th' injoyment of itself;
If you let slip time, like a neglected rose
It withers on the stalk with languish't head.
Beauty is Natures brag, and must be shown
In courts, at feasts, and high solemnities,
Where most may wonder at the workmanship.
It is for homely features to keep home,
They had their name thence; coarse complexions,
And cheeks of sorry grain, will serve to ply
The sampler, and to tease the huswifes wool.
What need a vermeil-tinctured lip for that,
Love-darting eyes, or tresses like the Morn?
There was another meaning in these gifts,
Think what, and be adviz'd, you are but young yet.

LADY

I had not thought to have unlockt my lips
In this unhallow'd air, but that this Jugler
Would think to charm my judgment, as mine eyes,
Obtruding false rules pranckt in reasons garb.
I hate when vice can bolt her arguments,
And vertue has no tongue to check her pride.
Impostor, do not charge most innocent Nature,
As if she would her children should be riotous
With her abundance; she, good cateress,
Means her provision onely to the good,
That live according to her sober laws,
And holy dictate of spare Temperance:
If every just man, that now pines with want,
Had but a moderate and beseeming share
Of that which lewdly-pamper'd Luxury
Now heaps upon some few with vast excess,
Natures full blessings would be well dispenc't
In unsuperfluous eeven proportion,
And she no whit encomber'd with her store;
And then the giver would be better thank't,
His praise due paid; for swinish gluttony
Ne'er looks to Heav'n amidst his gorgeous feast,
But with besotted base ingratitude
Cramms, and blasphemes his feeder. Shall I go on?
Or have I said enough? To him that dares
Arm his profane tongue with contemptuous words
Against the Sun-clad power of Chastity,
Fain would I something say, yet to what end?
Thou hast nor Eare, nor Soul to apprehend
The sublime notion, and high mystery,
That must be utter'd to unfold the sage
And serious doctrine of Virginity,
And thou art worthy that thou shouldst not know
More happiness than this thy present lot.
Enjoy your deer Wit, and gay Rhetorick,
That hath so well been taught her dazling fence,
Thou art not fit to hear thyself convinc't;

Yet should I try, the uncontrouled worth
Of this pure cause would kindle my rap't spirits
To such a flame of sacred vehemence,
That dumb things would be mov'd to sympathize,
And the brute Earth would lend her nerves, and shake,
Till all thy magick structures rear'd so high,
Were shatter'd into heaps o'er thy false head.

JOHN MILTON (1634)

64

LYCIDAS

In this Monody the Author bewails a learned Friend, unfortunatly drown'd in his Passage from *Chester* on the *Irish* seas, 1637; and by occasion foretels the ruin of our corrupted Clergy, then in their height.

Yet once more, O ye laurels, and once more
Ye myrtles brown, with ivy never-sear,
I come to pluck your Berries harsh and crude,
And with forc'd fingers rude,
Shatter your leaves before the mellowing year
Bitter constraint, and sad occasion dear,
Compels me to disturb your season due:
For *Lycidas* is dead, dead ere his prime,
Young *Lycidas*, and hath not left his peer:
Who would not sing for *Lycidas*? He knew
Himself to sing, and build the lofty rhyme.
He must not flote upon his watry bier
Unwept, and welter to the parching wind,
Without the meed of som melodious tear.
Begin then, Sisters of the sacred well,
That from beneath the seat of *Jove* doth spring,
Begin, and somwhat loudly sweep the string.
Hence with denial vain, and coy excuse,
So may some gentle Muse
With lucky words favour my destin'd urn,

And as he passes turn,
And bid fair peace be to my sable shrowd.
For we were nurst upon the self-same hill
Fed the same flock by fountain, shade, and rill.
    Together both, ere the high Lawns appear'd
Under the opening eye-lids of the morn,
We drove a field, and both together heard
What time the Gray-fly winds her sultry horn,
Batt'ning our flocks with the fresh dews of night,
Oft till the Star that rose, at Ev'ning, bright,
Toward Heav'n's descent had sloped his westering wheel
Meanwhile the Rural ditties were not mute,
Temper'd to th' Oaten Flute,
Rough *Satyrs* danc'd, and *Fauns* with clov'n heel,
From the glad sound would not be absent long,
And old *Damœtas* lov'd to hear our song.
    But, O the heavy change, now thou art gon,
Now thou art gon, and never must return!
Thee, Shepherd, thee the Woods, and desert Caves
With wilde Thyme and the gadding Vine o'ergrown,
And all their echoes mourn.
The Willows, and the Hazle Copses green,
Shall now no more be seen,
Fanning their joyous Leaves to thy soft layes.
As killing as the Canker to the Rose,
Or Taint-worm to the weanling Herds that graze,
Or Frost to Flowers, that their gay wardrobe wear,
When first the white thorn blows;
Such, *Lycidas*, thy loss to shepherd's ear.
    Where were ye Nymphs when the remorseless deep
Clos'd o'er the head of your lov'd *Lycidas*?
For neither were ye playing on the steep,
Where your old *Bards*, the famous *Druids* ly,
Nor on the shaggy top of *Mona* high,
Nor yet where *Deva* spreads her wisard stream:
Ay me, I fondly dream!
Had ye bin there—for what could that have don?
What could the Muse her self that *Orpheus* bore,

The Muse her self for her inchanting son
Whom Universal nature did lament,
When by the rout that made the hideous roar,
His gory visage down the stream was sent,
Down the swift *Hebrus* to the *Lesbian* shore?
　　Alas! what boots it with uncessant care
To tend the homely slighted Shepherds trade,
And strictly meditate the thankles Muse?
Were it not better don as others use,
To sport with *Amaryllis* in the shade,
Or with the tangles of *Neæra's* hair?
Fame is the spur that the clear spirit doth raise
(That last infirmity of Noble mind)
To scorn delights, and live laborious dayes;
But the fair Guerdon when we hope to find,
And think to burst out into sudden blaze,
Comes the blind *Fury* with th' abhorrèd shears,
And slits the thin spun life. But not the praise,
Phœbus repli'd, and touch'd my trembling ears;
Fame is no plant that grows on mortal soil,
Nor in the glistering foil
Set off to th' world, nor in broad rumour lies,
But lives and spreads aloft by those pure eyes,
And perfet witnes of all judging *Jove*;
As he pronounces lastly on each deed,
Of so much fame in Heav'n expect thy meed.
O Fountain *Arethuse*, and thou honour'd Floud,
Smooth-sliding *Mincius*, crown'd with vocall reeds,
That strain I heard was of a higher mood:
But now my Oate proceeds,
And listens to the Herald of the Sea
That came in *Neptune's* plea,
He ask'd the Waves, and ask'd the felon winds,
What hard mishap hath doom'd this gentle swain?
And question'd every gust of rugged wings
That blows from off each beakèd Promontory,
They knew not of his story,
And sage *Hippotades* their answer brings,

That not a blast was from his dungeon stray'd,
The Ayr was calm, and on the level brine,
Sleek *Panope* with all her sisters play'd.
It was that fatall and perfidious Bark
Built in th' eclipse, and rigg'd with curses dark,
That sunk so low that sacred head of thine.
    Next *Camus*, reverend Sire, went footing slow,
His Mantle hairy, and his Bonnet sedge,
Inwrought with figures dim, and on the edge
Like to that sanguine flower inscrib'd with woe.
Ah! Who hath reft (quoth he) my dearest pledge?
Last came, and last did go,
The Pilot of the *Galilean* lake,
Two massy keyes he bore of metals twain,
(The Golden opes, the Iron shuts amain)
He shook his Miter'd locks, and stern bespake,
How well could I have spar'd for thee, young swain,
Anow of such as for their bellies' sake
Creep and intrude, and climb into the fold?
Of other care they little reck'ning make,
Then how to scramble at the shearers feast,
And shove away the worthy bidden guest;
Blind mouthes! that scarce themselves know how to hold
A Sheep-hook, or have learn'd ought els the least
That to the faithfull Herdmans art belongs!
What recks it them? What need they? They are sped;
And when they list, their lean and flashy songs
Grate on their scrannel Pipes of wretched straw,
The hungry Sheep look up, and are not fed,
But swoln with wind, and the rank mist they draw,
Rot inwardly, and foul contagion spread:
Besides what the grim Woolf with privy paw
Daily devours apace, and nothing sed;
But that two-handed engine at the door
Stands ready to smite once, and smite no more.
    Return, *Alpheus*, the dread voice is past,
That shrunk thy streams; return, *Sicilian* Muse,
And call the Vales, and bid them hither cast

Their Bels, and Flourets of a thousand hues.
Ye valleys low, where the milde whispers use,
Of shades and wanton winds, and gushing brooks,
On whose fresh lap the swart Star sparely looks,
Throw hither all your quaint enameld eyes,
That on the green terf suck the honied showres,
And purple all the ground with vernal Flowres.
Bring the rathe Primrose that forsaken dies,
The tufted Crow-toe, and pale Gessamine,
The white Pink, and the Pansie freakt with jeat,
The glowing Violet.
The Musk-rose, and the well attir'd Woodbine,
With Cowslips wan that hang the pensive hed,
And every flower that sad embroidery wears:
Bid *Amaranthus* all his beauty shed,
And Daffodillies fill their cups with tears,
To strew the Laureat Herse where *Lycid* lies.
For so to interpose a little ease,
Let our frail thoughts dally with false surmise.
Ay me! Whilst thee the shores, and sounding Seas
Wash far away, where ere thy bones are hurld,
Whether beyond the stormy *Hebrides*,
Where thou perhaps under the whelming tide
Visit'st the bottom of the monstrous world;
Or whether thou to our moist vows deny'd,
Sleep'st by the fable of *Bellerus* old,
Where the great vision of the guarded Mount
Looks toward *Namancos* and *Bayona's* hold;
Look homeward Angel now, and melt with ruth.
And, O ye *Dolphins*, waft the haples youth.
  Weep no more, woful Shepherds, weep no more,
For *Lycidas* your sorrow is not dead,
Sunk though he be beneath the watry floar,
So sinks the day-star in the Ocean bed,
And yet anon repairs his drooping head
And tricks his beams, and with new spangled Ore,
Flames in the forehead of the morning sky:
So *Lycidas* sunk low, but mounted high,

Through the dear might of Him that walk'd the waves;
Where other groves, and other streams along,
With *Nectar* pure his oozy Locks he laves,
And hears the unexpressive nuptiall Song,
In the blest Kingdoms meek of joy and love.
There entertain him all the Saints above,
In solemn troops and sweet Societies
That sing, and singing in their glory move,
And wipe the tears for ever from his eyes.
Now *Lycidas*, the Shepherds weep no more;
Hence forth thou art the Genius of the shore,
In thy large recompense, and shalt be good
To all that wander in that perilous flood.
    Thus sang the uncouth Swain to th'Okes and rills,
While the still morn went out with Sandals gray,
He touch'd the tender stops of various Quills,
With eager thought warbling his Dorick lay:
And now the Sun had stretch'd out all the hills,
And now was dropt into the Western bay;
At last he rose, and twitch'd his Mantle blew:
To morrow to fresh Woods, and Pastures new.

JOHN MILTON (1637)

65

From *AN EGLOGUE ON THE NOBLE ASSEMBLIES*

Some melancholy swains about have gone
To teach all zeal their owne complection:
Choler they will admit sometimes I see,
But Fleagme, and Sanguine no Religions be.
These teach that Dauncing is a *Jezabell*;
And Barley-break, the ready way to Hell.
The Morrice Idols, Whitsun'-ales can be
But prophane Reliques of a Jubilee!

These in a Zeal, t'expresse how much they doe
The Organs hate, have silenc'd Bag-pipes too;
And harmlesse May-poles, all are rail'd upon
As if they were the towers of *Babilon*.
Some think not fit there should be any sport
I'th Country, 'tis a dish proper to th'Court.
Mirth not becomes 'em, let the sawcy swain
Eate Beef, and Bacon, and goe sweat again.
Besides, what sport can in their pastimes be
When all is but ridiculous fopperie?

THOMAS RANDOLPH (1638)

66

THE MILK-MAIDS EPITHALAMIUM

Joy to the Bridegroom and the Bride
That lie by one anothers side!
O fie upon the Virgin-Beds;
No loss is gain but Maiden-heads.
Love quickly send the time may be
When I shall deal my Rosemary!

I long to simper at a feast,
To dance, and kiss, and do the rest.
When I shall Wed, and Bedded be,
O then the qualme comes over me,
And tells the sweetness of a Theam
That I nere knew but in a dream.

You Ladies have the blessed nights,
I pine in hope of such delights:
And, silly Damsel, only can
Milk the Cows teats, and think on man,
And sigh and wish to taste and prove
The wholesome Sillibub of Love.

Make hast, at once twin-Brothers beare;
And leave new matter for a starre.
Women and ships are never shown
So fair as when their sails are blown.
Then when the Midwife hears you moan,
I'le sigh for griefe that I have none.

And you, deare Knight, whose every kisse
Reaps the full crop of *Cupids* blisse,
Now you have found confess and tell
That single sheets do make up hell.
And then so charitable be
To get a man to pitty me.

THOMAS RANDOLPH (1638)

67

A DIALOGUE BETWIXT TIME AND A PILGRIME

PILGRIME

Aged man, that mowes these fields.

TIME

Pilgrime speak, what is thy will?

PILGRIME

Whose soile is this that such sweet Pasture yields?
Or who are thou whose Foot stand never still?
Or where am I?

TIME

In love.

PILGRIME

His Lordship lies above.

TIME

Yes and below, and round about
Where in all sorts of flow'rs are growing
Which as the early Spring puts out,
Time falls as fast a mowing.

PILGRIME

If thou art Time, these Flow'rs have Lives,
And then I fear,
Under some Lilly she I love
May now be growing there.

TIME

And in some Thistle or some spire of grasse,
My scythe thy stalk before hers come may passe.

PILGRIME

Wilt thou provide it may?

TIME

No.

PILGRIME

Allege the cause.

TIME

Because Time cannot alter but obey Fates laws.

CHORUS

Then happy those whom Fate, that is the stronger,
Together twists their threads, and yet draws hers the longer.

AURELIAN TOWNSHEND (1653)

68

A PASTORALL DIALOGUE

SHEPHERD   NYMPH   CHORUS

SHEPHERD

This mossie bank they prest.

NYMPH

That aged oak
Did canopie the happy payre
  All night from the dampe ayre.

CHORUS

Here let us sit and sing the words they spoke,
Till the day breaking, their embraces broke.

Shepherd

See love, the blushes of the morne appeare,
  And now she hangs her pearlie store
    (Rob'd from the Easterne shore)
  I'th' Couslips bell, and Roses eare:
Sweet, I must stay no longer here.

Nymph

Those streaks of doubtfull light usher not day,
  But shew my sunne must set; no Morne
    Shall shine till thou returne;
  The yellow Planets, and the gray
Dawne shall attend thee on thy way.

Shepherd

If thine eyes guild my pathes, they may forbeare
  Their uselesse shine.

Nymph

My teares will quite
  Extinguish their faint light.

Shepherd

Those drops will make their beames more cleare,
Loves flames will shine in every teare.

Chorus

They kist, and wept, and from their lips and eyes
  In a mixt dew, of brinie sweet,
    Their joyes, and sorrows meet;
  But she cryes out.

Nymph

Shepherd arise,
  The sun betrayes us else to spies.

Shepherd

The winged houres flye fast, whilst we embrace,
  But when we want their help to meet,
    They move with leaden feet.

Nymph

Then let us pinion *Time*, and chase
The day for ever from this place.

SHEPHERD

Harke!

NYMPH

Aye me, stay!

SHEPHERD

For ever.

NYMPH

No, arise,
Wee must be gone.

SHEPHERD

My nest of spice.

NYMPH

My soule.

SHEPHERD

My Paradise.

CHORUS

Neither could say farewell, but through their eyes
Griefe, interrupted speach with teares supplyes.

THOMAS CAREW (1640)

69

THE ARGUMENT OF HIS BOOK

I sing of *Brooks*, of *Blossomes*, *Birds*, and *Bowers*,
Of *April*, *May*, of *June*, and *July*-flowers;
I sing of *May-poles*, *Hock-carts*, *Wassails*, *Wakes*,
Of *Bridegrooms*, *Brides*, and of their *Bridall-cakes*.
I write of *Youth*, of *Love*, and have accesse
By these, to sing of cleanly-*Wantonnesse*;
I sing of Dewes, of Raines, and, piece by piece,
Of *Balme*, of *Oyl*, of *Spice*, and *Amber-Greece*;
I sing of *Times trans-shifting*; and I write
How *Roses* first came *Red*, and *Lillies* White;
I write of *Groves*, of *Twilights*, and I sing
The court of *Mab*, and of the *Fairie-King*.
I write of *Hell*; I sing (and ever shall)
Of *Heaven*, and hope to have it after all.

ROBERT HERRICK (1648)

70

THE HOCK CART; OR, HARVEST HOME

To the Right Honourable Mildmay, Earl of Westmorland

Come, Sons of Summer, by whose toile,
We are the Lords of Wine and Oile;
By whose tough labours and rough hands,
We rip up first, then reap our lands
Crown'd with the eares of corne, now come,
And to the Pipe sing Harvest home.
Come forth, my Lord, and see the Cart
Drest up with all the Country Art.
See, here a Malkin, there a sheet,
As spotlesse pure as it is sweet;
The Horses, Mares, and frisking Fillies,
Clad all in Linnen white as Lillies.
The Harvest Swaines and Wenches bound
For joy, to see the *Hock cart* crown'd.
About the Cart, heare how the Rout
Of Rural Younglings raise the shout,
Pressing before, some coming after,
Those with a shout, and these with laughter.
Some bless the Cart, some kisse the sheaves
Some prank them up with Oaken leaves;
Some cross the Fill-horse, some with great
Devotion stroak the home-borne wheat;
While other Rusticks, lesse attent
To Prayers than to Merryment,
Run after with their breeches rent.
Well, on, brave boyes, to your Lords Hearth,
Glitt'ring with fire, where, for your mirth,
Ye shall see first the large and cheefe
Foundation of your Feast, Fat Beefe;
With Upper Stories, Mutton, Veale,
And Bacon, which makes full the meale,

Malkin, Cloth.   *Fill-horse*, Cart-horse.   *Upper Stories*, Calves' heads?

With sev'rall dishes standing by,
As, here a Custard, there a Pie,
And here all-tempting Frumentie.
And for to make the merry cheere,
If smirking Wine be wanting here,
There's that which drowns all care, stout Beere;
Which freely drink to your Lords health,
Then to the Plough (the Common-wealth),
Next to your Flails, your Fans, your Vats;
Then to the Maids with Wheaten Hats;
To the rough Sickle, and crookt scythe,
Drink, frollick boyes, till all be blythe.
Feed and grow fat; and as ye eat,
Be mindfull that the lab'ring Neat,
As you, may have their fill of meat.
And know, besides, ye must revoke
The patient Oxe unto the Yoke,
And all goe back unto the Plough,
And Harrow, though they're hang'd up now.
And, you must know, your Lords word's true.
Feed him ye must, whose food fills you.
And that this pleasure is like raine,
Not sent ye for to drowne your paine,
But for to make it spring againe.

ROBERT HERRICK (1648)

Frumentie, Wheat boiled in milk, and spiced with cinnamon.

71

CORINNA'S GOING A-MAYING

Get up, get up for shame, the Blooming Morne
Upon her wings presents the god unshorne.
    See how *Aurora* throws her faire
    Fresh-quilted colours through the aire:
    Get up, sweet Slug-a-bed, and see
    The Dew bespangling Herbe and Tree.

Each Flower has wept, and bow'd toward the East,
Above an houre since, yet you not dressed,
    Nay! not so much as out of bed;
    When all the Birds have Mattens said,
    And sung their thankful Hymnes: 'tis sin,
    Nay, profanation to keep in,
Whenas a thousand Virgins on this day
Spring, sooner than the Lark, to fetch in May.

Rise, and put on your Foliage, and be seene
To come forth, like the Spring-time, fresh and greene;
    And sweet as *Flora*. Take no care
    For Jewels for your Gowne or Haire:
    Feare not; the leaves will strew
    Gemms in abundance upon you:
Besides, the childhood of the Day has kept
Against you come, some *Orient Pearls* unwept:
    Come, and receive them while the light
    Hangs on the Dew-locks of the night,
    And *Titan* on the Eastern hill
    Retires himself, or else stands still
Till you come forth. Wash, dress, be briefe in praying:
Few Beads are best, when once we goe a-Maying.

Come, my *Corrina*, come; and comming, marke
How each field turns a street, each street a Parke
    Made green, and trimm'd with trees: see how
    Devotion gives each House a Bough
    Or Branch; each Porch, each doore, ere this,
    An Arke, a Tabernacle is,
Made up of white-thorn neatly enterwove,
As if here were those cooler shades of love.
    Can such delights be in the street
    And open fields, and we not see't?
    Come, we'll abroad, and let's obey
    The Proclamation made for May:
And sin no more, as we have done, by staying;
But, my *Corrina*, come, let's goe a-Maying.

There's not a budding Boy or Girle, this day,
But is got up and gone to bring in May.
    A deal of Youth, ere this, is come
    Back, and with *White-thorn* laden home.
    Some have dispatcht their Cakes and Creame
    Before that we have left to dreame:
And some have wept, and woo'd and plighted Troth,
And choose their Priest, ere we can cast off sloth:
    Many a green-gown has been given;
    Many a kisse, both odde and even:
    Many a glance, too, has been sent
    From out the eye, Love's Firmament:
Many a jest told of the Key's betraying
This night, and Locks pickt, yet w'are not a-Maying.

Come, let us goe, while we are in our prime,
And take the harmlesse follie of the time.
    We shall grow old apace and die
    Before we know our liberty.
    Our life is short, and our dayes run
    As fast away as does the Sunne:
And as a vapour, or a drop of raine
Once lost, can ne'er be found againe:
    So when or you or I are made
    A fable, song, or fleeting shade,
    All love, all liking, all delight,
    Lies drown'd with us in endlesse night,
Then while time serves, and we are but decaying,
Come, my *Corinna*, come, let's goe a-Maying.

ROBERT HERRICK (1648)

72

TO THE MAIDS TO WALK ABROAD

Come, sit we under yonder Tree,
Where merry as the Maids we'll be;
And as on *Primroses* we sit,
We'll venture, if we can, at wit;
If not, at *Draw-gloves* we will play,
So spend some minutes of the day;
Or else spin out the thread of sands,
Playing at *Questions* and *Commands*,
Or tell what strange Tricks Love can do,
By quickly making one of two.
Thus we will sit and talke, but tell
No cruel truths of *Philomell*,
Or *Phyllis*, whom hard fate forc't on
To kill her selfe for *Demophon*.
But fables we'll relate, how *Jove*
Put on all shapes to get a Love,
As now a *Satyr*, then a *Swan*,
A *Bull* but then, and now a man.
Next, we will act how young men wooe;
And sigh and kiss as Lovers do;
And talk of Brides; and who shall make
That wedding-smock, this Bridal-Cake,
That Dress, this Sprig, that Leaf, this Vine,
That smooth and silken Columbine.
This done, we'll draw lots who shall buy
And gild the Bays and Rosemary;
What Posies for our Wedding Rings,
What Gloves we'll give, and Ribanings;
And smiling at our selves, decree
Who then the joyning *Priest* shall be:
What short sweet Prayers shall be said,
And how the Posset shall be made

With Cream of Lillies, not of Kine,
And *Maiden's-blush* for spicèd wine.
Thus having talkt, we'll next commend
A kiss to each, and *so we'l end*.

ROBERT HERRICK (1648)

73

THE WAKE

Come, Anthea, let us two
Go to Feast, as others do.
Tarts and Custards, Creams and Cakes,
Are the Junketts still at Wakes:
Unto which the Tribes resort,
Where the businesse is the sport.
Morris-dancers thou shalt see,
Marian, too, in Pagentrie:
And a Mimick to devise
Many grinning properties.
Players there will be, and those
Base in action as in clothes;
Yet with strutting they will please
The incurious Villages.
Near the dying of the day
There will be a *Cudgell*-Play,
Where a *Coxcomb* will be broke,
Ere a good *word* can be spoke:
But the anger ends all here,
Drenched in Ale or drowned in Beere.
Happy Rusticks, best content
With the cheapest Merriment;
And possesse no other feare
Than to want the Wake next Yeare.

ROBERT HERRICK (1648)

74

THE FIRST WHITE AGE

Happy the first white age! when wee
Lived by the Earths meere Charitie;
No soft luxurious Diet then
Had Effeminated men,
No other meat, nor wine had any
Than the coarse Mast, or simple honey,
And by the Parents care layd up
Cheap *Berries* did the Children sup.
No pompous weare was in those dayes
Of gummie Silks, or Skarlet bayes;
Their beds were on some flowrie brink
And clear Spring-water was their drink.
The shadie Pine in the Suns heat
Was their coole and known Retreat;
For then 'twas not cut down, but stood
The youth and glory of the wood.
The daring Sailer with his slaves
Then had not cut the swelling waves,
Nor for desire of foreign store
Seen any but his native shore.
No stirring Drum had scarr'd that age,
Nor the shrill Trumpets active rage;
No wounds by bitter hatred made
With warm bloud soil'd the shining blade;
For how could hostile madness arm
An age of love to publick harm?
When Common Justice none withstood,
Nor sought rewards for spilling bloud.
O that at length our age would raise
Into the temper of those dayes!
But (worse than *Aetna's* fires!) debate
And Avarice inflame our state.

Alas! who was it that first found
Gold hid of purpose under ground,
That sought out Pearles, and div'd to find
Such pretious perils for mankind!

BOËTHIUS, *De Consolatione Philosophiæ*, Lib. II, Metrum 3,
translated by Henry Vaughan (1651)

75

A DIALOGUE BETWEEN THYRSIS
AND DORINDA

DORINDA

When Death shall part us from these Kids,
And shut up our divided Lids,
Tell me *Thyrsis*, prethee do,
Whither thou and I must go.

THYRSIS

To the *Elizium*.

DORINDA

Oh, where i'st?

THYRSIS

A Chast Soul can never mis't.

DORINDA

I know no way but one, our home;
Is our cell *Elizium*?

THYRSIS

Turn thine Eye to yonder Skie,
There the milky way doth lye;
'Tis a sure but rugged way,
That leads to Everlasting day.

DORINDA

There Birds may nest, but how can I,
That have no wings, and cannot fly?

THYRSIS

Do not sigh (fair Nimph) for fire
Hath no wings, yet doth aspire

Till it hit against the pole;
Heaven's the Center of the Soul.

DORINDA

But in *Elizium* how do they
Pass Eternity away?

THYRSIS

Oh, ther's neither hope nor fear,
Ther's no Wolf, no Fox, nor Bear.
No need of Dog to fetch our stray;
Our Lightfoot we may give away;
No Oat-pipe's needfull, there thine Ears
May feast with Musick of the Spheres.

DORINDA

Oh sweet! Oh sweet! How I my future state
By silent thinking Antedate:
I prethee let us spend our time to come
In talking of *Elizium*.

THYRSIS

Then I'le go on: There, sheep are full
Of sweetest grass, and softest wooll;
There birds sing Consorts, garlands grow,
Cold winds do whisper, springs do flow;
There alwayes is a rising Sun,
And day is ever but begun;
Shepheards there bear equal sway,
And every Nimph's a Queen of *May*.

DORINDA

Ah me, ah me.

THYRSIS

Dorinda, why do'st cry?

DORINDA

I'm sick, I'm sick, and fain would dye:
Convince me now that this is true;
By bidding, with me, all adieu.

THYRSIS

I cannot live without thee, I
Will for thee, much more with thee, dye.

DORINDA

Then let us give *Clorillo* charge o'th Sheep,
And thou and I'le pick poppies and them steep
In wine, and drink on't even till we weep;
So shall we smoothly pass away in sleep.

ANDREW MARVELL (1681)

76

AMETAS AND THESTYLIS MAKING HAY-ROPES

AMETAS

Think'st Thou that this Love can stand,
Whilst Thou still dost say me nay?
Love unpaid does soon disband:
Love binds Love as Hay binds Hay.

THESTYLIS

Think'st Thou that this Rope would twine
If we both should turn one way?
Where both parties so combine,
Neither Love will twist nor Hay.

AMETAS

Thus you vain Excuses find,
Which your selve and us delay:
And Love tyes a Womans Mind
Looser than with Ropes of Hay.

THESTYLIS

What you cannot constant hope
Must be taken as you may.

AMETAS

Then let's both lay by our Rope,
And go kiss within the Hay.

ANDREW MARVELL (1681)

77

THE MOWER AGAINST GARDENS

Luxurious Man, to bring his Vice in use,
 Did after him the World seduce:
And from the fields the Flow'rs and Plants allure,
 Where Nature was most plain and pure.
He first enclos'd within the Gardens square
 A dead and standing pool of Air:
And a more luscious earth for them did knead,
 Which stupifi'd them while it fed.
The Pink grew then as double as his Mind;
 The nutriment did change the kind.
With strange perfumes he did the Roses taint,
 And Flow'rs themselves were taught to paint.
The Tulip, white, did for complexion seek;
 And learn'd to interline its cheek:
Its Onion root they then so high did hold,
 That one was for a Meadow sold.
Another World was search'd, through Oceans new,
 To find the *Marvel of Peru*.
And yet these Rarities might be allow'd,
 To Man, that sov'raign thing and proud;
Had he not dealt between the Bark and Tree,
 Forbidden mixtures there to see.
No Plant now knew the stock from which it came;
 He grafts upon the Wild the Tame:
That the uncertain and adult'rate fruit
 Might put the Palate in dispute.
His green *Seraglio* has its Eunuchs too;
 Lest any Tyrant him out-doe.
And in the Cherry he does Nature vex,
 To procreate without a Sex.
'Tis all enforc'd; the Fountain and the Grot;
 While the sweet Fields do lye forgot:

Where willing Nature does to all dispence
   A wild and fragrant Innocence:
And *Fauns* and *Faryes* do the Meadows till,
   More by their presence than their skill.
Their Statues polish'd by some ancient hand,
   May to adorn the Gardens stand;
But howso'ere the Figures do excel,
The *Gods* themselves with us do dwell.

ANDREW MARVELL (1681)

78

From DAMON THE MOWER

How long wilt thou, fair Shepheardess,
Esteem me, and my Presents less?
To Thee the harmless Snake I bring,
Disarmed of its teeth and sting;
To Thee *Chameleons* changing hue,
And Oak leaves tipt with hony dew.
Yet Thou ungrateful hast not sought
Nor what they are, nor who them brought.

I am the Mower *Damon*, known
Through all the Meadows I have mown.
On me the Morn the dew distills
Before her darling Daffadils.
And, if at Noon my toil me heat,
The Sun himself licks off my Sweat.
While, going home, the Ev'ning sweet
In cowslip-water bathes my feet.

What though the piping Shepherd stock
The plains with an unnum'red Flock,
This Sithe of mine discovers wide
More ground than all his Sheep do hide.
With this the golden fleece I shear
Of all these Closes ev'ry Year.

And though in Wooll more poor than they,
Yet am I richer far in Hay.

Nor am I so deform'd to sight,
If in my Sithe I looked aright;
In which I see my picture done,
As in a crescent Moon the Sun.
The deathless Fairyes take me oft
To lead them in their Danses soft;
And, when I tune my self to sing,
About me they contract their Ring.

How happy might I still have mow'd,
Had not Love here his Thistles sow'd!
But now I all the day complain,
Joyning my Labour to my Pain;
And with my Sythe cut down the Grass,
Yet still my Grief is where it was:
But, when the Iron blunter grows,
Sighing I whet my Sythe and Woes.

While thus he threw his Elbow round,
Depopulating all the Ground,
And, with his whistling Sythe, does cut
Each stroke between the Earth and Root,
The edged Stele by careless chance
Did into his own Ankle glance;
And there among the Grass fell down,
By his own Sythe, the Mower mown.

Alas! said He, these hurts are slight,
To those that dye by Loves despight.
With Shepherds-Purse, and Clowns-all-heal
The Blood I stanch, and Wound I seal.
Only for him no Cure is found
Whom *Juliana's* Eyes do wound.
'Tis death alone that this must do:
For Death thou art a Mower too.

ANDREW MARVELL (1681)

79

THE NYMPH COMPLAINING FOR THE
DEATH OF HER FAUN

The wanton Troopers riding by
Have shot my Faun and it will dye.
Ungentle men! They cannot thrive
To kill thee. Thou ne'er didst alive
Them any harm: alas nor cou'd
Thy death yet do them any good.
I'm sure I never wisht them ill;
Nor do I for all this; nor will:
But if my simple Pray'rs may yet
Prevail with Heaven to forget
Thy murder, I will Joyn my Tears
Rather than fail. But O my fears!
It cannot die so. Heavens King
Keeps register of everything:
And nothing may we use in vain.
Even Beasts must be with justice slain,
Else men are made their *Deodands*.
Though they should wash their guilty hands
In this warm life-blood, which doth part
From thine, and wound me to the Heart,
Yet could they not be clean; their Stain
Is dyed in such a Purple Grain.
There is not such another in
The World to offer for their Sin.

Unconstant *Sylvio*, when yet
I had not found him counterfeit,
One morning (I remember well)
Tied in this silver Chain and Bell,
Gave it to me; nay and I know
What he said then; I'm sure I do.

Deodands, Forfeits for crimes.

Said he, Look how your Huntsman here
Hath taught a Faun to hunt his Dear.
But *Sylvio* soon had me beguil'd.
This waxed tame, while he grew wild,
And quite regardless of my Smart,
Left me his Faun, but took his Heart.

     Thenceforth I set myself to play
My solitary time away,
With this; and very well content
Could so mine idle Life have spent.
For it was full of sport; and light
Of foot, and heart; and did invite
Me to its game: it seemed to bless
Itself in me. How could I less
Than love it? O I cannot be
Unkind t'a Beast that loveth me.

     Had it liv'd long, I do not know
Whether it too might have done so
As *Sylvio* did; his Gifts might be
Perhaps as false or more than he.
But I am sure for ought that I
Could in so short a time espie,
Thy Love was far more better then
The love of false and cruel men.

     With sweetest milk, and sugar, first
I it at mine own fingers nurst.
And as it grew, so every day
It wax'd more white and sweet than they.
It had so sweet a Breath! And oft
I blusht to see its foot more soft,
And white, (shall I say than my hand?)
NAY, any Ladies of the Land.
     It is a wond'rous thing, how fleet
'Twas on those little silver feet

With what a pretty skipping grace,
It oft would challenge me the Race:
And when't had left me far away,
'Twould stay, and run again, and stay,
For it was nimbler much than Hinds;
And trod, as on the four Winds.

I have a Garden of my own,
But so with Roses over grown,
And Lillies, that you would it guess
To be a little Wilderness.
And all the Spring time of the year
It onely loved to be there.
Among the beds of Lillyes, I
Have sought it oft, where it should lye;
Yet could not, till it self would rise,
Find it, although before mine Eyes.
For, in the flaxen Lillies shade,
It like a bank of Lillies laid.
Upon the Roses it would feed,
Until its Lips ev'n seem'd to bleed:
And then to me 'twould boldly trip,
And print those Roses on my Lip.
But all its chief delight was still
On Roses thus its self to fill:
And its pure virgin Limbs to fold
In whitest sheets of Lillies cold.
Had it liv'd long, it would have been
Lillies without, Roses within.

O help! O help! I see it faint
And die as calmely as a Saint.
See how it weeps! the Tears do come
Sad, slowly dropping like a Gumme.
So weeps the wounded Balsome: so
The holy Frankincense doth flow.
The brotherless Heliades
Melt in such Amber Tears as these.

I in a golden Vial will
Keep these two crystal Tears; and fill
It till it doth o'reflow with mine;
Then place it in *Diana's* shrine.

Now my Sweet Faun is vanish'd to
Whether the Swans and Turtles go:
In fair *Elizium* to endure,
With milk-white Lambs, and Ermins pure.
O do not run too fast: for I
Will but bespeak thy Grave, and die.
    First my unhappy Statue shall
Be cut in Marble; and withal,
Let it be weeping too: but there
Th' Engraver sure his Art may spare;
For I so truly thee bemoane,
That I shall weep though I be Stone:
Until my Tears, still dropping, wear
My breast, themselves engraving there.
There at my feet shalt thou be laid,
Of purest Alabaster made:
For I would have thine Image be
White as I can, though not as Thee.

ANDREW MARVELL (1681)

NOTES

(The numerals refer to the numbering of the poems in the text.)

1. One of the lamentably few poems of its kind to survive, this song is perhaps only a fragment. It has a conventional opening (see Introduction, p. 32), and is a cultivated exercise in a theme which, after great refinement in courtly hands, reverted to the folk. It is one of a group of songs in MS Harleian 2253. It may have concealed religious significance.

2. Henryson's poem is also a literary version of native non-classical Pastoral. The setting is unfeignedly Scots. The interest in Courtly Love (stanza three) is characteristic of the author of *The Testament of Cresseid.*

3. This shepherd is unliterary; the poet's effort has been to set a 'real' English shepherd in the context of the Nativity theme. In this the poem resembles the famous *Wakefield Shepherds' Play (Secunda Pastorum).*

4-6. This group is extracted from the various collections of popular ballads of the sixteenth and seventeenth centuries. The poems are not, of course, strictly Pastorals at all. One can only guess at the degree of similarity between them and their rustic ancestors, which are a basic ingredient of Pastoral, like those lost poems which appealed so fruitfully to Theocritus. Here, of course, they are sophisticated by literary influences and townee attitudes. No. 4 is a townsman's maying-song, showing a typical interest in rustic love, though a very different one from Tasso's. No. 5 is a high-spirited but quite 'literary' treatment of the Golden Age theme, here exploited for satirical purposes which become very explicit in the second part, not here reprinted. No. 6 is a popular descendant of the theme of No. 1. The theme of the maid with the bashful or ignorant lover is very ancient, and the author makes a rather self-conscious reference to the Venus and Adonis story. (*Cf.* the first half of No. 2.)

7. Daphnis is a recurrent pastoral name. He was originally a hero in Sicilian mythology. See the First Idyll of Theocritus. The song-

contest is a stock feature of classical Pastoral; see No. 10. This, and No. 8, are drawn from the first English translation of Theocritus, which included only six of the Idylls. See Introduction, pp. 20–22.

8. The Argument shows how easily, given the readiness of the period to read all poetry for its concealed meanings, the critic could extract an apparently perverse and improbable doctrine from an ancient poem. The Emblem is an addition in the Spenserian manner (*Shepheardes Calendar*, 1579). There is an interesting list of pastoral deities and heroes. Those most frequently mentioned in pastoral poetry are Endimion, Adonis, and Ganymede (to whom there is allusion here). The nymph spits thrice to avert a bad omen.

9. This is a truly seminal poem. See Introduction, p. 27. Beaumont's readings are not always those of the modern translator, but the sense is fairly clear, except in the closing lines, which, as they stood in Virgil, were certainly not Messianic. Virgil's latest translator has: ". . . no one who has not given his mother a smile has ever been thought worthy of his table by a god, or by a goddess of her bed." (*Virgil: The Pastoral Poems*, translated by E. V. Rieu, 1949.) The meaning of the passage is still in dispute. The myth of the Cumæan sybil is recounted in Ovid, *Metamorphoses*, XIV, 132 ff. She was a very aged prophetess of ecstatic utterance (see *Æneid* VI, 77 ff.), and her recorded sayings were preserved by an order of priests for consultation in national emergencies. The original collection was destroyed by fire in 83 B.C. Later commentators dwelt on the similarity between the sybilline prophecies here set forth by Virgil, and the Messianic prophecies of the Old Testament, especially Isaiah's (*Isaiah* ix). The Maid is Astræa (see No. 11). Lucina is the goddess of childbirth. Tiphys was the helmsman of the Argo, the ship in which Jason and his heroes sailed in quest of the Golden Fleece. Linus was a musician, killed by Apollo for the same boast with which the poet here challenges Pan. Many of the problems raised by this poem are considered by H. J. Rose in his *Eclogues of Vergil* (see Bibliography); but the extent of even its modern bibliography is enormous.

10. A song-contest imitated from No. 7. See Rose, *op. cit.*, pp. 139 ff. It has been suggested that Virgil subtilizes the contest by making the songs of Thyrsis slightly less perfect than those of Corydon. Lybethrian—of Libethra, a cave frequented by the Muses. Priapus, said to be the son of Bacchus and Venus, was the divine protector of orchards. The bay-tree (laurel) was held to be proof against lightning.

11. Not Pastoral, but the most famous simple statement of the theme of the Golden Age. The passage occurs in Book I of the *Metamorphoses*. I have retained Sandys' Notes. Compare with No. 9 for correspondence of detail. Later works drawing upon this *locus classicus* are noted in their place below.

12. The inclusion of this rather dreary poem, in a metre for which we have lost the taste, is a concession to history. Mantuan was popular, and familiar to all educated people. He had formerly been translated by Barclay. See Introduction, p. 30.

13. See Introduction, p. 31. This short poem is characteristic of Sanazzaro, who was, for some reason, more imitated than translated. Drummond was the most far-ranging of Elizabethan verse-translators. See Kastner's edition (2 vols., Manchester University Press, 1913). *Myncius*, a tributary of the Po (see No. 64).

14. The first chorus in *Aminta*, the most celebrated of Italian pastoral dramas, by Torquato Tasso, author of the *Gerusalemme Liberata*. *Aminta* was published in 1581, having been acted eight years earlier. The play, and this chorus more than any other part of it, was well known and often translated into English; this little-known version by Reynolds compares favourably with the others. These lines are the central modern expression of the "soft primitivist" attitude to the Golden Age theme. They posit a natural kind of love, virtuous though unimpeded by civilized conventions, and attribute the decline from that ideal to Honour. The sentiments of this passage were later put to a less ingenuous use by seventeenth-century exponents of naturalistic ethics; perhaps the best example is Carew's *A Rapture*. See the note on this in Rhodes Dunlap's edition of Carew (Oxford University Press, 1949). The concluding lines of this extract are a close paraphrase of Catullus, *Carmen*, 5.

15. For Guarini, see Introduction, p. 31. The passage is closely related to No. 14, although Guarini was fond of proclaiming his originality; nevertheless, it implies a reproof to the doctrine of Tasso, and presents a much more moral paradise than the older poet's. The translator, Fanshawe, has produced a paraphrase rather than a strict translation. He is best known as the translator of the

Portuguese epic poet Camoẽs. The connexion between these poems (14 and 15) and those of Virgil and Ovid (9 and 11) will be obvious.

16. An early literary Pastoral, which appeared in *Tottel's Miscellany* (1557) and in *Englands Helicon* (1600), from which it is here reprinted. The latter work attributes it (probably wrongly) to the Earl of Surrey. Discussing this work in relation to the later Pastoral, W. W. Greg wrote:

> Happily the seed of Phillida's coyness bore fruit, and the amorous pastoral ballad or picture, a true *idyllion*, became a recognized type in English verse. It certainly owed something to foreign pastoral models, and, like the bulk of Elizabethan lyrics, a good deal to Italian poetry in general; but in its freshness and variety, as in its tendency to narrative form, it asserts its independence of any rigid tradition, and justifies us in regarding it as an outcome of [a] native impulse. . . .[1]

17. Googe exactly imitates Mantuan, and uses the fourteener like Turberville. He has a patent ecclesiastical allegory. *Selye* is an interesting word in connexion with pastoral poetry. The *Oxford English Dictionary* distinguishes three senses in which during our period it was "very extensively used," adding that it is sometimes "difficult to decide what shade of meaning was intended." They are: (i) deserving of pity, helpless, defenceless (conventionally applied to sheep); (ii) weak, feeble, frail; (iii) unlearned, unsophisticated, rustic, ignorant. The word carries the poet's feeling of superior standing, learning, and sophistication, as well as his sense of the uncomplicated nature of rustic life.

18. *The Shepheardes Calender* (1579) was admitted even among contemporaries to be the first great English poem of the Renaissance. It was the first major work of Spenser, highly experimental, but none the less assured, and the work of a poet moving easily within the pastoral convention. Spenser professes his debt to the French poet Marot, though he is reticent about Mantuan, to whom he apparently owed much. He was also familiar with the critical precepts of the *Pléiade*, the major movement in French poetry after Marot, and his use of the native northern dialect may be an attempt to anglicize a well-known doctrine of the *Pléiade*, rather than a deliberate attempt to imitate the Doric of Theocritus. I have left in one specimen of E.K.'s glosses; the identity of this commentator is a matter of perennial dispute, and he may have been Spenser himself. There is

[1] *Pastoral Poetry and Pastoral Drama*, p. 77.

so much to be said about *The Shepheardes Calender* that it is best here to say very little, and to leave the student to consult the edition of W. Renwick (Oxford University Press, 1930) or the Variorum edition referred to in the Bibliography. The August Eclogue is in the tradition of Nos. 7 and 10. "As treated here, it is almost—though unintentionally—an allegory of the new poetry: the simple swains sing merrily enough, but a grave, elaborate, Italianate song of *Colin's* hushes them in admiration, their simple impromptu is overshadowed." (Renwick, p. 206.) Cuddie's song is a sestina like that of Sidney (No. 24).

19. This theme derives from Virgil and Mantuan, and the poem, like the Argument which precedes it, has a special reference to Spenser's object of making available in English everything the Renaissance considered best in poetry. The reference to the bringing of "the white beare to the stake" is an allusion to the crest of Robert Dudley, Earl of Leicester, which was a bear and a ragged staff; Spenser wrote of the Dudley family in a lost poem.

20. Imitated from an eclogue by Marot. The identity of *Dido* is quite unknown; for disputes about the identity of Rosalind and other characters in the poem, see the editions cited above.

fishes hask: "The sonne reigneth, that is, in the signe Pisces all November. A *haske* is a wicker pad, wherein they use to cary fish." (E.K.) In fact this is incorrect; the sun is in Pisces in February, not November. This poem is a pastoral elegy in the tradition of the First Idyll of Theocritus, the epitaph of Moschus, the poem which follows, and *Lycidas*.

21. This pastoral elegy, Spenser's second lament for the death of Sir Philip Sidney, appeared in 1595 together with similar poems by other hands. Sidney was killed in 1586. Spenser is adapting, not the classical poets, but Ronsard, in whose version of the Adonis story he must have detected elements which corresponded to the story of Sidney. It is, of course, wrenching the Adonis myth to have Stella die after her lover. The poem really ends with a 'Lay,' supposed to be by the Countess of Pembroke. This I have cut. Apart from its value as a pastoral elegy this poem is an interesting comment on the almost universal identification of Sidney with the perfect Renaissance courtier.

22. For comment upon this Canto see Introduction, p. 41, and the Variorum edition of Spenser. The Sixth Book of the *Faerie Queene* is the Book of Courtesy. Ostensibly Sir Calidore demonstrates that the true courtier is at ease in all company. Spenser uses the theme, common in early French lyrical poetry, of the encounter of a courtier with rustic games and rustic purity; he also uses the theme, related to the important pastoral motives of Shakespeare and Milton, of the lost royal child and the triumph of nurture (Calidore) over nature (Corydon). The reader will recall the importance of these themes in Shakespeare's final Comedies. In the same Book, there is a Salvage Man; he is a progenitor of Caliban.

23–28. Sidney's Pastoral is individual, and, like all his work, experimental. Few poets have so deliberately explored kinds and forms; his *Arcadia*, though it owes its title to Sanazzaro, who also outlined the form, is a work of great originality and depth. Like Spenser, it was Sidney's ambition to show that English was a language worthy and able to be the medium of the highest poetry, and of all kinds of poetry. The poems here included are examples of his explorations. No. 23 is an interesting rationalization of the poet-shepherd figure. No. 24 tries the difficult sestina form (*cf.* Spenser's experiment, No. 18), with a splendid degree of success. *Serene:* the heavy dew-fall which often accompanies tropical sunsets. No. 25 is a melodious variation on native ballad—and Theocritean themes. No. 26 has a peculiarly beautiful lyric gravity, later caught by Lord Herbert of Cherbury, and occasionally by one or two others, but nevertheless rare. Only the setting of this poem is pastoral; but there are hints of pastoral situations in Stella's reference to "tirant honour" (*cf.* Tasso's chorus, No. 14) and in the faint reflection of Theocritus, Idyll XXVII, though the outcome there is, of course, different. *Cf.* also No. 25, though in the present poem the values are explicitly courtly. Stella was Penelope Devereux, who married Lord Rich. No. 27 exhibits two recognized varieties of rustic, the true Pastoralist and the 'salvage man' who lived the life of nature, like a beast (Greek θηρίον wild beast), competing before Diana of the woods (an allegorical designation of the virgin Queen Elizabeth) for that native English pastoral prize, a May-lady. No. 28 is more conventional, and uses Pastoral as a transparent allegorical veil. Dyer and Greville were poets and friends of Sidney—the first greater in reputation than his scanty extant works appear to warrant; the second a major poet, and Sidney's first biographer. Note Sidney's preoccupation with alternate single- and double-rhymes.

29. This poem, by Sidney's sister, is an example of the pastoral of compliment. It was not unusual to compare Elizabeth to Astræa (see Nos. 9 and 11) with rich implications for the poets—*Iam redit et virgo* ... ("The Maid returns ..."). The Countess of Pembroke was a learned lady who achieved fame as the friend and patron of poets.

30. Marlowe's highly decorated lyric is, like those of Barnefield included below (Nos. 41 and 42), a development of a conventional pastoral theme in the language of erotic fantasy which so interested the Elizabethans.

31. The best-known of several 'replies,' which include one by Donne; not certainly Raleigh's.

32. This description of love in pastoral terms begins with the Platonic higher order of love, before it deals with that which "reacheth but to dust." *ten months* was a usual Elizabethan expression for the period now generally reckoned as nine calendar months; it may be a reminiscence of No. 9.

33. Greene wrote much excellent pastoral verse. Note the pun in stanza two and the reference to the notion that meteors were exhalations from the earth in stanza three.

34. Not, perhaps, characteristic of Lodge; but one of the finest of all Elizabethan lyrics. Its themes are conventional, but stanza four should deter those who simplify the story of Elizabethan poetry by making a clean break with Donne. "Prevent the concurrence of falling bodies at the centre of the sphere; cause a vacuum; benight day; remove the *raison d'être* of everything." All this can happen before Mutability is conquered. In stanza fourteen the reference is to Alexander the Great, who, when Apelles was painting his portrait, covered with his finger a small scar on his face.

35. Drayton was a professional poet, voluminous, laborious, and skilful. He was, particularly at the start of his career, much under the influence of Spenser. *Idea, The Shepheardes Garland,* is a Spenserian imitation. Here in one eclogue are his versions of the Golden Age (see Nos. 9 and 11, 5, 14, and 15), and his famous "Dowsabell," a characteristic English pastoral love-encounter, very sophisticated in its artificial simplicity, and with elements of both *pastourelle* and Theocritus (Idyll XXVII). There are many reminiscences of Spenser (including some of No. 19), and, as the reader will see, of Nos. 9 and 11. Drayton's countryside is Warwickshire; his metre is that of Chaucer's *Sir Thopas. Lemster* = Leominster. *Isumbras* is a reference to a fourteenth-century romance. For Colin and Rosalind

see *Shepheardes Calender, January, June, August* (No. 18), and *December*. Drayton is somewhat unusual in that he excludes religious and political allegory; but he is conventional in employing the Golden Age as an occasion for satire on contemporary affectations—painting, borrowed hair, deformed fashions, and so on. The reference to Tamburlaine was probably suggested by Marlowe's plays. Tamburlaine was a Scythian shepherd.

36. This version was probably known to Keats. The account of perpetual Eden, with its fruitful Spring, is connected with the classical theme of the Golden Age, and usually calls forth a reference to the apples of the Hesperides. See Spenser, *Faerie Queene*, II, 12; III, 6; Milton, *Paradise Lost*, VI; and Marvell, *Bermudas*, *The Garden*, etc. This poem strictly belongs to the Elizabethan genre of the erotic mythological fantasia, but it has interesting pastoral elements. There is a mixture of English and classical lore. Menalus is a mountain in Arcadia; the trees are allocated to Gods as in Virgil, Eclogue VII (No. 10). *Barley-break* is defined as *O.E.D.* as "an old country game . . . originally played by six persons (three of each sex) in couples; one couple being left in a middle den termed 'hell' had to catch the others who were allowed to separate or 'break' when hard pressed, and thus to change partners. . . ." This favourite pastoral game is frequently referred to in a manner leaving no doubt that an innuendo is intended. (Cf. *Now is the Month of Maying*.)

37. The opening line is imitated from Spenser, and so is much of the remainder, *e.g.*, the reference to "the fishes hask" (see note on No. 20). A competent Spenserian imitation probably influenced also by Drayton.

38. Breton's Pastorals are extremely distinguished; he had a true sense of the bitter-sweetness of the situation. This is a literary variation of the *pastourelle*, modest, gay, and localized. It was sung during an entertainment given to Queen Elizabeth by the Earl of Hertford at Elvetham in 1591.

> On Wednesday morning, about nine of the clock, as her Majestie opened a casement of her gallerie window, there were three excellent Musitians, who, being disguised in auncient countrey attire, did greet her with a pleasant song of Corydon and Phillida . . . it pleased her Highnesse, after it had beene once sung, to command it againe. . . .

39. One of the most exquisite of all pastoral lyrics. Breton's Preface to *The Passionate Shepheard* is of interest:

Faire Shepheardesse, pardon your poore Swaine, who seeing the faint feeding of his pining flock, and hopeless to recover the droping Lambes of his best folde, knowing such to be the divine Nature of your vertue, as wil suffer nothing to perish, that you are able to preserve: doth beseech you . . . to give them for the heart sicknesse a little grazing in the ground of your least grace, in which prospering (by your favour) they shal live but to your service . . . . *Pastor Fido*—Guarini.

41–42. Barnefield uses the Pastoral primarily for sugared variations on its themes; his success can hardly be denied. The blend of native and classical elements, and the richness with which his fancy invests the pastoral properties, combine to make his poems uniquely attractive at first glance, though he has little to say about the pastoral situation; he shows how superbly the themes can be made to sound. In No. 41, *Cyparissus* was a youth loved by Apollo, who accidentally killed one of the god's favourite stags. Pining away for grief, he was changed by Apollo into a cypress. (Ovid, *Metamorphoses*, X, v, 121.) In No. 42, *Ladon* is a river in Arcadia (*cf.* No. 62). For the significance of the theme of the shepherd-king, see Introduction, p. 18. Colin, Astrophel, Amintas, and Rowland stand for Spenser, Sidney, Watson, and Drayton.

43. The identity of J.M. has not been discovered. The theme of this lyric is that of Nos. 9, 11, 15, 35, 36, etc.

44. Elizabethan song was greatly affected by the fashion of Pastoral; a very high proportion of madrigals employ the pastoral properties, sometimes in a perfunctory way, sometimes quite elaborately blending classical elements with native rural scenes and events.

45. This poem uses beggars as pastoral figures, as Fletcher does in his play, *The Beggars Bush*. Other playwrights used gipsies in a similar way. The deviation is a characteristic of later Pastoral, which sometimes shunned the increasingly 'literary' shepherd when it had something unusual to say. The jocose reference to sheep (fleas) emphasizes the deviation.

46–47. These poems are the work of a poet who possessed an extraordinary metrical virtuosity and control of tone. The first is a skilful *vante*, the refrain ambiguously epigrammatic.

48–50. Fletcher's play was an ambitious attempt to naturalize in English the elaborate pastoral tragi-comedy of Guarini, whose theories are referred to in the Introduction (p. 31).

51. This charming conversation shows Fletcher's sensitivity to the social implications of Pastoral, and is included as a valuable contemporary comment on the town-country tension.

52. This passage, which is at the heart of *The Winter's Tale*, gives in the words of Polixenes the orthodox critical doctrine of the relationship between Art and Nature. Perdita's thesis is, philosophically, dubious; but her refusal to listen to the explanation of Art as a force of Nature is in the end justified by Shakespeare's distinction between two kinds of Nature, which he works out in *Cymbeline*, *The Winter's Tale*, and *The Tempest*. Perdita is a princess in the care of a shepherd; in this she resembles Pastorella (see No. 22). Like Pastorella, the gentle savage in Spenser, and the sons of Cymbeline, Perdita's 'nature' is evidently noble despite the 'natural' meanness of her surroundings.

53. Jonson's play was never finished. His Prologue informs the audience of his intention to present them "with such wool As from meere *English* Flocks his Muse can pull"; *meere* means 'pure.' Jonson's design is to rival Greece and Rome, the characteristic nationalist objective of the Renaissance poet. He chooses as his theme the ancient English pastoral motive of Robin Hood; he laments the death of the true country life, and blames the Puritans. *Cf.* No. 65 and Introduction, p. 38.

54. An example of Jonson's classical mood, which Herrick refined. The Masque of this name was presented at Court in 1620. Reference may be made to another of Jonson's masques, *The Golden Age Restor'd* (1615), as illuminating the prevalent literary conception of the Golden Age.

55. Passerat is, roughly speaking, a French Herrick. He was read in this country. This is a fairly close translation by Drummond (published posthumously) of a comic pastoral dialogue. *Cf.* No. 6. The original opens:

> *Elle:* Pastoureau, m'aimes-tu bien?
> *Lui:* Je t'aime, Dieu sçait combien.
> *Elle:* Comme quoi?
> *Lui:* Comme toi,
>   Ma rebelle
>   Pastourelle, etc.

This is virtually mock-pastoral, not far removed from Gay.

56. *The Shepheard's Hunting* was written when Wither was in gaol, paying for his satire *Abuses Stript and Whipped*. This passage is not representative of the book as a whole, which is openly allegorical. In l. 62 one might risk an emendation—for *West* read *East*. He means ivory. *Need* (three lines further on) is the reading of the text, but Sidgwick was right to print *meed*. *Cups of turned maple-root* are the Spenserian "mazers."

57. Many of the Christmas games here referred to are obsolete, and in some cases no one knows what they were. They were frowned upon and to some extent suppressed by the Puritans—Wither's 'churls.'

58. *Britannia's Pastorals* is an ambitious poem of considerable length. (The Third Book was published posthumously.) It is a narrative Pastoral with a complex allegorical plot, Spenserian in outlook and manner. Here Fida sees Truth arising from the corpse of her hind, which has been murdered by Riot. The hind is an emblem of considerable complexity, with elements of Virgil, *Aeneid* VII, of the *Song of Solomon*, and of Petrarch. See *Epigram* 1, *Theatre of Worldlings*, in Spenser's *Minor Poems* (edited by de Selincourt), p. 483; and No. 79. The references to Christian pastoral imagery are here explicit. Arachne rashly competed with Minerva at weaving, and was turned into a spider.

59. Although this song is quite well-known, Browne is one of the poets here included who have been very imperfectly studied. After the publication of Book I, John Davies of Hereford advised Browne to

> ply this pastoral vein, for it may well contain
> The richest morals under poorest show . . .
> Thus do I spur thee on with sharpest praise,
> To use thy gifts of Nature, and thy skill,
> To double-gild Apollo's brows and bays,
> Yet make great Nature Art's true sovereign still.

60. Two complementary pastoral attitudes, expressed in the pleasantly conceited Spenserian manner of the author and his circle. The piscatory eclogue probably originates in the twenty-first Idyll of Theocritus, but its first modern exponent was Sanazzaro. *Rots*—disease of Sheep.

61. Milton had a scholarly attitude to Pastoral, but his "lubber fiend" is an English Puck.

62. These songs are from an earlier masque than *Comus. Ladon* is a river in Arcadia; *Lycaeus* a range of mountains there; *Cyllene, Maenalus,* and *Erymanth* are also Arcadian mountains. *Syrinx,* a nymph, was turned into a reed when pursued by Pan, who haunted the Arcadian mountains.

63. *Comus* (1634), though called *A Mask,* and in the tradition of that courtly entertainment, is also in the tradition of the English Pastoral of Sidney, Spenser, Shakespeare, and Fletcher. In this passage Milton makes Comus give superb expression to the 'naturalist' attitude to the wealth and fertility of the world. Fletcher had done much the same thing in Act V of *The Faithful Shepherdess,* but the difference between Fletcher and Milton is that the latter provides the Lady with an answer in terms of a Temperance of more than Spenserian exaltation, whereas Fletcher's Priest is, discon-certingly, baffled: "You're better read than I, I must confess, in blood and lechery."

64. *Lycidas* appeared in a volume of thirteen elegies called *Obsequies to the Memory of Edward King,* in 1637. It is the last great pastoral elegy in the tradition of the First Idyll of Theocritus, and the Tenth Eclogue of Virgil. It would be hopeless to attempt any account here of the vast number of echoes of previous poetry, both ancient and modern, and it is at this stage probably unnecessary to attempt a refutation of Johnson's criticisms. (See Introduction, p. 13). Nobody disputes the famous passage in *Rasselas*; it is true that shepherds have neither the occasion nor the vocabulary for poetic speculation. But the reader should know how far beside the point Johnson's remarks are; they show how necessary it is for a modern reader to make the acquaintance of the whole tradition of Pastoral before he judges individual examples. Milton avails him-self in particular of one element in the tradition—namely, that by a natural shift in emphasis from the dead 'shepherd' to the 'shepherd' who laments him, the poem may have a serious autobiographical element. Milton was not a close friend of King's, and in his Latin pastoral elegy for Diodati, the *Epitaphium Damonis,* there is more interest in the subject of the lament than there is in *Lycidas.* The name Lycidas occurs first in Theocritus. The long digression on the corruption of the Church is a traditional element, which originated with Petrarch and was developed by Mantuan and Spenser. The catalogue of flowers is found in many poets from Theocritus to Spen-ser. They are 'literary' flowers, and could not have been assembled at one time. But the commentary which the modern reader of this poem so badly needs must be sought elsewhere. The poem can perhaps best be seen in terms of the tradition in T. P. Harrison's anthology, *The Pastoral Elegy* (see Bibliography).

65. This poem may be compared with No. 58. Randolph excelled in the erotic eclogue when this variety became specially fashionable (under French influence; it is not a far step from the Golden Age to libertinism, as the French writers showed).

66. This poem is more characteristic of Randolph, whose best pastoral poetry is somewhat salacious in character. It is a pastoral epithalamium, neat and sophisticated, but still ultimately descending from the Eighteenth Idyll of Theocritus.

67. This exquisitely refined poem represents a new note which Pastoral achieved in English after the middle of the seventeenth century. The reader will note a similarity of tone to several of the later poems. The pastoral constituents are perverted to serve a more or less esoteric purpose, and there is a constant controlled dissonance between the apparent simplicity of the theme and the intense sophistication of the imagery. *Cf.* No. 78.

68. Another poem that shows how serious poets were extending Pastoral to include new objectives. Carew has an explicitly pastoral setting; he uses the medieval *alba* (a song of lovers parting at dawn) as Shakespeare does in *Romeo and Juliet* and, ironically changed, in *Troilus and Cressida*; but the poem's conclusion, with its allusions to the *Song of Solomon*, reminds us that the Pastoral has become for him and other poets of the time a vehicle for many metaphysical and emblematical subtleties. Carew's *A Rapture*, which is not included here, has great interest as a libertine version of the Golden Age theme, somewhat in the manner of Donne's naturalist poems, and resembling superficially the mood of Marvell's *To His Coy Mistress*. It is a deliberate perversion of the theme as stated by Tasso (No. 14) and treated a little later by Guarini (No. 15).

69–73. Herrick is in the Jonsonian line of what might be called metropolitan classicism, but somewhat affected by the superb refinement of later Pastoral, which is in a sense a kind of decadence. His countryside is Devon; he sings of maypoles; but his *tessitura* is a sort of counter-tenor—pure, with a suggestion that the objects and emotions under consideration are not strictly his own affair. Herrick's central paradox is "cleanly wantonness." He sometimes posed as a modern Martial, and he has the technique and the longings of a voluntarily minor poet in a Silver Age. The theme of No. 70 was first explored by the French poets Saint-Amant and Racan; these poets were read by Mildmay Fane's circle, which included Marvell. No better example exists than No. 71 of the poignancy a traditional poet can find in 'conventional' themes. Here, and in Carew and Marvell, is poetry about poetry; a purely original restatement, made possible by a fine alteration in sensibility, of the pastoral theme. The most obvious literary debt is to Catullus. In No. 72, Phyllis was the daughter of the King of Thrace, who destroyed herself when her lover Demophon went home to Athens. No. 73 is another example of the quality mentioned above with reference to No. 71—the delight in sheer technical control of the restatement.

74. This poem of Boëthius is an influential statement of the Golden Age theme, illustrated by the poems of Virgil, Ovid, Tasso, and others above. Vaughan's famous poem *The Retreat* alludes to it. In that poem Vaughan richly develops this basic pastoral theme with his private imagery of Eden, Fall, and Redemption, in a mood not far removed from that of Marvell in No. 77. I have placed it here to show that another version of the Golden Age theme was fertile as late as 1651.

75. Marvell is not good material for puzzle-solvers, and the slipperiness of his meanings does not encourage a search for a complete solution. In this poem he seems to be commenting obliquely upon such poems as No. 68, just as in *The Garden* he is commenting upon and transforming the favourite themes of the French *libertins*. It would, however, be rash to treat the poem as being even principally a conversion of Carew's materials for a higher (in the Platonic sense) purpose. The religious and secular ingredients are not separable.

76. Ancestors of this poem will be found earlier in the book; what is new is the play of Marvellian wit.

77. This is, partly, a comment upon Randolph's poem *Upon Love fondly refused for Conscience' Sake*. It is in the same metre, simulating the Latin elegiac.

The gard'ner grafts not only apples there,
    But adds the warden and the pear.
The peach and apricot together grow;
    The cherry and the damson too;
Till he hath made by skilful husbandry
    An entire orchard of one tree.
So lest our paradise perfection want,
    We may as well inoculate or plant.

Here the argument is used as part of a libertine effort at seduction, but Marvell is making a serious statement, on the side of Perdita rather than that of Polixenes, concerning the Art-Nature opposition. (See No. 52.) An orthodox statement of the position, using the same imagery, which was traditionally associated with the theme, may be found in Puttenham's *Arte of English Poesy*: "The Gardiner by his arte will . . . make the single gillifloure, or marigold, or daisy, double; . . . a bitter melon sweete; a sweete apple soure; a plumme or cherrie without a stone . . . any of which things nature could not doe without mans help and arte." A statement on Marvell's side may be found in Montaigne's essay *Of Cannibals*. Man's Fall corrupted Nature (*cf.* the insistence of Vaughan, and of Milton in Book IV of *Paradise Lost*, on this point), and the garden is an emblem of that corruption; the Mower stands outside it in fields which are made to emblematize unfallen Nature. All this is a mere suggestion of the complexity of the Mower figure. See No. 78. The *Marvel of Peru* is *Mirabilis Jalapa*.

78. The Mower becomes even more mysterious here. See W. Empson's extraordinary analysis in *Some Versions of Pastoral*. Death is a mower, and all flesh is grass. Just as the poet himself assumes a quasi-blasphemous martyr-pose in *Appleton House*, and the fawn is momentarily a Christ-symbol in No. 79, so the Mower (who belongs to the unfallen world) sheds his blood for love. The herbs mentioned were used to staunch the flow of blood from wounds.

79. See note to No. 58. One of the most 'artificial' and complex of Marvell's poems. The analyses offered in Empson's book, and in M. C. Bradbrook and M. G. Lloyd Thomas, *Andrew Marvell* (Cambridge University Press, 1940), are helpful up to a point, but much more is to be done in the way of historical analysis. This poem probably represents the furthest and most mysterious development of English pastoral poetry. It was impossible to go further; there had to be a new start.

BIBLIOGRAPHY

The following is a short list of books which the reader might usefully consult for further study. It does not, of course, pretend to be a full bibliography of the subject.

CHAMBERS, E. K.: (editor) *English Pastorals* (London, 1895). An anthology with a good historical introduction.

GREG, W. W.: *Pastoral Poetry and Pastoral Drama* (London, 1906). This is the standard history of English pastoral poetry and drama.

DOVER WILSON, J.: *Life in Shakespeare's England* (Cambridge, 1911). There is a Penguin edition of this valuable anthology.

RENWICK, W. L.: *Edmund Spenser* (London, 1925).

EMPSON, W.: *Some Versions of Pastoral* (London, 1936). A speculative and exciting inquiry into the pastoral element—very broadly defined—in English literature, from the Miracle Plays to *Alice in Wonderland*.

HARRISON, T. P.: (editor), *The Pastoral Elegy* (Austin, Texas, 1939). A scholarly anthology of this branch of pastoral from Theocritus to Arnold, with introduction and notes.

The Variorum Spenser, Minor Poems, Vol. I, edited by E. Greenlaw and others (Oxford University Press, 1943). A great collection of fact and opinion concerning Spenser's poetry, including the pastoral poems.

THEOCRITUS: *The Idylls*, translated by R. C. Trevelyan (Cambridge, 1947). A very fine modern translation.

VIRGIL: *The Pastoral Poems*, translated by E. V. Rieu (Penguin, 1949). A prose translation, with a valuable essay on each eclogue.

Englands Helicon (1600), edited by Hugh Macdonald (London, 1950). A handsome and cheap modern edition of the most pastoral of the great miscellanies.

SOURCES OF THE TEXTS

1. Harleian MS. 2253; K. Sisam, *Fourteenth Century Verse and Prose* (Oxford University Press).
2. *Poems*, edited by R. Harvey Wood (Oliver and Boyd).
3. Balliol MS. 354; *Anglia*, xxvi.
4. *The Pepys Ballads*, edited by H. Rollins (Harvard University Press), Vol. I.

5. *The Pepys Ballads,* edited by H. Rollins (Harvard University Press), Vol. II.

6. *The Pepys Ballads,* edited by H. Rollins (Harvard University Press), Vol. II.

7. *Sixe Idillia, that is, sixe small, or Petty Poems, or Æglogues, chosen out of the right famous Sicilian Poet Theocritus . . .*

8. See No. 7.

9. *Poems,* edited by A. H. Grosart (Fuller Worthies Library).

10. *Virgils Eclogues translated into English.*

11. *Ovids Metamorphoses Englished.*

12. *The Eclogues of Mantuan.*

13. *Poems,* edited by L. E. Kastner (Manchester University Press).

14. *Torquato Tassos Aminta Englisht.*

15. *Il Pastor Fido, the Faithfull Shepheard.*

16. *Englands Helicon* (1600, 1614). Text from edition of 1614.

17. *Eglogs, Epytaphes, and Sonettes* (1563).

18. Text from Globe edition (Macmillan).

19. Text from Globe edition (Macmillan).

20. Text from Globe edition (Macmillan).

21. Text from Globe edition (Macmillan).

22. Text from Globe edition (Macmillan).

23. *Englands Helicon* (1600, 1614). Text of 1614.

24. *The Countesse of Pembrokes Arcadia,* edited by A. Feuillerat (Cambridge University Press).

25. *Englands Helicon* (1600, 1614). Text of 1614.

26. *Englands Helicon* (1600, 1614). Text of 1614.

27. *Englands Helicon* (1600, 1614). Text of 1614.

28. *Davison's Poetical Rhapsody,* edited by H. Rollins (Harvard University Press).

29. *Davison's Poetical Rhapsody,* edited by H. Rollins (Harvard University Press).

30. *Englands Helicon* (1600, 1614). Text of 1614.

31. *Englands Helicon* (1600, 1614). Text of 1614.

32. *Englands Helicon* (1600, 1614). Text of 1614.

33. *Menaphon* (1589); *Englands Helicon* (1600, 1614).

34. *Phillis* (1593); *Englands Helicon* (1600).

35. *The Works of Michael Drayton,* edited by J. W. Hebel (Basil Blackwell), Vol. I.

36. *The Works of Michael Drayton,* edited by J. W. Hebel (Basil Blackwell), Vol. I.

37. *Davison's Poetical Rhapsody,* edited by H. Rollins (Harvard University Press).

38. *Englands Helicon* (1600, 1614). Text of 1614.

39. *The Passionate Shepheard,* Pastoral 4.

40. *Englands Helicon* (1600, 1614). Text of 1614.

41. *Poems,* edited by A. Grosart (1876).

42. *Poems*, edited by A. Grosart (1876).
43. *Englands Helicon* (1600, 1614). Text of 1614.
44. *Englands Helicon* (1600, 1614). Text of·1614.
45. *Davison's Poetical Rhapsody*, edited by H. Rollins (Harvard University Press).
46. *Works*, edited by P. Vivian (Oxford University Press).
47. *Works*, edited by P. Vivian (Oxford University Press).
48. *The Works of Beaumont and Fletcher*, edited by A. Glover and A. R. Waller (Cambridge University Press), Vol. II.
49. *Works*, edited by A. Glover and A. R. Waller (Cambridge University Press), Vol. II.
50. *Works*, edited by A. Glover and A. R. Waller (Cambridge University Press), Vol. II.
51. *Works*, edited by A. Glover and A. R. Waller (Cambridge University Press), Vol. I.
52. The First Folio (1623).
53. *Works of Ben Jonson*, edited by C. H. Herford and P. Simpson (Oxford University Press), Vol. VII.
54. *Works*, edited by C. H. Herford and P. Simpson (Oxford University Press) Vol. VII.
55. *Poems*, edited by L. E. Kastner (Manchester University Press).
56. *The Shepherds Hunting.*
57. *Faire-Virtue, The Muse of Phil'arete, etc.*
58. *Britannias Pastorals.*
59. *Britannias Pastorals.*
60. *Poetical Works of Giles and Phineas Fletcher*, edited by F. S. Boas (Cambridge University Press), Vol. II.
61. *Poems* (1645).
62. *Poems* (1645).
63. *Poems* (1645).
64. *Poems* (1645).
65. *Poems* (1638). Text from second edition (1640).
66. *Poems* (1638). Text from second edition (1640).
67. *Poems*, edited by E. K. Chambers (Clarendon Press).
68. *Poems*, edited by Rhoades Dunlap (Oxford University Press).
69. *Hesperides* (1648).
70. *Hesperides* (1648).
71. *Hesperides* (1648).
72. *Hesperides* (1648).
73. *Hesperides* (1648).
74. *Works*, edited by L. C. Martin (Oxford University Press).
75. *Poems*, edited by H. Margoliouth (Oxford University Press).
76. *Poems*, edited by H. Margoliouth (Oxford University Press).
77. *Poems*, edited by H. Margoliouth (Oxford University Press).
78. *Poems*, edited by H. Margoliouth (Oxford University Press).
79. *Poems*, edited by H. Margoliouth (Oxford University Press).